Russian Law in Transition
Law and Institutional Change

Soili Nystén-Haarala

KIKIMORA PUBLICATIONS

Series B : 21 Helsinki 2001

Russian Law in Transition

ISBN 951-45-9902-0
ISSN 1455-4828

Aleksanteri Institute
Graphic design: Vesa Tuukkanen

Gummerus Printing
Saarijärvi 2001

Contents

Acknowledgements

Writing a book on Russian law in transition has been my dream for a long time. Unfortunately, a law scholar working in a law faculty can usually consider such research only as a hobby. Interdisciplinary approaches to law as well as studying rapidly changing legal systems are mostly regarded as less important research lying outside the hard core of mainstream legal studies. However, Russian law cannot be understood without studying it in its economic, social, political and historical context. It is not the details that are interesting in Russian law, but the transitory development itself. I am convinced that every lawyer could learn more about law, if it was studied as an institution and a developing process.

The interest within the institutional framework study of the Forestry Project at the International Institute for Applied Systems Analysis (IIASA) in Laxenburg, Austria made it possible to write this book. I would like to express my gratitude to those who contributed to the completion of my research reports and this book, namely Sten Nilsson, Counselor to the Director and Leader of the Forestry Project, Lars Carlsson and Mats-Olov Olsson, all of whom helped me with their valuable comments. I am also grateful to the other members of the project who, together, form an encouraging interdisciplinary working group.

I am also grateful to my "home institute" the Law Faculty of the University of Lapland in Rovaniemi and especially to the then Dean of the faculty, Professor Terttu Utriainen, who encouraged me to take leave of absence and spend time at IIASA to write this book. The focus of the University of Lapland on Russian studies has made it possible for me to also lecture on Russian law at my home university. I am most grateful to M.Sc (Soc.Sc.) Mare Rantaniemi, who coordinated an EU/Interreg project "Working with Russia" at the University of Lapland. Her support has been invaluable for this book. Heartfelt appreciation also goes to Professor Juha Tolonen at Vaasa University, who guided me toward the long path of studying Russian law. He is the one to thank for helping me choose to make a hobby a profession. Without his encouragement, I might long ago have turned to easier paths of legal studies.

I am also thankful to many Finnish colleagues, representing various disciplines, for all the interesting discussions on the problems of transition. One particularly rich source of inspiration has been the Aleksanteri Institute in Helsinki. The Institute's Master's Programme and Graduate School in Russian and East European Studies have provided extremely motivating intellectual surroundings for lecturing and doing research on Russian Law.

My sincerest thanks also go to my colleagues at the Institute of State and Law of the Russian Academy of Sciences in Moscow, especially Vice-Director of the Institute, Professor Irina Ikonitskaya, who kindly introduced me to Russian land law. I am also grateful to the teachers of the Law Faculty of the Pomor State University in Archangel who participated in a Tempus/Tacis project, which I coordinated along with writing this book. I have learned a lot about Russian law from my Russian colleagues. The Russian comments outside the legal studies have also been most fruitful for understanding transition. I am most grateful to Dr. Dmitri Furman at the Institute of Europe of the Russian Academy of Sciences in Moscow, who found time to comment on the chapter concerning constitutionalism and federalism.

I gratefully acknowledge IIASA not only for providing the surroundings to concentrate on my research but also for financial support. Thanks are especially due to Shari Jandl of the Forestry Project, who not only reliably and effectively assisted me with the English language but also edited the book, as well as to Martina Jöstl and Anka James of the Publications Department, who took care of the layout and diagrams, respectively. All the remaining errors are naturally my own.

Last but not least, I want to express gratitude to my family. My husband, Eino, provided me with the opportunity to concentrate on my work and bore the responsibility for the children and the household. I dedicate this book to Eino and our sons, Ville and Jaakko. Probably because I was not at home very much, our sons have grown up to be independent and caring young men, of whom any mother would be proud. My desire is to dedicate more time to them even if new challenges of transition studies have still to be discovered.

Soili Nystén-Haarala
Laxenburg, April 2001

Abbreviations

AktG	Aktiengesetz (German Joint Stock Companies Act)
CC	The Civil Code of the Russian Federation (Grazhdanskii kodeks)
CIA	Central Intelligence Agency, United States of America
DEM	Deutsche Mark (German Mark)
EU	European Union
FIGs	Financial-Industrial Groups
GKI	Gosudarstvennyi komitet RF po upravleniyu gosudarstvennym imushchestvom (State Committee of Property)
GmbH	Gesellschaft mit beschränkter Haftung (German Limited Liability Company)
GmbHG	Gesetz betreffend die Gesellschaften mit beschränkter Haftung (German Limited Liability Companies Act)
ICC	International Chamber of Commerce (Paris)
IIASA	International Institute for Applied Systems Analysis, Laxenburg, Austria

KGB	Komitet Gosudarstvennoi Bezopasnosti (Soviet Intelligence Agency)
Komm.	Kommentarii (Commentary)
NEP	New Economic Policy
NTV	Nezavisimoe Televidenie (Independent Television)
OECD	Organization for Economic Co-operation and Development
ORT	Obshchestvennoe Rossiiskoe Televidenie (Public Russian Television)
OVR	Otechestvo – vsya Rossiya
OYL	Osakeyhtiölaki (Finnish Joint Stock Companies Act)
PrC	Private Company (Britain)
RF	Russian Federation
Ross. Gaz.	Rossiiskaya gazeta
RSFSR	Russian Socialist Federal Soviet Republic (Rossiiskaya Sotsialisticheskaya Federativnaya Sovetskaya Respublika)
SSSR	Soyuz Sovietskikh Sotsialisticheskikh Respublik
UNCITRAL	United Nations Conference on International Trade Law
US	United States (of America)
USSR	Union of Soviet Socialist Republics
ZAO	Zakon ob aktsionernykh obshchestvakh (Russian Law on Joint Stock Companies) and Aktsionernoe obshchestvo zakrytogo tipa (Closed Joint Stock Company)

1

LAW AND TRANSITION— AN INTRODUCTION

1.1 Transition and Institutions

After the collapse of communism, Russia has been in a process of fundamental socioeconomic transformation, which can be described as transition to a market economy, democracy and the rule of law. A similar fundamental transformation is going on in the post-communist countries of Central and Eastern Europe. Even if these post-communist countries are all different, their main problems of transition are the same. The transformation process has not been as easy and technical as the first reformers and many foreign advisers may have thought in the beginning. Even if there has been a rapid change and a lot has been achieved, there is still a long and thorny road to the final objectives of transition. The result may also be a peculiar Russian version of a market economy, democracy and the rule of law.

The standpoint of this study is the belief that Russian problems are institutional. Institutions are the rules of the game and without them there is no economic or social activity. The most important role of institutions is to reduce uncertainty by establishing a stable structure for human interaction. Institutions facilitate the interaction between people and organizations. They are essential for keeping transaction costs on a socially acceptable level (North, 1992).

As North and Thomas (1973) have shown in their studies of economic history, the results of changes usually differ from what was originally intended, because institutions play an important role in change. Institutions tend to resist change. Since moral values and attitudes of people change only slowly, radical changes from above are not going to be successful if they are not widely accepted in society. Too radical changes may even have a deteriorating effect on the general respect of law. In transition, law is an important tool in transforming society into a new trail and an institution, which itself, should be transformed. This makes law a difficult tool in managing transition.

Law constitutes the official rules of the game, which can be enforced by coercive legal rules. An inadequate and contradictory legal framework has often been blamed for the chaotic circumstances, where industry and commerce must try to transform in Russia.[1] The legal framework is far from perfect but a lot has already been achieved to create modern legislation for the needs of a market economy and democracy. Most of the problems exist, however, in enforcement or legal norms. Implementing new official rules in Russia's extraordinary environment does not produce similar results to those in established democratic market economies. Changing legal rules does not yet bring society to the level of a market economy, democracy and the rule of law. Informal institutions have to support the formal ones. Unofficial rules of the game—"the rules in use"—are at least as important as formal legal rules (Pejovich, 1998:23; Crawford and Ostrom, 1995). Law is an institution working within a larger institutional framework of enforced norms, routines, conventions and traditions. Law does not function in a vacuum but within the institutional framework of society. For this reason, a holistic view is necessary to understand transition and the role of law in this process.

According to abundant empirical research it seems that the rules of the game, both official and unofficial, are vague and that the absence of trust in business relations is usual (e.g., Suomen, 1998;

---

[1] Inadequate and obscure law seems to be the first and foremost target of criticism among foreign businessmen working in the Russian markets (see e.g., Ollila, 1999:31–35). According to IIASA's empirical research concerning forest companies in several regions of Russia, Russian managers themselves regarded tax and business legislation as well as violations of contracts as their main problems in business (Carlsson *et al.*, 2000:7).

Kortelainen, 1997; Törnroos and Nieminen, 1999). The crucial problem in developing the rule of law in Russia is the absence of trust (see Fell, 1999). In the Soviet Union, law was repressive and arbitrary. People did not have trust in their legal system. However, trust has to be re-established but it is not easy when the economy is in a chaotic situation and when a hectic political power struggle is going on. It should not be forgotten that the new legal system is not created from nothing but should replace the former socialist system, which was based on communist so-called democratic centralism, one-party dictatorship as well as on a centrally planned economy. Institutions such as law are inherited from the Soviet past and as such they can even constitute a block for transition.

1.2 Legal Studies and Change

Even if law is both an important tool in transition and an institution in transition, there is no legal theory explaining change. Mainstream legal studies understand law as a system of norms and the task of legal studies as explaining the correct application of norms especially in courts. Kelsen's norm hierarchy represents the purest and most endogenic legal positivism. Legal norms are applied depending on their position in the hierarchy of norms, which is based on a ground norm (Kelsen, 1968; 1991).[2] A hierarchy of norms is positive law, which according to Kelsen is the foundation of every society. Order is based on a normative system, which can be created in any kind of society. Therefore legal positivism also attracted V.I. Lenin and the Bolsheviks. Especially attractive was the idea that the state is the ultimate source of law and that there is nothing above the state to limit its legislative power, since legal positivism separated law from morals.

---

[2] Autonomy of law is one of the cornerstones of legal studies, especially in the mainstream legal positivist approach. See Hart (1978), a modern "softened" version of legal positivism emphasizing autonomy of law. Aarnio describes typical features of Finnish legal positivism in the following way. Legal information is sought in law and legal studies. All knowledge based on experience is rejected (Aarnio, 1975). Sociologist and economic approaches to law challenge the closed character of legal studies.

Legal theory was called the theory of state and law in the Soviet Union to emphasize that the two cannot be separated from each other, and that it is the state that is the ultimate source of law. The difference to a rule of law country was that the rulers did not understand law to bind them as well. Law was a weapon in the hands of the ruling class, which could direct the state in any direction that was beneficial to the rulers themselves (Berman, 1996; Alekseev, 1999). Law was only for the citizens to obey. Order governed by law in such a society is "dictatorship of law" for the citizens. It is at least better than disorder.

When law is understood to be only a technical construction, which can be changed at any time, it can be claimed that Russian law has changed completely. Legislation has been modernized and especially civil (private) law can already, from the legislative point of view, be called the law of a market economy. The problems, however, mostly lie in enforcement and weak application of the law. Law that is not followed is not effective. Legal scholars representing legal realism claim that law is more than only a system of norms, but that it becomes law when it is implemented and when it actually binds. Therefore, legal realists study either how people feel that law binds them or how the authorities or judges implement law (Ross, 1966).[3] From this point of view the common saying that there is no law in Russia becomes understandable. Law, which does not matter, is hardly a law at all. From the legal realistic point of view law is not endogenous but is considered to function in its context.

Studying foreign legal systems is understood in legal studies to be an issue of comparative law. Comparativists compare legal systems either to aid the legislator or a judge. Comparative law is also used for the purpose of unification or simply to provide legal studies with

---

[3] One of the founders of sociological law, Eugen Ehrlich, stressed that law is binding only when it really is implemented and followed (Ehrlich, 1967). Realism, which Ross called ideological realism, is based on this idea. Scandinavian realism emphasizes that law is a social phenomenon. American realism (Roscoe Pound, Karl Llewellyn), which Ross calls behavioristic realism, is also based on the same basic idea as Ehrlich's sociological law. American realists, however, saw that law is enforced when authorities implement it. They observed the behavior of authorities. Ross, himself emphasizes the ideology of judges.

new approaches and solutions (Zweigert and Kötz, 1992:15–27). Comparative law uses a classification of legal systems into different legal families as a tool in comparisons. There are typical styles and features attached to different families. Usually it is understood that a comparative study must compare two or more legal systems in a systematic way. In legal systems, which are close to each other and where the economic and political systems are similar, a comparative study can concentrate on one or a few specific legal norms. Comparative studies can be quite technical comparisons of legal norms in different countries. On the other hand, the mainstream comparative doctrine emphasizes that law has to be studied in its context. Comparative law is close to legal sociology and legal history (Zweigert and Kötz, 1992). David (1978) even emphasizes the significant role of ideologies.

The comparative method also enables studying change. Especially legal history and a historical aspect concentrate in change. Otherwise legal studies usually assume law as a stable system. Also comparative studies are more often studies of stable legal systems than studies of change. The classification of legal families provides a tool for studying and comparing legal systems. Transition in post-communist countries has, however, challenged the classification of legal families. Socialist law was considered to form one family of law with a similar ideology and style. After the collapse of communism in Europe, the socialist family was dropped, for example in the new edition of Zweigert's and Kötz's influential textbook on comparative law, and only now can it be seen in which direction each of the legal systems is going to develop. There are, however, other comparativists, who consider that post-socialist countries still form one legal family on the grounds of similar problems of transition (Cruz, 1995). It is of secondary value, whether we regard countries of transition to form a legal family or not. What matters is that problems of transition are similar in each of these countries (Tolonen, 1996). Their legal traditions before socialism were different and the impact of the socialist system was different in each country. However, every country that has to transform its economic, legal and political system to a market economy, democracy and the rule of law, face similar problems.

There is, however, no theory on transition in comparative legal studies. Comparative law is important for those countries that are in transition. They can find more developed solutions in the law of market economy countries. They can use foreign law to support the legislator or even judges. But, what can a study comparing a transition country with a more advanced market economy offer to the latter? Russian solutions in legislation and case studies hardly interest Western legislators or judges in developing their own domestic law. Therefore a systematic and technical comparison is not necessarily a reasonable study method. Transition is of more profound and theoretical interest to more developed market economies. Transition challenges the stable approach to law and makes us ask what law actually is. Transition can increase our knowledge concerning the role of law in change and the relations of law to economy and power structures. However, we can acknowledge the value of studying law in transition only if we see law in its context and not merely as a mechanical system of norms.

1.3 Can Institutions be Changed?

Since there is no theory on transition in legal studies, such theories have to be found elsewhere. Also neoclassical economics uses stable theories. Theories, which focus on change, can be found in institutional economics. Institutionalists have criticized the reforms in post-communist countries of not taking institutions into account and presupposing the existence of an already well functioning institutional framework (e.g., Stiglitz, 1999; Carlsson *et al.,* 2000). The result of the reforms has been that the old habits and attitudes have modified the intended reforms into something, which cannot be called either socialism or a market economy. A *virtual economy* is what Gaddy and Ickes (1998) started to call the economy, which is a mixture of a pretended market economy and inheritance of socialism.

The same applies to democracy and the rule of law. They can also be called virtual. The concept "dictatorship of law", which was launched by President Putin, is some kind of virtual rule of law, an attempt to establish order but with arbitrary means. Dictatorship of law is based on the idea that the state creates the system of norms, which citizens then have to obey. It is still far from democratic rule of law, which can challenge the rule makers and is based on trust. If courts, judges and the police are not trusted, law can be only a system forced upon the people from above. Real development of the rule of law requires that also informal institutions change and support the legal system.

As Putnam (1993:183) illustrated in his study of Italian transformation, history changes slowly and current changes are decided by historical circumstances. This clear and obvious fact does not, however, mean that change is impossible or that failure is predictable due to historical reasons.

The crucial difficulty in transition is that the situation in Russia is far from ordinary. Economic reforms failed, politics are corrupt, and economic crime is common in everyday life. All these failures are connected with one another thereby forming a vicious circle. Before the vicious circle can be broken, the reasons for its existence must be realized.

The obvious vicious circle of transition gives weight to the unpleasant conclusion, which some scholars have drawn, claiming that it is impossible to develop democracy, a market economy and the rule of law at the same time (e.g., Tolonen, 1996; Elster, 1993). Law, economics and politics are usually studied separately. Therefore, we do not know enough about their interaction. Central and Eastern European countries are now laboratories where the dynamics of this interaction can be observed. These countries have been forced to rebuild the ship at sea (Elster *et al.*, 1998). Social scientists, economists and legal scholars have a lot to learn about the transformation process. The crucial question of transformation is whether the vicious circle can be broken and how.

The question whether institutions can be changed and how, cannot be answered in this book; it can only be discussed. Institutions tend to maintain old mentalities and cultural habits, which again might prevent institutions from changing. Before anything can be said about whether or not institutions can be changed, we have to know how they function. The author shares the institutionalists' point of view and the presupposition that the existing institutional setup in Russia is hindering the development of the rule of law, a market economy and democracy (Carlsson *et al.*, 2000).

North (1997:2) suggests the following four institutional features that are associated with low-cost transaction and credible

commitment, which are essential for the functioning of any market economy:
- the cost of measuring,
- the size of the market,
- enforcement of rules, and
- attitudes and perceptions.

The cost of measuring deals with the fact that when no or poor standards exist with regard to the quality of goods and services, the behavior of agents etc., every single transaction might be subjected to endless deliberations. The same applies when property rights are ill defined. For example, in Russia property rights are poorly defined and common rules of behavior in business are poorly developed. The absence of trust and unclear rules raise transaction costs.

The second feature, according to North, is the size of economy. When interpersonal exchange dominates, friends, relatives, or clans are the main players. When markets grow, exchange becomes more impersonal and more elaborate ways of constraining the parties might occur. In a market economy, market competition is able to constrain the actors.

The enforcement of rules is the third feature. The legal system performs the function of solving the disputes between parties as a third party. It should also be emphasized that the cheapest enforcement occurs when people have internalized certain conducts of behavior as norms. In long-term business cooperation the parties may also have developed other third party solutions or supported their mutual relations with credible commitments and hostages (Williamson, 1985). In Russia a lot of hopes are vested in the court system. Effective enforcement is, however, only developing. It should also be emphasized that the courts are not the best possible means for solving contractual or inter-organizational disputes even if they are needed as the ultimate appeal mechanism (Williamson, 1985; Nystén-Haarala, 1998).

The fourth feature deals with the mentality and ways actors think. Cultural aspects, Soviet thinking modes and the peculiar attitude to power have often been mentioned as obstacles for transition (e.g., Kennaway, 1997; Jensen, 1997). There is a collectivist attitude, which is vested in institutions and pulls the development in another direction. In this connection the problem of trust is essential (Rose *et al.*, 1998; Huemer, 1998). Attitudes and perceptions are connected with the enforcement of legal rules. Legal principles do not necessarily change with the legal rules. Legal principles, which do not reflect the values and social norms of the people, are difficult or impossible for the legal machinery to apply (Tolonen, 1992). Attitudes and perceptions are not yet at the level of the principles of a market economy, democracy and the rule of law, but old principles still have an important effect hindering the enforcement of new legal rules.

1.4 Aim and Structure of the Study

Assessing Russia's performance is possible simply by comparing it to the situation in Western countries. Such a method is not unfair or impolite, since Russia has clearly expressed that the objectives are a market economy, the rule of law and democracy. The evaluation criteria should be seen as a set of "basic principles". The fundamental evaluation criteria are the very basic requirements that guarantee a sustainable development for the whole economy. The conditions are as follows:[4]

- Constitutional rules are acknowledged and transparent.
- The structure of property rights is settled and well defined, i.e., private actors can acquire property or obtain the right to utilize property for their own benefit.
- Rules and regulation from official authorities are regarded as legitimate and apply equally to similar actors.
- The market decides the price of property and goods.
- Decision-making regarding collective choice and operational rules is decentralized.
- Private investors can realize the returns on their investments.
- Rules are enacted aimed at preventing the devastation of natural resources.
- Legitimate authorities take measures against violations of rules.

---

[4] These are the evaluation criteria used in case studies conducted within the institutional framework study of the Forestry Project at IIASA (see, e.g., Carlsson *et al.*, 2000; Carlsson *et al.*, 1999; Fell, 1999).

The aim of this study is to describe Russian transitional processes towards the rule of law, a market economy and democracy from the legal point of view by applying a holistic approach and using the above-mentioned criteria in the evaluation. The study also has another aim. The focus is on the role of law in these processes. It is worth assessing what are the opportunities and the limits of law and how it is connected with the predominant institutional setup.

The author shares the idea that efficient markets are built from below with the assistance of the political structure but that the central figures in this development are the managers of individual firms (cf., Carlsson *et al.*, 1999). In establishing the rule of law courts are important, but the legal centralist emphasis on courts must be rejected (cf., Williamson, 1985; Nystén-Haarala, 1998). In establishing the rule of law, civil society and informal institutions are at least as important as the formal hierarchy of norms. It is therefore not enough to only describe the legal rules, but to also try to understand the problems of implementing them.

Ostrom has introduced an idea of three important layers in change (Crawford and Ostrom, 1995). She thinks that effective transition must occur on all levels of society. The level of the constitution is important because the main principles of society are found there. Implementation of the rules on the level of citizens and firms is the second level, and the third level is the operational day-to-day level of citizens and firms. All these levels are important and interact. Ostrom's layers are similar to a legal realist approach to law. Legislation and its implementation cannot be separated. The grass-root level is crucial in the development of informal rules and business culture because it is the grass-root level, which has to adapt most to the changes in the environment.

This study is divided into three main chapters. The focus of chapter two is on the legal framework on the constitutional level. Constitutionalism and federalism are defined in the constitution but their real meaning is revealed when the rules are applied. This chapter mainly focuses on the general level of the rule of law, which provides firms with the general framework for business.

Chapter three focuses on property rights, which have a significant role to play in economic efficiency. The property rights system is also very much a political issue. Privatization and regulation of property rights in Russia has been given from top-down. Credibility and persistence of property rights is significant in economic development and constitute an important framework for the operation of firms. In addition, this chapter focuses both on the political choices—the struggle in society—and also touches upon the firms, which operate within the developing framework of property rights facing the problems with local authorities and the court system.

Chapter four concentrates on the rules regulating the functioning of firms. Development of corporate governance and the transition in the functioning of a firm is of major importance in understanding the hindrances for development towards a market economy.

These three chapters can also be read individually, since they were originally written as interim reports at the International Institute for Applied Systems Analysis (IIASA). Together the three chapters aim at providing a general view on the legal framework for business in Russia. The rule of law and constitutionalism are not only designed for the relations between the state organs. They form the general framework for business, which can be assessed from the point of view of trust in politics and the legal system. Property rights probably play the most important role in economic efficiency. The system of property rights constitutes a significant framework for business operations. Company law in chapter four represents the legal framework for intra-organizational rules of firms.

References

Aarnio, Aulis (1975). *Laki, teko ja tavoite. Tutkimus tavoitteellisuudesta lain tulkinnassa ja sen soveltamisessa (Law, Action and Goal. Research on Goal-orientation in the Interpretation of Law and Its Implementation).* Lainopillisen ylioppilastiedekunnan kustannustoimikunta. Forssa (in Finnish).

Alekseev, S.S. (1999). *Pravo, azbuka, teoriya, filosofiya. Opyt kompleksnogo issledovanya (Law, the Elements, Theory and Philosophy).* Statut, Moscow (in Russian).

Berman, Harold J. (1996). The Struggle for Law in Post-Soviet Russia. In: A. Sajo (ed.) *Western Rights? Post-Communist Application.* Kluwer, pp. 41–55.

Carlsson, Lars, Nils-Gustav Lundgren and Mats-Olov Olsson (1999). Forest Enterprises in Transition—Business Behavior in the Tomsk Forest Sector? Interim Report IR-99-010. International Institute for Applied Systems Analysis, Laxenburg, Austria.

Carlsson, Lars, Nils-Gustav Lundgren and Mats-Olov Olsson (2000). Why is the Russian Bear Still Asleep After Ten Years of Transition? Interim Report IR-00-019. International Institute for Applied Systems Analysis, Laxenburg, Austria.

Crawford, Sue E.S. and Elinor Ostrom (1995). A Grammar of Institutions. *American Political Science Review*, 89 (3), September, pp. 582–600.

Cruz, Peter de (1995). *Comparative Law in a Changing World*. Cavendish, London.

David, Réne (1978). *Les grands systèmes de droit contemporains (The Great Systems of Contemporary Law)*. 7th Edition, Dalloz, Paris (in French).

Ehrlich, Eugen (1967) *Recht und Leben: Gesammalte Schriften zur Rechtstaatsachenforschung und zur Freirechtslehre (Law and Life: Collected Works of Research on the Rule of Law and Jurisprudence of Free Law)*. Ausgewählt und eingeleitet von Manfred Rehbinder. Duncker and Humbolt, Berlin (in German).

Elster, Jon (1993). The Necessity and Impossibility of Simultaneous Economic and Political Reform. In: D. Greenberg and S.N. Katz (eds.) *Constitutionalism and Democracy. Transitions in the Contemporary World*. Oxford University Press, New York, pp. 267–274.

Elster, Jon, Claus Offe and Ulrich K. Preuss (1998). *Institutional Design in Post-communist Societies. Rebuilding a Ship at Sea*. Cambridge University Press.

Fell, Astrid (1999). On the Establishment of Trust in the Russian Forest Sector. Interim Report IR-99-054. International Institute for Applied Systems Analysis, Laxenburg, Austria.

Gaddy, Clifford G. and Barry W. Ickes (1998). Beyond the Bailout: Time to Face Reality about Russia's Virtual Economy. *Foreign Affairs*, 77, pp. 53–67.

Hart, H.L.A. (1978). *The Concept of Law*. Oxford University Press, Oxford.

Huemer, Lars (1998). *Trust in Business Relations. Economic Logic or Social Interaction*? Borea Förlag, Umeå.

Jensen, Donald N. (1997). Patrimonialism in Post-Soviet Russia. Radio Free Europe/Radio Liberty (RFE/RL) Newsline. Downloaded from the Internet: http://www.aa.net/~russia/mentor/palmentor.html (18 February 1998).

Kelsen, Hans (1968). *Puhdas oikeusoppi (Jurisprudence of Pure Law)*. Original Title: Reine Rechtslehre. Helsinki (in Finnish).

Kelsen, Hans (1991). *General Theory of Norms*. Translated by Michael Hartney. Clarendon, Oxford.

Kennaway, Alexander (1997). The Mental and Psychological Inheritance of Contemporary Russia. The Euro-Atlantic Foundation. Downloaded from the Internet: http://xs4all.freenet.kiev.ua/NATO/eaf/papers/ mental.html (22 February 1998).

Kortelainen, Jarmo (1997). Crossing the Russian Border. Regional Development and Cross-border Cooperation in Karelia. Institute of Geography, University of Joensuu, Joensuu, Finland.

North, Douglass C. (1992). *Institutions, Institutional Change and Economic Performance.* Cambridge University Press.

North, Douglass C. (1997). The Contribution of the New Institutional Economics to an Understanding of the Transition Problem. The United Nations University, World Institute for Development Economics Research (UNU/WIDER) Annual Lecture, 7 March, Washington University, St. Louis.

North, Douglass C. and R.P. Thomas (1973.) *The Rise of the Western World: A New Economic History.* Cambridge, USA.

Nystén-Haarala, Soili (1998). *The Long-term Contract. Contract Law and Contracting.* Finnish Lawyers Publishing, Helsinki.

Ollila, Timo (1999). Itä-Lapista Venäjälle. Tutkimus Itä-Lapin yritysten liiketoiminnasta Venäjän markkinoilla 1990-luvulla (Research of Business Activities of Enterprises of Eastern Lapland in the Russian Market in the 1990s). Working Paper 29, Publications of Social Sciences Center, University of Lapland (in Finnish).

Pejovich, Svetozar (1998). *Economic Analysis of Institutions and Systems.* Kluwer, London.

Putnam, Robert D. (1993). *Making Democracy Work.* With Robert Leonardi and Raffaella Y. Nanetti. Princeton University Press.

Rose, Richard, William Mishler and Richard Haerpfer (1998). *Democracy and its Alternatives.* Polity Press, Oxford.

Ross, Alf (1966). *Om ret og retfærdighed (Law and Justice).* Nyt nordisk forlag Arnold Busck, Copenhagen (in Danish).

Stiglitz, Joseph E. (1999). Whither Reform? Ten Years of the Transition. World Bank Annual Conference on Development Economics, Washington, DC, 28–30 April.

Suomen lähialueet. Tilastokeskus (1998). (Regions Bordering Finland). 3, Centre of Statistics, Finland (in Finnish).

Tolonen, Hannu (1992). Rules, Principles and Goals: The Interplay Between Law, Morals and Politics. *Scandinavian Studies in Law, 1991,* Vol. 35, pp. 270–293. Stockholm Institute for Scandinavian Law. Almqvist and Wicksell, Uppsala.

Tolonen, Juha (1996). Legal Aspects of Transformation. A General View. Proceedings of International Symposium on Law, Economics and Business in the Melting Pot, 11–12 March 1996. Copenhagen Business School, Law Department and Tokai University, Research Institute of Social Sciences, pp. 127–141.

Törnroos, Jan-Åke and Jarmo Nieminen (eds.) (1999). *Business Entry in Eastern Europe. A Network and Learning Approach with Case Studies.* B 4, Kikimora Publications, Helsinki, Finland.

Williamson, Oliver E. (1985). *Economic Institutions of Capitalism: Firms, Markets, Relational Contracting.* Free Press, New York.

Zweigert, Konrad and Hein Kötz (1992). *An Introduction to Comparative Law.* Translated from German by Tony Weir. Clarendon Press, Oxford.

2

DEVELOPMENT OF CONSTITUTIONALISM AND FEDERALISM IN RUSSIA

2.1 Introduction

2.1.1 Constitutionalism, the Rule of Law and Democratic Federalism

In Anglo-Saxon legal culture the principle of the rule of law was developed in the 19th century. The rule of law meant that even the highest lawmaking authority might not lawfully infringe certain basic principles of justice. The source of those basic principles of justice was found in the English constitution, which is embodied in a chain of certain historical documents beginning with the Magna Carta of 1215 reaching until the Bill of Rights of 1689, as well as in English common law (Berman, 1996).

The concept "constitutionalism" is of American origin and still sounds strange even to English ears (Berman, 1996:45). Constitutionalism is defined as keeping government in good order. The government is bound by rules laid down in advance of its actions. Constitutionalism implements the rule of law, bringing about predictability and security in relations between individuals and the government by defining, in advance, the powers and limits of that government (Alexander, 1998:4; Kay, 1998:17–19). The Americans added into the notion "rule of law" an emphasis on its foundations in written federal and state constitutions that proclaimed civil liberties such as freedom of religion, speech, press and assembly. The philosophy of American constitutionalism rests on an implicit theory of natural law.

The Americans also introduced a governmental system of checks and balances, entrusting to the judicial branch of government supreme authority to guard the constitution. This added a new dimension to the rule of law concept, since it meant that in appropriate cases any citizen in any court could invoke it against the legislature itself. According to British tradition it is the parliament, which is sovereign and has the highest authority.

The roots of the rule of law are deep in the history of Western legal thinking. Berman (1983) claims in his book "Law and Revolution" that the rivalry between the Catholic Church and the States, which he calls the Gregorian Revolution, developed a new type of citizenship in Western culture. Because of several sources of legal power, these powers had to be limited and the citizens were allowed to challenge the power.

In the United States the idea of several sources of law was further developed in federalism. The core of American federalism is the states, which form the federation, not the federation governing its parts from above. Different sources of power have limited authority, which is measured with legal and political competence and no one has the "ultimate word" of the sovereign. Justice is not a willful submission to authority, but a reasoned contention. The governmental authority is governed by a due process of law, which can be controlled. Federalism and the power of the states rest on a developed civil society controlling the state power from bottom-up (Ostrom, 1987:67–70).

The Russian legal system has, however, been more influenced by continental European legal tradition. The German *"Rechtsstaat"* concept was developed simultaneously with the Anglo-Saxon rule of law in the early 19th century. In a *Rechtsstaat* the supreme political authority should be based on, governed by, and bound by the law it made. This classical *Rechtsstaat* idea is formulated in Weber's (1978) formal rationality, which means that predictability and formal justice can be reached by following strictly formal legal rules. Weber, however, also saw the possibility of substantive rationality, but the starting point should still be the strict application of formal rules. It created predictability, which is needed for economic activity. The most notable difference to the Anglo-Saxon concept, which stressed the limits of governmental power, is that the *Rechtsstaat* reflected positivist legal theory emphasizing the state as being the only origin of legal norms. Legal positivism separated law from politics, but both the presupposition that political leaders are bound by law and the "Protestant" individualistic legacy of challenging the legal system and the state power existed.

The positivist *Rechtsstaat* concept influenced Russian lawyers at the end of the 19th and early 20th centuries. The legal positivist idea of the State being the only and ultimate source of law appealed to the Bolsheviks, who adopted it as the official Soviet legal theory (Alekseev, 1999; Berman, 1996). The Bolsheviks, however, did not consider themselves to be bound by law, but rather used law as a weapon to coercively change Russian society to correspond to their own communist ideals. During the Stalinist Era, the Soviet State systematically violated its own laws. Stalin's successors continued along the same line. Thus, the *Rechtsstaat* ideology was used in a centralist way. Even though the constitution guaranteed the Soviet republics sovereignty and national minorities autonomy, the ultimate source of law existed at the federal center and was defined by the Communist Party, which had taken the position of the tsar.

On the other hand, legal romanticism existed among Soviet lawyers. This romanticism saw the potential in law to develop a better society with legal methods (Alekseev, 1999). Even if such an attitude could be called romanticism in the Soviet Union, it was actually to a great extent dreaming of original Kelsenian legal positivism and a *Rechtsstaat*. Such romanticism is actually elitist by nature. The idea is that specialists have an important role in developing society. It was also only brave dissidents, who could challenge the existing rules. The role of individuals was so significant because of the absence of a civil society. In a society lead by specialists law governs society when law is left to lawyers who can create rules, which others then have to obey. Law and the rights of citizens stemmed from the government and its Leninist ideology. A good government was regarded as one able to take care of its citizens and offer them social and economic benefits in exchange for their political rights. The citizens themselves had no right to challenge the state power.

It was in the beginning of *perestroika* that the conception *"pravovoe gosudarsvo"* was brought into Soviet legal theory. This simply meant a return to the original *Rechtsstaat* idea according to which the state is bound by the laws, which it has previously promulgated and can only modify or repeal them by previously promulgated lawful procedures. Gorbachev also adopted, according to both American and German examples, the Constitutional Court as a judicial body to check the constitutionality of laws. After the new Russian constitution of 1993, there has been a modern written legal source for interpreting constitutionality—the Russian principles of human rights and the rule of law. The Constitutional Court has played a significant role in developing constitutionalism because the new Constitution left many important issues open. Among the unsolved crucial questions are the principles of Russian federalism.

It seems obvious that, after the collapse of communism in Eastern Europe, American constitutionalism has become a model for both Russia and post-communist Central European countries. A written constitution and especially the judicial control of a Constitutional Court are understood as a necessity for constitutionalism (cf., Shulzhenko, 1995:116). American constitutionalism can, however, not be the model through which Russian constitutionalism should be assessed, since the *Rechtsstaat* conception and legal positivism are closer to Russian tradition. The other even more significant difference in traditions is that there is no history of Russian rule of law but a history of more or less dictatorial autocratic rule (Istoriya…, 1999:260; Alekseev, 1999:56).

Russian legal history has a lot in common with Western legal history, but there is one significant difference. In the Orthodox Christian world the church was always under the rule of the earthly sovereign, who represented God on earth. Different rival sources of law never developed, and therefore citizenship did not develop in the Western way either. In Russian tradition, citizens are obedient subordinates who can complain and a good tsar may listen to them, but a citizen is not allowed to challenge the state power.

There were some reformer tsars. Catherine the Great was interested in the ideas of Enlightenment, but she did not build more than a façade in Russia. Peter the Great tried to westernize Russia. The most significant reformer was, however, Aleksandr II who, before he was assassinated, managed to free the peasants from slavery and push through legal reforms. Constitutional monarchy existed for a while and constitutional democracy was tried before the revolution crushed it. Russian history of democracy is a history of delayed reforms and rule of law, which never managed to develop. Finally, the communists managed to develop a fallacy of constitutionalism, a repressive legal system and society without trust in the law and the judicial system (Istoriya..., 1999:260).

The problems not only include the absence of tradition but also the exceptional circumstances in Russia with corruption, crime, economic failure and social problems. Therefore, it is obvious that constitutionalism cannot function according to the highly developed and well-established American model due to the exceptional circumstances prevailing in Russia. Legal and political culture has to develop simultaneously with legal rules. This is the real challenge for Russian transition.

Even if in many parts of the world constitution is regarded as a formal legitimizer of political power and not as a guarantor of rights to the citizens there are, however, some minimum requirements, which can be set for constitutionalism to function. Rules should be acknowledged and transparent. Decision-making should be decentralized and rules and norms regarded as legitimate. It is not enough that the formal setting is correct with all the bodies of modern constitutionalism. It is the actual legitimacy that counts. At this stage of development constitutionalism and the rule of law can already offer a predictable environment and transparent rules of the game for industry and commerce.

2.1.2 Aim and Structure of this Chapter

The purpose of this chapter is to describe the Russian transitional process towards constitutionalism, decentralization and the rule of law by applying a holistic approach.

The starting point of the analysis is that the main reasons for the bad functioning or failure of constitutionalism are not simply legal technicalities but depend on the broader institutional framework: unstable economy, underdeveloped politics and corruption. Adopting a new constitution does not yet make a fundamental transformation. Legal and political culture must also be transformed.

Russian problems are institutional and the crucial difficulty in transition is that the situation in Russia is far from ordinary. Economic reforms failed, politics are corrupted, and economic crime is common in everyday life. All these failures are connected with one another forming a vicious circle. Before the vicious circle can be broken, the reasons for its existence must be realized. It is in this context that it is essential to discuss the rule of law.

The reforms have changed the Russian socialist economy into a virtual economy, which was definitely not the objective. We can also question whether the rule of law is also "virtual" at the existing stage of Russian transition. Another difficult question that is focused on in this study is the role of law in transition, its limits, dependency on the surrounding society, and predominant institutional setup.

Even if the rights of an individual are the crucial question of constitutionalism, this study focuses only on the analysis of the legal framework, which constitutes a minimum requirement for the rule of law, and should be able to offer adequate predictable rules of the game for industry and trade.

The first part of this chapter focuses on the separation of powers between the federal legislative, executive and judicial organs. The constitution of 1993 is presidential and emphasizes the executive power. However, the balance between the state organs has not yet been found. The Federal Constitutional Court has a significant judicial role in interpreting the unclear and disputed constitution.

The second part of this chapter aims at analyzing the development of federalism. Russian federalism has traditionally contained an inner conflict between official centralism and unofficial decentralism. If this conflict cannot be solved, economic growth is effectively blocked.

The third part of this chapter briefly focuses on the attempts to introduce another form of decentralization—local self-governance in Russia.

2.2 The Power Struggle on the Federal Level and the Constitution

2.2.1 Origins of the Russian Constitution

2.2.1.1 Background of the Power Struggle after the Collapse of the Soviet Union

The Russian Federation was born as the successor of the collapsed Soviet Union. The collapse was finalized with an agreement between the Presidents of Russia, Ukraine and Belorussia on 8 December 1991 (The Minsk Treaty). The Russian Socialist Federal Soviet Republic (RSFSR), a former part of the Soviet Union, continued its existence from 1 January 1992 as a new independent state called the Russian Federation and as the state successor of the Soviet Union responsible for the commitments of the Soviet Union. The Russian Federation carries on all the international treaties that were signed and ratified by the Soviet Union. This was one of the reasons why the United States demanded nuclear weapons to be moved from Ukraine and Kazakhstan to the territory of the Russian Federation. The other new states had to accede to international treaties and join international organizations.

There were several reasons for the collapse of the Soviet Union. The gradual reforms of the economy and the leading party, which Mikhail Gorbachev tried to push forward in a new political atmosphere of *glasnost* "openness", proved to be inadequate. When the Soviet citizens were finally allowed to criticize the state and the powerful Communist Party, the dams were broken and the prohibited nationalist feelings burst out. The total collapse of the economic system, which was based on pretended success, was suddenly visible to everybody.

The Union broke up even if the majority of the RSFSR had voted to retain the Union in March 1991. According to an opinion poll of 1994, 68% of the respondents thought that the Minsk Treaty was the wrong decision and only 16% were convinced that it was the right decision.[5] Furthermore, 76% of the respondents thought

---

[5] According to another more recent opinion survey in 1999, 31% of the respondents saw the collapse of the Soviet Union as inevitable. Still, a great

that the disintegration of the USSR worsened living standards (Rose and Haerpher, 1994:41). However, for Boris Eltsin who won the presidential elections of the Russian Republic in June 1991, the splitting up of the Union gave him the opportunity to start economic and political reforms in Russia. He also received the full support of the leaders of the Western market economies, who regarded him as the guarantor of transformation into democracy, a market economy and the rule of law. It was the proposed signing of the Union Treaty on 20 August that prompted the attempted putsch, and its failure gave Eltsin and the Russian authorities victory. In the flush of victory Eltsin even banned the Communist Party, which he himself had served for decades. The ban of the communist party, however, caused a lot of criticism and the Constitutional Court found it inconsistent with the constitution (see section 2.2.4.4).

The Russian Republic did not have its own "republican elite" like the other republics. Therefore, the USSR federal agencies became Russian institutions as did most of the ministries, too. The new federation inherited a large and cumbersome federal bureaucracy, of which the officials were accustomed to thinking in Union terms and obeying party orders. Republican elites in other Soviet republics were as authoritarian, but not as federal and center-oriented as the former USSR federal bureaucracy. Even if the governmental organs had earlier been only ceremonial or bureaucratic organs and the party, which had decided everything no longer existed, there was both institutional and organizational continuity. The re-modeling that occurred was the introduction of a presidency.[6] Under the old model,

---

majority (55%) of the respondents thought that the collapse of the Union should and could have been avoided. Almost half of the respondents of this survey (48%) also thought that the former Soviet republics are not capable of surviving and will be dependent on Russia also in the future (Kääriäinen and Furman, 2000b:66).

[6] Presidency was first introduced to the Soviet Union during Gorbachev's era. The president (chair of the Congress) was earlier a ceremonial figure, and the General Secretary of the Party led the country with the Politburo. Gorbachev was the first party leader who let himself be elected by the Congress as a president. Legal specialists proposed this change and Gorbachev hesitated because he thought that the Presidency did not belong to the Soviet conception (Kuznetsov, 1996).

Eltsin had worked as the chair of the Congress and its smaller Supreme Soviet, elected among the deputies, with a presidium of ministers and committee chairs to draft legislative proposals and to put them before the Soviet of Congress.

The new model separated the executive from the legislature. Since the executive was earlier officially submitted to the legislature, the separation of powers seeded a potential conflict between the legislature and the executive. In the new model, the president proposed leading ministers to the Congress, which could reject them as well as presidential legislative proposals. The president directed policy making but also the role of the Congress and its Supreme Soviet became much more significant. The deputies of the Congress, which had been elected with the Communist Party controlled elections, constituted the potential to oppose the reforms.

At the beginning of 1992, Eltsin authorized price reforms and started the privatization program with his decrees without collaborating with the Congress. This shock therapy soon started inflation, which cut the savings of the citizens. The people, who had wished that democracy would bring a better life, were disappointed. The enthusiasm for democracy and a market economy started to cool. The regions found themselves in a new situation, where the federation now controlled the resources of the former Union, and where the reformers talked about decentralization. Three important issues namely, (1) the direction of economic reforms, (2) the nature of the federation, and (3) the relationship between the president and the congress lead to a power struggle and finally a total clash at the federal center.

By December 1992, the congress started to challenge both the presidential powers and the reforms. President Eltsin had to sacrifice Prime Minister Egor Gaidar and dismiss him. The reforms, however, continued under Viktor Chernomyrdin, and so did the conflict between the president and congress. The chair of the Supreme Soviet, Ruslan Khasbulatov, whose career in Moscow was dependent on his post and whose own home region Chechnya was one of the most separatist republics, had no other possibility than to encourage the power jealousy of the deputies. Most of them had no party or any other organization to support them when their careers as deputies would be over. The deputies knew that in the new environment most of them might not have the chance to be re-elected.

It would, however, be unfair to label the aspirations of the deputies with pure power jealousy. There was a legal basis for the claims of the Supreme Soviet for a leading role since, according to the then existing constitution of 1977, the Congress was the most important state organ. Sovereignty of the parliament is one established form of democracy existing, for example, in England. The leading role of the Supreme Soviet in Russia is, however, understood to have the same meaning as in 1917 when all of the power was demanded to be given to the Soviets.

In April 1993, President Eltsin tried to solve the deadlock with a referendum in which he was given a clear majority of votes in support of his policy. Eltsin had already threatened the congress several times before with a referendum. He counted on his popularity and Russian willingness to support their leader when asked and not depend upon their personal opinions about the dispute. Results of an opinion survey made in June and July 1993 showed that the opinions of the citizens on the debated issue were quite dispersed. About 30% were in favor of a strong congress, which should have the power to stop the president taking actions that it objects. Another 30% were in favor of a strong presidency. The rest would have preferred some kind of checks and balances and no supremacy of any state organ (Rose *et al.*, 1993:38).

The Russian political elite showed its incompetence of reaching a compromise. The Supreme Soviet did not change its position. Nor did Eltsin try to find a compromise, but used his victory in the referendum to legitimize his "more democratic" standpoint. A new constitution was needed, but the drafting process did not make any progress. The president had set his drafting committee, while the Supreme Soviet worked with its own competing draft. Such round-table discussions as the post-communist Central European countries organized to draw the whole population, including the opposition of the former communist rulers, to take part in the decisive historical turning point of values, morals and philosophy would not have been possible in the bitter power struggle circumstances in Russia.

Eltsin broke the deadlock by dissolving parliament in September 1993. Whether the president had the right to dissolve parliament is still a disputed issue among Russian lawyers (see section 2.2.4.4). However, from a purely legal point of view dissolving the organ, which according to the constitution was the sovereign, was actually a presidential *coup d'état*, which lead to an armed conflict. Some of the deputies refused to leave their posts and found armed forces to defend them. There was a hectic struggle behind the curtains for the support of the army. Eltsin even won this struggle and the armed forces stormed the parliament building, the so-called White House in October 1993.

Compared to the developments in post-communist Central European countries, such as Poland, Hungary and Czechoslovakia, there are differences in both the values and means of introducing democracy. In those countries, the people saw change as a return to their earlier European values (Skapska, 1999a). Multiethnic Russia, which had been unified with the help of superpower mentality, had lost Eastern Europe, the Union and, as the Russians soon found out, also its significant international position. Instead, it had gained only an unstable economy and a shaky "democratic" governmental structure with a hectic power struggle. The Russians are clearly aware of their genuine cultural character. Opinion polls show that a great majority of Russians (78%) in the poll prefer to develop Russia according to their own traditions. Only 22% of the respondents answered that Russia should rather be developed according to Western European traditions (Rose and Haerpher, 1994:23).

Another significant difference between Russia and the above-mentioned post-communist Central European countries is that in the latter a non-communist opposition already existed, while the power struggle in Russia occurred between former communists who seem to be people drawn to politics to get economic and social benefits from the party.[7] The unwillingness of the communist bureaucracy to refrain from power and the fear of losing both the earlier benefits and the fruits of privatization caused other even more violent struggles in such former Soviet republics, where the nationalist

---

[7] However, according to Skapska in Poland the historical moment to create a constitution as a new social contract was lost. The post-communists, who won the next elections because of their heavy criticism of the results of the shock therapy of the government formed by the coalition of Solidarnost and the new conservative, took over the constitutional process leaving the opposition out of the drafting process (Skapska, 1999b). Communist uncompromising and authoritarian mentality in dealing with politics does not change easily.

movement managed to get into power. *Coups* and civil wars in Georgia, Azerbaijan and Tajikistan are typical examples of the authoritarian mentality of the *nomenklatura* and unwillingness to accept other fractions in power. Only the Baltic States are an exception; the former communist leaders accepted to wait for the next elections. Roeder (1994), in his article analyzing authoritarian and oligarchic tendencies in post-soviet states, claims that the Soviet bureaucracy preferred an autocratic leader to keep its own position secured. This is most certainly a significant factor hindering development towards democracy, a market economy and the rule of law.

Authoritarian rule is typical in all post-soviet states. In Russia, President Eltsin was determined to push the reforms ahead to make it impossible to return to communism. The principles of democracy were forgotten in the power struggle. Similar situations are well known from Latin America where democracy has been sacrificed for economic reforms. Latin American experiences also show that democracy has been even more difficult to develop after its rude rejection. It is often claimed that economic reforms will slow down or stop if they are not pushed ahead determinedly or even dictatorially. In democratic circumstances shock therapy is definitely going to face resistance (Elster, 1993). President Eltsin, however, chose a pretended democracy and authoritarian leadership instead of either an open dictatorship or democracy.

In the Russian environment, Eltsin's choice may not have been a conscious choice between different alternatives but a result of path-dependent development. Authoritarianism is a tradition in Russia and the Soviet Union. The attitude to state power is totally different from Western approaches. The ultimate power center of the state always has the last word. The citizens are obedient subordinates who can complain but cannot challenge the state power. While in the United States constitutionalism is regarded as limitations of the state power, the state in the Soviet Union existed to take care of the needs of the obedient citizens. Berman (1983) shows, in his study on the formation of the Western legal tradition, that the rivalry between the church and the states developed a new type of citizenship in Western culture, where citizens could challenge the power. The development, which started from what Berman calls the Gregorian Revolution, gradually developed into the rule of law and democracy. Leaning on Max Weber's famous "Die protestantische Ethik und der 'Geist' des Kapitalismus" from 1904/05, he also claims that the Protestant revolution in the 16th century shifted the development into a more individualist trail allowing liberalism and capitalism to grow.

In Russian Orthodox Christian tradition, only one absolute power center existed, which did not allow its subordinates to challenge the earthly power, which also represented God on earth. Stalin was able to use this mentality of the people and threaten them with terror. Intellectuals, who had or could have had differing opinions, were made examples of what happens when one might want to challenge the power. The memory of the terror still makes people fear that it may repeat itself. President Eltsin, on the other hand, was supposed to be a good tsar, who puts things in order. When he withdrew from power asking the people "to forgive his failure", the same hopes were vested in Vladimir Putin.

2.2.1.2 *"Eltsin's" Constitution—Legacy of Authoritarian Rule*

Elections for a new Federal Assembly were announced for December 1993 and a new presidential constitution was drawn up.[8] The reformers, however, lost the elections and failed to win a majority in the new parliament. The peace between the executive and legislative was an uneasy one. As a result of the fight, the executive rule strengthened. The result of the elections shows that not only the economic reforms had disappointed the people but also that the bloodshed at the White House had been a deep disappointment to many Russians. "Democracy" had brought them bloodshed and economic difficulties. The president, who had resorted to arms, was the same man who had become a hero of the unarmed resistance against the putsch in August 1991.

The constitution, which had been drafted under the presidential administration, was accepted in a referendum on 12 December 1993. The citizens were asked whether or not they accepted the

---

[8] The first commentary on the constitution, which was written by the specialists who drafted it, explains that the draft was chosen because it was more "juridical" than its competitors (Konstitutsiya..., 1994).

constitution. Textbooks of constitutional law explain that the referendum was considered to be the most democratic way to accept the constitution (Shulzhenko, 1995). The reason for using a referendum was, however, that President Eltsin could not push his constitution through in the Supreme Soviet in a parliamentary procedure. The text of the constitution was officially published only on 9 November 1993. The citizens had a whole month to become acquainted with the constitution. There was no time for wide democratic discussions. The constitution was introduced with an attack, leaving the citizens only an opportunity to vote either for or against President Eltsin. In such situations, Russians tend to support their leader. Knowing that elections and referendums in the Soviet Union was simply a ritual to legitimize already made decisions and that in elections the citizens were supposed to show loyalty to the state power, the results of the referendum turned out to be even worse for President Eltsin.[9] Almost half of the voters did not bother to go to the polls and almost half of those who did, voted against the president. The result of the referendum also reflected the dispute between Eltsin and regional leaders. People in the provinces, especially those with non-Russian majority, tend to rely on their regional leader.

According to the Presidential Decree on Referendum (N. 1633) of 15 October 1993, the constitution had to be supported by more than half of the voters. The Central Election Committee announced that 56.63% of those entitled to vote participated in the referendum and that 58.6% of them voted in favor of the constitution. From these figures, Eltsin's critics calculated that only about one fourth of the voters actually accepted the constitution.[10] It is not difficult to agree that in spite of the formally democratic way to introduce the constitution—a referendum—the legitimacy of it is rather low. It hardly received the needed support from the citizens, who could not have been well informed about the contents of the basic legal

---

[9] The results of the elections can also be interpreted that when people were no longer compelled to go to the polls, they did not bother to do so.

[10] Anatolii Lukyanov, chair of the Duma Committee of Legislation and Court Reform, even suggested that the referendum did not fulfill the requirements of the law on elections and that there were "millions of extra votes included" (Lukyanov, 1999).

document that they were asked to support. Besides, they were unsure whether a constitution matters at all. According to an opinion survey half a year after the elections, 57% of the respondents did not believe that the constitution would ensure a lawful and democratic state and only 17% thought that it would. 79% of the respondents who did not vote in the referendum explained that the primary reason was that it would not make any difference. 56% of those who did not vote admitted that they did not understand what it was all about (Rose *et al.*, 1993:38–39, 46).

The referendum formally legalized the constitution. Since the citizens were only formally drawn into the process, the constitution cannot be called a "Social Contract" of the new society, unless it is accepted that a social contract can be forced upon the citizens. However, the idea of a social contract itself as with the other ideals of Enlightenment, which constitute the foundation of existing European and North American constitutions, were neither born in a democratic process nor without bloodshed. Introducing "Eltsin's constitution" reflects traditional Russian understanding of the citizens as obedient subordinates. The omnipotent state changed the basic document containing the division of state powers and the aspirations of the state to take care of its citizens. The citizens could participate in the process by casting their vote for the new basic document.

Drafting a constitution in such a short time is a remarkable achievement by Russian constitutional specialists. However, such a constitution does not necessarily reflect the widely shared values of the population or an agreement of the political elite on the division of political power and economic resources in the huge multicultural and multiethnic state. It is a typical constitution of a young and still shaky democracy with a fierce power struggle. Political power was more important than legality, but this fact has not been openly admitted. Rather, it has been disguised in a pretended rule of law and pretended democracy. The word democracy suffered a serious inflation in the power struggle between the legislature and the executive. Democracy is understood cynically as a slogan covering autocratic rule.

2.2.2 Powers of the President

2.2.2.1 *Strong Presidential Power*

Legislative power in the Russian Federation belongs mainly to the Federal Assembly, which has two chambers: the Federal Council and the State Duma. The president is the head of the executive power but also has important legislative and nomination powers. The government works under the president and is responsible both to him and the State Duma. The President can dismiss the Government, but he can also dissolve the State Duma when he disagrees with its lack of confidence in the government. The modern judicial control, which is typical in Central and Eastern European countries in transition, also exists in Russia. The Constitutional Court is the judicial organ, which can resolve disputes between federal state organs as well as federal and regional organs and consider the consistency of legal norms with the constitution. The court also examines the constitutionality of laws in a concrete case upon the request of individual citizens.

The presidential nature of the Russian constitution is clearly a result of the power struggle, which the president won. Strong presidential power seems to be quite typical for young and unstable democracies. Carl Schmitt favored strong presidency for the Weimar Republic because he saw that in exceptional circumstances there has to be one person who can act quickly to defend the fundamental rights of the nation (Dyzenhaus, 1997:70). The Weimar Republic had a strong presidency but President Hindenburg was too weak to defend the weak democracy against an even stronger aspirant to power. Perhaps transition to democracy does not only need a strong leader but also enough democrats? In Russia, there is a huge bureaucracy willing to support authoritarian rule, for which democracy may constitute a threat.

In France, de Gaulle supported similar ideas of strong leadership to pilot the country through difficulties. In Latin America, strong presidency is also typical causing heavy power struggles for the presidency. The disadvantage of a strong presidency is that it is very much dependent on the personality of the president. A power-seeking president may start to act in a dictatorial way. Critics of a strong presidency referred to foreign examples and saw that a strong presidency tends to hinder parliamentarism to develop (Kulyabin,

1992). As a compromise, the presidential term was limited to two four-year terms to prevent the president acting in a dictatorial way (Konstitutsiya..., 1994). A strong presidency also seems to be a system, which is difficult to abolish.[11] Authoritarian rule is quite persistent to changes.

A strong presidency itself is a new phenomenon in Russia (see section 2.2.1.1). Strong leadership, however, is not new in Russia. Eltsin actually continued the style of party secretaries and those of the tsars before them. The need for a strong authoritarian leader is an established tradition and something that people start to long for when they are lost and need someone to make decisions for them. Opinion surveys, however, show that the Russians do not necessarily trust a strong presidency. In 1996, only 4% of the respondents accepted that the president was ruling by decrees without any parliamentarian veto, 44% accepted the rule by decree but with parliamentarian veto, 31% rejected the rule by decree and approved parliament overruling the president, and 21% rejected either unilateral power ruling by decree or vetoing. In the same poll, 65% of those questioned were in favor of some kind of checks and balances (Rose, 1996). Compared to the survey of 1993, it seems that the disappointment in President Eltsin showed increasing distrust in a strong presidency. Those who preferred a strong parliament remained about the same, but those who trusted a strong presidency earlier seemed to have been disappointed (cf., Rose *et al.*, 1993). Rose (1996), however, interprets the results that they do not necessarily prove that a strong presidency itself is rejected or that the people would consider some other alternative. The trust in President Putin before the presidential elections, without knowing anything about his political or economic program, shows that people are ready to put their trust in a new Savior with the likely result of being disappointed again.

---

[11] In Finland, where a strong presidency was established as a result of the civil war in 1918, it was abolished only with the new constitution of 2000. One reason for the long survival of the strong presidency was the threatening foreign political situation, which was explained to require a strong leader above the political parties. In fact, this expression meant that democracy could not always have been taken into account.

2.2.2.2 Presidential Elections

The president is elected for four years (article 81 of the constitution). The candidates must be at least 35 years old and have had a permanent residence in Russia during the last 10 years. The elections are general, direct and free. If there are more than two candidates and no one receives a majority of the votes, a second election must be held between the two candidates who received the most votes. According to the constitution, the same person cannot be elected for more than two terms. Limiting the presidential term was considered to be important because the Russian president has so much power that unlimited terms could make him a lifelong "dictator" (Konstitutsiya..., 1994).

A new and extremely detailed act on presidential elections was passed on 31 December 1999 (No. 228). It regulates, in a detailed manner, the pre-election campaign and rules for sponsoring the candidates. Sponsorship and advertising by state or municipal officials, army officials, and other than Russian citizens or organizations are forbidden. The act also forbids any propaganda against the unity of the federation, the constitutional structure (!) or containing social, racial or nationalist hatred or any other misuse of publicity (article 53).

The background for these rules is President Eltsin's rallying for the second round and defamation of his competitors. The *oligarchs* whose wealth stems from dubious privatization and who found it appropriate to threaten people with a return to communism sponsored the campaign. The present rules for campaigning are such that anything negative said about the competitors may, in principle, cause a lawsuit. The new rules actually improve the possibilities of a sitting president who receives free publicity because of his official tasks. He already has the advantage of his existing power.[12]

---

[12] The then Acting President Putin's popularity, on the other hand, was based on the Chechen War, which was carried on with the help of a propaganda campaign against an ethnic group—the Chechens. Furthermore, President Putin's decision not to publish his program before the elections thereby preventing it from being "torn apart" in the campaign reflects the Kremlin's leadership strategy of counting on the people's readiness to support a leader simply because he is the leader. Tsar Boris chose a successor who is hopefully going to be a "good tsar".

2.2.2.3   *The President and the Government*

According to article 83 of the constitution, the president appoints the head of the government with the consent of the State Duma. The president chooses a candidate and presents him to the Duma, who can either accept or refuse him within one week. If the Duma does not accept the candidate, the president must make another proposition. If the Duma disapproves of the candidate three times, the president can order new parliamentary elections (article 111). This system enables a fast nomination of the prime minister. The threat of premature elections is a strong weapon in making the Duma agree with the president. The first commentary of the constitution explains that this provision is to make sure that the parliament and the president agree on the candidate (Konstitutsiya…, 1994:483).

In 1998, President Eltsin used the possibility of threatening to have new elections in order to force the Duma to accept his candidate. When he chose Kirienko and the Duma disapproved, he proposed the same candidate two more times. Twice the Duma disapproved, but finally approved so as to avoid new elections. Refusing to change his candidate after the disapproval of the Duma is quite an interesting interpretation of article 111 from President Eltsin. It is not mentioned in the constitution that it should be a different person each time. President Eltsin's interpretation, which has become the leading interpretation, however, contradicts the original idea of the drafters of finding a compromise.

The president also appoints the ministers upon the proposal of the chairman of the government. There is no such practice that the government should represent the majority of the parliament. In fact, it seems that it is personal relations that count most. This is possible because the party system is still so weak in Russia. The ministers do not represent their party in the first place, but the president. The prime minister is a humble assistant to the president. According to article 83, the president can also preside at sessions of the government as well as overrule government decrees. President Eltsin very often used these powers, too.

President Eltsin also used to dismiss and appoint ministers according to his own wishes. According to the constitution, the president is entitled to dismiss the government even in the absence of a lack of confidence from the Federal Assembly. President Eltsin used this power in 1998 when he dismissed Chernomyrdin's government. Also, the Duma has the parliamentary right to dismiss the government by giving its lack of confidence. However, in such situations, the president has the right to dismiss the Duma if he disagrees with its lack of confidence. Such provision reduces parliamentarism to a minimum and the role of the government to a tool of the president.

2.2.2.4 The President and Legislative Power

The president also has a lot of power in the legislative process. Firstly, he has the initiative right for federal acts to the Federal Assembly (article 104). The initiative right is widely spread in Russia. It is also given to the Council of the Federation or its representative, the State Duma or its deputy, the government, as well as similar organs of the subjects of the federation.[13] Also, the Supreme Court, the Supreme Arbitration Court and the Constitutional Court have the same initiative right. Even if the initiative for laws is widely spread, the president has the best resources for drafting them. The presidential administration has been active in initiating laws, which have been better drafted than those of many other initiators. The widely spread initiative right produces drafts of various quality as well as drafts that sometimes compete with each other.

Before any act passed by the Federal Assembly comes into effect, the president has to sign and confirm it (article 107). If he refuses to sign the act within 14 days, the draft law has to be sent back to the Federal Assembly. The Federal Assembly can break the veto of the president by accepting the draft with a qualified majority of two-thirds of the votes in both chambers. In such circumstances, the president has to sign the act within seven days. A refusal to sign under these circumstances on the ground of irregularities in the voting has been held as unconstitutional by the Constitutional Court in April 1998 (6 April, No. 11, P).

---

[13] The common concept for the republics, regions, territories, cities and areas is "subject of the federation" see section 2.3.1.3.1.

President Eltsin used his veto rights often, but the Federal Assembly was seldom able to break his veto. This was due to the absence of political consensus in the State Duma.[14] While President Eltsin had to struggle with the Duma, which often had different ideas about legislation, President Putin managed to pave the way for a strong and quite undisputed presidency mainly by creating a new party "Unity", the only program of which is to support the sitting government.[15]

The most important of the president's legislative powers has obviously, in practice, been the power to give decrees (*ukaz*) and regulations (*rasporyazhenie*) (article 90). Usually decrees are used for the most important enactments and regulations for individual administrative matters. In the hierarchy of norms, presidential decrees are under the federal laws (*zakon*). Above the laws there is the constitution, which laws and other norms are not supposed to contradict. In the hierarchy of norms, presidential decrees supplement federal laws with more detailed rules that, however, should not contradict the law above.

Under presidential decrees there are governmental decrees (*postanovlenie*) and regulations (*rasporyazhenie*). As a rule, decrees are normative and regulations treat routine administrative matters. The president has the power to repeal governmental decrees if he finds them contradicting the constitution, federal laws or presidential decrees. Ministries, state committees and other departments issue decrees, instructions and regulations, which are not a matter of constitutional regulation. Ministers can issue orders (*prikaz*) and instructions (*instruktsiya*). Earlier, such administrative regulations were important but nowadays the large number of more detailed

---

[14] In the Duma, elected in 1995, the presidential veto was a powerful weapon because of the absence of political consensus in the State Duma. The Communists and the Liberal Democrats would have had a qualified majority had they only been able to agree on breaking the president's veto. Those parties, however, detest each other and were, therefore, unable to resist the president.

[15] In the elections of the State Duma in 1999, the "Kremlin Party" won 77 seats, which made it the second largest party after the Communists, who received 113 seats. A great number of independent deputies (100) gave more influence to the power party "Unity".

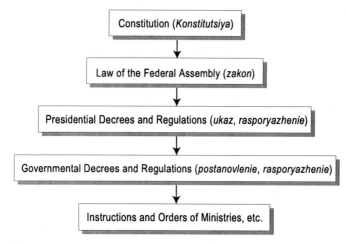

Diagram 2.1: *Hierarchy of Federal Norms.*

parliamentary laws and presidential decrees has diminished their importance.

Presidential decrees have gained an extraordinary status in Russia because there are gaps in legislation. In many important fields of jurisdiction, there is no legislation or the legislation stems from the Soviet period. In such cases, the country has been governed by the decrees of the president. Such a decree is supposed to be intermediary until the law of the Federal Assembly has been passed. The Constitutional Court has accepted this practice due to gaps in legal norms (30 April 1996, No. 11, P). Eltsin was, however, often accused of misusing his power by refusing to sign the new law prepared by the parliament only to continue the lifetime of his decrees.[16] The privatization of state enterprises was governed by presidential decrees even though a law existed.

President Eltsin even widened the presidential veto with his own interpretation of the constitution. Citing article 80 in part two

---

[16] Of the 897 laws passed by the Duma over the period 1994–1997, 262 (25.9%) were vetoed at least once by the Council of the Federation and 263 (29.3%) were vetoed at least once by the president. Furthermore, the Council of the Federation vetoed 30 bills more than once and the president exercised multiple vetoes 23 times (Remington, *et al.*, 1998:301).

of the constitution, which describes the president as the guarantor of the constitution, he took the right to return without signature any piece of legislation that he believed to be unconstitutional or if "procedural violations" were committed in its passage. In practice, the president can return any bill he does not like and can therefore block legislation even without having to use the official veto right. The constitutional court has denied only the use of such unofficial veto in such cases where the Federal Assembly has broken the veto of the president.

Presidential decrees also enter an astonishingly wide range of subjects. There is, for instance, a decree on the legal system presenting the division of different branches of the law, an issue that would belong to jurisprudence in most countries. The president signs his decrees independently without the consent of the government or the corresponding minister. The drafters of presidential decrees work for the presidential administration and are appointed by him.

On the other hand, President Eltsin also used his veto right several times quite wisely in acting as the guarantor of human rights (article 80.2). The Law on the Freedom of Religion is one good example. This law was corrected to a more equal form after Eltsin's veto. The first law, which Eltsin refused to sign, favored the Orthodox Church so much that representatives of other churches regarded it as unequal and violating the principle of the constitution that Russia is a secular state, which does not favor any particular religion. Another example of a law that Eltsin vetoed on the basis of violating human rights is one that would have forced every foreigner entering the Russian Federation to take an "aids test".

2.2.2.5 Nomination Power and Other Important Powers of the President

The president also has the power to nominate the candidates for the Constitutional Court, the Supreme Court, and the Supreme Arbitration Court of the Federation (article 83, e). It is the Council of the Federation that appoints this high judiciary. The same goes with the Procurator General (see section 2.2.4.3). According to the constitution the president appoints all the other judges of federal courts. To ensure the separation of executive and judicial powers, a collegium of judges approves the candidates before the appointment of the president. Such nomination power is not regarded as supremacy of executive power over the judicial one but reflects the idea of the president functioning above the whole political system.

In practice, the Federal Assembly has rejected the candidates nominated by the president several times. Eltsin also used his power to propose dismissals of high judiciary. Dismissing the Procurator General Yurii Skuratov in January 1999, who was too eager to investigate financial transfers of the family members of the president and those of his assistants to Swiss banks, caused a scandal. The official reason for dismissal was exceeding his authority, which was seasoned with a secretly shot sex video of Mr. Skuratov with prostitutes that was broadcasted on national television news. With the video, the Kremlin suggested that the Procurator General may also have connections with the organized crime and was not more reliable than those whom he investigated. The Council of the Federation did not agree with Eltsin. In December 1999, the Constitutional Court, however, approved that the president had the right to suspend the Procurator General during the investigations of potentially exceeding his authority even without the consent of the Council of the Federation (1 December 1999, No. 17, P).

The president also appoints the Security Committee (article 83, g). This organ, lead by the president, became very important during the Chechen War. The Security Committee made all the important decisions concerning the war without the consent of parliament. Such an arrangement means, in practice, that the president can direct military operations within Russian territory against the Russian population when he considers that the unity of Russia is threatened. According to the constitution, the president has the power to introduce an extraordinary situation in the Russian Federation or in a particular locality, but he must immediately notify the Council of the Federation and the State Duma. The Chechen War was, however, started in 1994 on the basis of secret Presidential Decrees without introducing an extraordinary situation and without notifying parliament. The Constitutional Court found Eltsin's decrees not contradicting the constitution because he acted to defend the unity of Russia. The decision of the court was not unanimous and the dissenting opinions show that the judges have a high respect for the rule of law. The majority of them, however, seemed to have been more concerned in maintaining the legacy of the executive than opening the dangerous discussion on the limits of power and the rights to challenge power when the unity of the federation is at stake (see section 2.3.1.3.4).

The president also nominates his own administration (article 83, i, j). He governs a huge bureaucratic administration with a lot more personnel than the parliamentary administration. This administration prepares drafts for laws and presidential decrees. Also the coordination and supervision of the executive power of the subjects of the federation is located in the presidential administration. Such a huge administration guarantees the president good resources to lead the country. The presidential administration has gradually developed into a super agency governing the whole executive power in the federation and in its subjects.

As the head of state, the president represents Russia in international relations and directs its foreign policy (article 80.4). The president conducts negotiations with foreign states and signs international treaties, instruments of ratification, etc. (article 86). He is also the Supreme Commander-in-Chief of the Armed Forces of the Federation (article 87.1). The president confirms the Basic Provisions of the Military Doctrine (article 83, h). He also appoints and dismisses the high command of the Armed Forces (article 83, k). The president has the right to declare a military situation, which he must immediately inform the State Duma and the Council of the Federation about (article 87.2). However, he does not have the right to declare war.

2.2.2.6 *The Future of a Strong Presidency*

At the end of 1997 there was a discussion on constitutional reform.[17] One of the most important reforms considered was to diminish the power of the president and strengthen the role of parliament. There was even a draft for changing the constitution in the Duma in 1998,

---

[17] V.L. Sheinis, a deputy in the Duma, launched the discussion (Sheinis, 1997). A lot of specialists in constitutional law took part in the discussion. Finally, even some specialists, who worked in the presidential administration, recommended drafting a completely new constitution (Satarov and Krasnov, 1999).

but the Duma rejected it.[18] There are a lot of legal specialists who consider that such strong powers of the president leave almost no room to develop parliamentarian democracy in Russia.[19] The arguments that were expressed against a strong presidency before introducing the constitution of 1993 have proved their value. A strong presidency was then already argued to lead to half-democracy and authoritarianism (Kulyabin, 1992). Authoritarian rule, once established, is not likely to easily change into a balanced democracy. There is a huge presidential administration backing authoritarian leadership and the gains of a strong presidency.

President Eltsin interpreted his powers quite widely and even exceeded them when he felt that he had a good reason. His wide interpretations of the constitution also paved the way for a strong presidency in the future. Russians seem to complain about authoritarian mentality, at least when the president is not able to solve the economic and social problems of Russia. Complaints about President Eltsin's rule by decrees did not, however, prevent Acting President Putin from succeeding by using the image of a strong president.[20]

In other post-communist European countries, reforms and their results have lead to changes of government. In Russia, President Eltsin dismissed and appointed one government after another but directed the policy himself. Even if economic reforms have been lead by a strong president, in spite of the resistance of the Federal Assembly, economic policy has not been steady and firm. President

---

[18] After President Eltsin's resignation, new parliamentary and presidential elections, there is still a draft on constitutional reforms. During his election campaign, President Putin took part in the discussion suggesting that the presidential term should be extended to six years. President Putin's success in the elections created a new political environment, where the president's opinion on his powers is a crucial factor in the direction the potential constitutional reform should take.

[19] Nersesyants (1999:380–382) put this opinion by clearly stating that the excessive powers of the president make the separation of powers asymmetric and unbalanced and is the main weakness of the Russian constitution.

[20] A typical Russian phenomenon was that Putin's image and power encouraged ordinary people to turn to his election campaign office with their own personal social problems.

Eltsin chose to try to keep his own popularity at the cost of changing governments and a jumpy economic policy. Even if his leadership was autocratic, he was not immune to the opinions of the people. Opinion surveys show that the Russians largely blamed President Eltsin, the government and the presidential administration for the economic problems. Only the mafia (whatever the respondents may have understood by mafia) scored even "better" in being responsible for the economic problems (Rose, 1996:12–13). However, in spite of all the complaining, the people eagerly elected the same corrupt Kremlin power clique to stay in power even in the absence of any economic program.

Even if presidential powers were to be diminished, changing the constitution is very difficult. It would require no less than a three-quarter majority of the total number of the members of the Council of the Federation and no less than two-thirds of the total number of deputies of the State Duma and, of course, the signature of the president within 14 days (article 108). In addition, a change of constitution does not come into force before the two-thirds of the legislative organs of the subjects of the federation have approved the change (article 136). Changing the constitution was deliberately made difficult to prevent constant changes in the constitution, which the earlier Supreme Soviet had made with a two-third majority, and to also secure authoritarian presidential power in the future. It is not likely that presidential powers will be diminished during President Putin's regime against his will. Besides, a strong presidency has become popular among the Russian people and the president has even strengthened his power. However, because the constitution is so difficult to change, President Putin has had to use other than constitutional means to strengthen his power.

2.2.3 A Parliament without Parliamentarism

2.2.3.1 *Structure of the Federal Assembly*

According to the constitution, the two chambers of the Federal Assembly are equal but have different powers. In enacting legislation the State Duma is, in practice, more important since the process starts there.

The model for the structure of the Council of the Federation has obviously been the United States Senate. In the Russian press the Council of the Federation is often called the Senate and its members senators. The members, two from each subject of the federation, represent the interests of the regions. According to the constitution, one of the members representing the subject comes from the legislative and the other from the executive body of the State Authority (article 94). The constitution does not regulate how the members are chosen. The members were elected for the first Council of the Federation under the new constitution. Even then, 67% were officials of regional and local governments. Their term was, however, only two years. In June 1995, a new law made the Council of the Federation a permanent organ, the members of which are the head of the legislative organs and the heads of the executive organs from each of the subjects. This means that there are no general elections and changes of individual members occurring every year. However, the Council cannot be dissolved. It is, in principle, always in session but in practice the heads of the subjects of the federation are busy with leading their own regions. The rise in the status of the Council made it less effective in the legislative process. The new law also increased the power of the president. By 1995, the president had done a lot to make governors loyal to him in each corner of the federation (see sections 2.3.1.2 and 2.5).

The State Duma consists of 450 deputies and is elected every four years. The elections are held on the basis of the federal law on the Elections of Deputies of the State Duma of 2 June 1999 that was passed to replace the previous law of 21 June 1995, which had been in force for only four years. Half of the deputies (225) are elected according to the majority rule from one-man constituencies. The other half (225) is elected according to proportional vote. This compromise between two electoral systems was already created with the electoral law of 1995.

The new electoral law regulates detailing the registration of candidates, the duties and contents of the electoral committee, rules for financing the campaign, and advertising on television, in a similar way as the presidential electoral law (see section 2.2.2.2). According to Russian lawyers a detailed law should establish clear rules.[21] However, detailed regulation does not necessarily lead to the rule of law. In the last elections in 1999, the election committee applied strict rules of sponsorship and the obligation to inform about all sources of income to arbitrarily drop some candidates from the list, but did not apply the rules to every candidate in the same way. In this way, the election committee managed to drop a lot of Zhirinovskii's liberal democratic candidates from the lists with the help of obscurities in formalities.

Financially, the Federal Assembly is autonomous, determining its own expenses in the state budget. It also determines its own internal structure and procedures being guided only by the constitution itself. In practice, the chambers sit separately, in different buildings in Moscow and also have their own support personnel. The reason for the sharp separation is that the chambers should work autonomously (Parlamentskoe..., 1999) and not be able to unite to challenge the president.

The constitution requires that both chambers form committees and commissions to prepare and give advance consideration to draft laws and hold hearings. There are a lot of committees and commissions and each member or deputy must serve on at least one committee.[22] The State Duma elects the chairmen of the committees and commissions. In the Council, the election is done at a session of the committee. If the contents of the government do not have to reflect the result of the elections of the Duma, the distribution of the chairmanship of the committees and commissions do not either. The election of the chairman and the chairs of the commissions and committees caused a scandal in the Duma, which started its work in 2000. President Putin's party,[23] Unity (Bears), allied with the communists and elected communist Gennadii Seleznyov the chairman, shared the chairs among themselves and left the others almost without anything (Russia Today, 2000a,b). Specialists of constitutional law have, however, suggested that the memberships

---

[21] Matejkovich's (1998) opinion is expressed in the context of regulating the parliamentary and governor's elections of the subjects of the federation.
[22] A complete list of parliamentary committees and commissions can be found in Parlamentskoe... (1999:49).
[23] The party leader is Mr. Sergei Shoigu.

and chairs of committees and commissions should be delivered according to the principle of proportional representation of each party, arguing that in other countries such a rule exists even without any legal regulation (Gorobets, 1998:34). Russian politics, however, does not cultivate skills of cooperation and compromise. It even seems that harsh authoritarian crushing of enemies is regarded as successful leadership in Russian underdeveloped political culture.

2.2.3.2 The Legislative Process

In principle, the Federal Assembly is independent in enacting legislation. However, the powers of the Federal Assembly are not unlimited. Some laws can be adopted by referendum, bypassing parliament, and during a military or extraordinary situation laws may be suspended. The Constitutional Court may declare laws of the parliament unconstitutional. International treaties may take precedence over laws. The president has a veto right to laws, which a two-third majority of both chambers can break. There are also certain laws on finances, which may be enacted only when government has submitted an opinion regarding them.

The legislative process of the Russian federation may be divided into eight major stages (1–8). Legislative initiative (1) is rather widely spread. However, all draft laws must originate in the State Duma, including those initiated by the Council of the Federation. Draft laws are registrated and supervised by the State Duma.

Excluding the law on the budget, laws undergo three readings in the State Duma (2). The basic provisions of the draft law are discussed during the first reading. The Duma may adopt the law at the first reading and establish a time for the second reading, reject the law, or in principle even adopt it as final at the first reading. Amendments to the first draft are sent to the committee responsible for the draft. The revised draft is then submitted to the Duma for the second reading accompanied by the tables of rejected and supported amendments. The version adopted at the second reading is then sent to the committee, which edits the draft to eliminate internal contradictions and correct style. After this task is completed the draft is sent again to the Council of the State Duma within seven days for inclusion in the agenda. After the third reading the draft cannot be

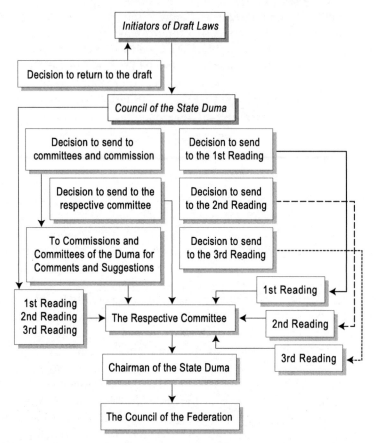

Diagram 2.2: *Legislative Process in the State Duma.* Source: *Parlamentskoe…, 1999:106.*

returned for further amendments or discussion as a whole. A majority of votes is required to adopt a federal law and a two-third majority for a federal constitutional law.[24] A constitutional law is one that touches the constitutional rights and duties of the citizens.

---

[24] A constitutional law concerns a question that has not been taken into account in the constitution and is a law, which would require changes or amendments to the constitution (Krestyaninov, 1995). Such a law requires a two-third majority in the State Duma and a three-quarter majority in the Council of the Federation (article 108).

After being adopted at the third reading, the draft is sent to the Council of the Federation (3) within five days (article 105 (3)). If the law involves expenditures to be covered from the federal budget, the draft law has to include the opinion of the government.

According to article 105 (4) of the constitution, the Council of the Federation must consider federal laws within a 14-day period. According to article 106, federal laws relating to the federal budget, federal taxes and charges, financial, currency, credit, and customs regulation, monetary emission, ratification and denunciation of international treaties, the status and defense of the state boundary of Russia, and war and peace have to be considered by the Federal Council. Other federal laws, which the Council has not considered within the 14-day period, are sent to the president for signature and promulgation. In practice, this period has been impossible to comply with. The Constitutional Court interpreted the constitution in March 1995 (23 March, No. 1, P) considering that the 14-day period refers only to the commencement of consideration by the Council of the Federation. It is not required that consideration be completed within that period. There have been plans to change the constitution to extend the period. Especially after the law of 1995 that made the heads of the subjects of the federation permanent members of the Council of the Federation, the short consideration period in practice diminishes the power of the Council.

A law rejected by the Council of the Federation is sent to a conciliation commission, which is formed from representatives of each chamber (4). The commission considers only those provisions of the law, which were the subject of disagreement and seeks to work out agreed provisions in the form of a unified text.

The decrees adopted by the conciliation commission are sent to the State Duma within five days (5). Only proposals contained in the protocol of the conciliation commission are discussed in the Duma. No amendments going beyond those proposals are considered.

The State Duma votes upon each proposal of the commission individually and each must obtain the majority of the total number of deputies of the chamber. The law adopted in the version of the conciliation commission is then sent to the Council of the Federation.

If the Council of the Federation rejects the law at the second consideration, or the State Duma did not accept the proposals of the conciliation commission and disagreed with the decision of the Council of the Federation to reject the law, the law is put to a vote in the State Duma in its original form before the conciliation procedures. If no less than two-thirds of the deputies vote in favor of the law, it is considered adopted and sent within five days to the president for signature.

If a law is considered and does not receive the required majority, the rejection is formalized by a decree of the Council of the Federation. This decree contains a list of provisions, which the council considers should be discussed with the State Duma or by a conciliation commission between the two chambers. It is sent to the Duma within five days. If the Duma adopts the law a second time, taking into account all of the proposals of the Council of the Federation, it is returned to the respective committee of the Council which confirms acceptance of the proposals and recommends

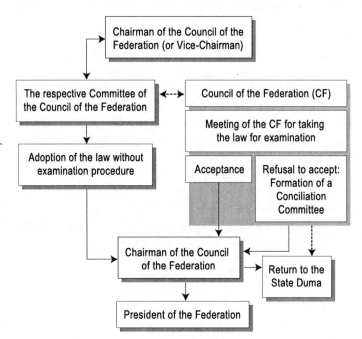

Diagram 2.3: *Legislative Process in the Council of the Federation.*
(Source: Parlamentskoe..., 1999:114).

approval of the law without further plenary discussion. If the Duma accepts only some of the proposals, the law is reconsidered as though it were an entirely newly adopted text.

Under the constitution if the president of the Russian Federation rejects a federal law within 14 days of receiving it for signature, the State Duma gives a second consideration to the law (6) within ten days. The Duma can either approve the law in the version proposed by the president with a simple majority or overrule the veto with a two-third majority.

Overriding the presidential veto has to be considered also in the Council of the Federation where it requires also a two-third majority of the members (7). Approval of the law vetoed by the president is sent in the form of a decree to the president, who is obliged to sign and promulgate it. The signature and promulgation of the president is the last stage of the legislative process (see section 2.2.2.4).

The budgetary process is even more complicated and requires four readings in the Duma. The federal budget, which in the Russian Federation is twice as large as the regional and local budgets together but only about the same size as that of the Netherlands, raises a lot of discussion and struggle. Therefore, it is very seldom decided on time and the expenditure has to occur on the basis of alleged budget at least during the first quarter of the year (Parlamentskoe..., 1999:121–124). The revenue of the federal budget for the budgetary year 1997 was 712,635 billion rubles and the expenditure 839,489 billion rubles (Byudzhetnaya..., 1999). There are, however, a lot of extra budgetary funds, which do not show in these figures (Kirkow, 1996).

2.2.3.3 Other Powers of the Federal Assembly

The Council of the Federation has special competence concerning the changes of the boundaries between subjects of the federation (article 102, a), confirming presidential decrees on introducing military or extraordinary situations (article 102, b; c), and possible use of armed forces beyond Russian territory limits (articles 102, d). The Council of the Federation also appoints the highest ranking judges and the Procurator General from the candidates nominated by the president (articles 102, g; h). The Council can also terminate the presidential term (article 102, e) but not without the consent of the State Duma (Konstitutsiya..., 1994:457). The Council of the Federation also has powers to impeach the president on the basis of an accusation put forward by the Duma for treason or committing another grave crime (article 102, t). In practice, the impeachment weapon is impossible to use. However, it was tried against President Eltsin. Some members of the Duma raised the impeachment process against the president for starting the Chechen War but they did not find enough support in the Duma.

The State Duma appoints the Ombudsman for Human Rights (article 103, e) and the chairman of the Central Bank (article 103, c). The latter is proposed for candidacy by the president and the former by the president, the Council of the Federation, or deputies of their associations. The State Duma can also proclaim amnesty (article 103, t).

The most important powers of the State Duma outside the legislative process are also limited in favor of the president. The prime minister is appointed by the president, which has to be approved by the Duma (article 103, a). The same goes with the situation when the State Duma has expressed a lack of confidence in the government (article 117) (cf., section 2.2.2.3).

2.2.3.4   A Weak Party System, Corrupt Politics and the Weak Duma

According to Russian constitutional specialists, the mandate of the deputy from his constituency is nowadays free, not imperative. The constitution is silent about this issue, but earlier the deputies were responsible for the electors and could even be recalled when failing to fulfill their promises. Nowadays, they are not dependent on the opinions and wishes of the voters from their own electoral district (Butler, 1999).[25] There is no party discipline either. The parties are no more than clubs of people who have gathered around a strong personality. The only real party with permanent grass-root level

---

[25] There are, however, some opinions expressed that since there is no law, which would have ended the imperative mandate, it cannot be clear whether or not it exists (Vedeneev, 1995).

support is the Communist Party, which relies on the pensioners, and other groups who have lost their earlier economic and social security.

Parties, which are clubs around some influential individuals, are created and die with the charisma or political influence of the leader.

Former Prime Minister Viktor Chernomyrdin's party "Our Home Russia" already lost in the elections of 1996 and in 2000 managed to get only seven seats, all from the one-man constituencies in the gas producing regions of Northern Siberia.

Creation of a "Kremlin Party" (Unity) with no other program than supporting the existing Kremlin policy and President Putin, explains a lot about the Russian political environment. Unity became the second largest party in the elections of 2000, probably due to the media control of the government and the popularity of Acting President and Prime Minister Putin, which was based on the dirty war in Chechnya.

Primakov's and Luzhkov's party, OVR, based its campaign on digging out the scandals connected with the corruption and money laundering of the so-called Kremlin family consisting of president Eltsin's family members and close assistants. The Kremlin was, however, more successful in its defamation campaign against the critics. The case concerning possible money laundering of the Kremlin family was closed and the Procurator General suspended for investigations of possibly exceeding his authority. As soon as Mr. Putin became acting president, he gave President Eltsin immunity as a former president. It was actually the first decree, which he signed in his office after being appointed to the acting presidency (No. 1763 of 31 December 1999).

Since both the party system and civil society are weak, corruption is widespread and open. The Russians do not seem to respect party politics. In many opinion surveys, people give the opinion that a deputy should be a good specialist, preferably a professional lawyer or an economist (Rose *et al.*, 1993:39). People seem to vote for a person instead of a party. In the elections of 2000, 100 out of the 225 seats from one-man constituencies went to independent non-party candidates. The great amount of independent deputies only exceeds the power of "the Kremlin party" and the bureaucracy of the presidential administration.

The common opinion of the Duma among the people is that it is a weak and corrupted organ that cannot work properly.[26] Russians actually do not trust any political organ. According to an opinion survey, only 13% of the respondents answered that they trusted the Duma; 14% declared trust in the president (Eltsin), and only 7% trusted the parties (Rose, 1999:21). Corruption is one reason why strong leadership is tolerated in Russia. The parliament is no better. The president represents state power more clearly; he is the personified state power, the modern-day tsar. Eltsin, however, lost his popularity and the same is probably going to happen to Putin, too.

One typical phenomenon has been that criminal bosses, or people who are afraid of criminal investigations, try to get seats in the Duma because the deputies have immunity against criminal investigations.

In the elections of 2000, two *"oligarchs"*, whose role in the privatization process has been dubious namely Boris Berezovskii and Roman Abramovich, managed to gain immunity against poten-tial criminal investigations. During Primakov's government, there was already a warrant against Berezovskii, but Primakov's attack on the *oligarchs* and illegalities in the privatization process lead to the dismissal of his government.

The general opinion in Russia seems to be that either most officials (53% of the respondents) or almost all (36% of the respondents) are corrupt and that, in comparison with Soviet times, corruption has increased a lot (52% of the respondents) (Rose, 1998:37). The Russians seem to have adapted to corruption—it has become part of their culture. A survey comparing attitudes in Russia, the Czech Republic, and Korea showed that Russians were most likely to pay bribes and use connections. 38% of the Russian respondents declared that they would be likely to pay bribes to get into university, 44% were likely to bribe to get a flat, and 62% were likely to bribe when there was a delay in obtaining a government

---

[26] According to Russian political scientist, Boris Kagarlitskii, votes can be bought in the State Duma. When the approval of Mr. Kirienko for prime minister was sought in the Duma, the decisive vote could be bought for 30,000 dollars. Usually votes cost between 2,000 and 3,000 dollars. Another corrupt practice is that enterprises can buy authorization from a person responsible from the parliamentary committee (Kagarlitskii, 1999).

permit. Almost half of the Czechs and Koreans would have written a letter to the head of the office, which Russians thought would make no difference (Mishler and Rose, 1995). It is typical in Russia that corruption is admitted openly. Corruption is, in principle, disapproved but people still admit openly that they are ready to bribe because it is the easiest and sometimes the only way to get things done.

Corruption and alienation of citizens from the political system does not encourage the desperately needed emergence of a civil society to control politics. Earlier, civil institutions, other than those that were party controlled and established, would have been illegal but now when the citizens are allowed to form free civil institutions they do not care for such an activity. According to Putnam (1993) social capital of the people should be able to be turned into political activity through learning to cooperate and trust in the people in voluntary civil organizations. There are a lot of social networks among Russians and many surveys show that trust is common among relatives and friends. People seem to help even their friends' friends with devoted altruism without requiring reciprocal favors. However, Russians generally have a low level of trust in other people. In a comparative survey, only 34% of the Russian respondents said that they tended to trust other people, while the rate was 55% in the Czech Republic and 77% in Korea (Rose and Shin, 1998:16). Russians have learned, and are learning all the time, not to trust in political organizations. Democracy requires trust in political institutions, but why should people trust in untrustworthy institutions?

The way out of corrupt politics cannot be centralism and the strengthening of presidential powers. Choosing such an authoritarian way does not break the vicious circle of corrupt politics. On the contrary, a strong authoritarian presidency weakens the parliament and the parties and is, in itself, one reason for the miserable situation.

2.2.4 The Judicial Power of the Federation

2.2.4.1 *The Federal Courts*

2.2.4.1.1 *Introducing Regional First Instance Courts*

According to the constitution the court system is federal in Russia. Thus, the courts from the first to the third or fourth instance are all federal. The federal law of 31 December 1996 regulating the court system, however, recognizes also regional courts. They can be courts of the first instance (*mirovye sudi*) and are also regulated by regional legislation. Appeals from a regional court to the federal courts are available but how it happens and to which level is not yet certain. The subjects of the federation have, however, not started to establish their own competing regional court systems except in Chechnya.[27] Making *mirovye sudi* regional is, however, one of the compromises giving the regions more weight but making them partly responsible for the costs. As a result, a lot of hopes have been put on these new courts both because of their regional nature and for historical reasons. Local first instance courts were first introduced in Russia with the reforms of Aleksandr II in 1864[28] but were abolished by the Bolsheviks. The overall experience of these courts was positive according to Russian legal scholars (Stetsovskii, 1999; Malyi, 1999).

There is a federal law on regional first instance courts from 17 December 1998. These courts, however, have not yet started to function. There should also be a law on the regional level, but the primary reason why these courts cannot function yet is that the

---

[27] Chechnya is also an example of double standards in legal systems. Both official Soviet legal norms and their own traditional law exist, which is primary especially in the countryside. Traditional law had nothing to do with criminal organizations, which created their own norms. However, a young man, who is already used to double standards, is probably more likely to accept criminal standards, in addition to exchange of wealth and security, which the official state can not provide. Unfortunately, double standards and subcultures were not studied in the Soviet Union because they did not officially exist (see, e.g., Chesnov, 1999).

[28] The legal reform of Aleksandr II was profound. The reform clarified the court system and introduced the jury to criminal cases according to the French example. Aleksandr II also abolished serfdom.

present Codes of Criminal and Civil Procedure do not contain regulations for a procedure, which is required in such first instance courts. In regional courts, only one judge examines minor criminal and civil cases. In the modern version, the judge is required to have legal education. Salaries should be paid from the federal budget but the facilities are financed from the regional budget.

2.2.4.1.2   Courts for Commercial Disputes

The federal courts are divided into two different systems—ordinary courts and courts for commercial disputes. The latter are for disputes between commercial enterprises, individuals and enterprises, and enterprises and the State. There were already commercial courts in the Tsar's Russia that settled cases dealing with bills of exchange and other commercial matters. In 1931, when the planned exchange of goods system was introduced on an obligatory written-form basis, economic courts were established to settle the disputes between State enterprises. These courts started to be called arbitration courts; they were permanent courts administrative in nature. The arbitration court system was preserved after the collapse of the planned economy, since the judges of arbitration courts were regarded as the only judges with at least some kind of experience in business transaction disputes although within a planned economy. Preserving the arbitration courts and turning them into commercial courts was actually a result of successful lobbying by the judges. Most of the cases in arbitration courts deal with taxation but a lot of cases dealing with breaches of contracts, company law disputes, and bankruptcies are also taken before arbitration courts. Other civil law (mostly family law), criminal, and administrative cases go to ordinary courts.

The structure of the arbitration court system is regulated in the Law on Arbitration Courts of 28 April 1996. The arbitration courts function on four different levels and the country is divided into arbitration districts. The highest instance is the Supreme Arbitration Court in Moscow, which gives binding regulations to the arbitration courts, instructions and even rules of interpretation in concrete cases. Like the Supreme Court, the Supreme Arbitration Court also has the initiative in drafting laws and they both give statements and comments on draft laws. Under the

Supreme Arbitration Court there are 10 *kassatsiya* courts, under which there are 85 *appellyatsiya* courts in centers of the subjects of the federation. The first instances are called *arbitration* courts and they are situated in towns in *appellyatsiya* districts.

Commercial arbitration in the western meaning of the concept also exists. In Russian it is called *treteiskii sud*, which can be either on an *ad hoc* basis or in a permanent board, such as the Board of Arbitration at the Moscow Commercial and Industrial Chamber. *Ad hoc* arbitration is rare, but local chambers of commerce have permanent boards where judges can be selected. A separate law on arbitration does not exist. The Russian *treteiskii sud* system is regulated in the Civil Code (article 11), in a temporary decree on *treteiskii suds* settling economic disputes of 1992, and in the Law on Arbitration Courts of 1996. The Moscow Chamber of Commerce settles international commercial disputes and functions according to the rules, for which the model has been the UNCITRAL arbitration rules. It can compete successfully with other international arbitration boards such as in Stockholm or the ICC board in Paris. It is considerably less expensive than its western competitors and the quality of the judges is supposed to be high.

2.2.4.1.3   Ordinary Courts and Court Procedure

Ordinary courts function in three instances. The first instance is the *rayon*-level court. The appeal level is a *city court* in big cities or *oblast courts* in oblasts. The highest instance is the Supreme Court of the Russian Federation in Moscow.

Both Russian civil and criminal procedure is oral. The decisions, however, are often based on written documents and it is therefore important not to rely on the oral procedure. The principle of *lis pendens* is not quite established in Russia. There can be several competing decisions from different courts on the same case. This problem is, however, diminishing. Human rights organizations have repeatedly paid attention to the long pretrial detentions. The judge is entitled to send a case back for investigation several times, if he thinks that the case has been badly prepared by the prosecutor. In practice, pretrial detentions can extend to several years. Suspects often confess only in order to get better conditions in the ordinary prisons (Country…, 1999).

Jury trials have been introduced in Altai, Krasnodar and Stavropol territories as well as in Ivanovsk, Moscow, Rostov, Ryazan, Saratov and Ulyanovsk regions. Jury trials are known in Russian legal history; they were used in the 16th century and from 1864 until the Bolsheviks abolished them in 1918. They were reintroduced during the transition period in the RFSFR constitution as an amendment. The present constitution guarantees that an individual, who is accused of a crime, has the right to a jury trial (article 20, 47).

There are 12 members in a jury, which agree on a verdict of guilty or not guilty in criminal cases. In those regions where juries are introduced they function both on the *rayon* and appeal levels. Jury trials are regulated in the Criminal Procedural Code. Juries can even be used in more serious crimes without the consent of the accused. There are plans to limit the number of cases brought before juries due to high costs. On the other hand, they are going to be introduced to regions where they are not yet in use (Stetsovskii, 1999).

Even if the jury trials in the United States are regarded as one of the cornerstones of democracy, they are unfamiliar in the continental legal tradition relying on professional judges. There is a lot of skepticism towards the jury system but the official opinion is that democracy has worked in the jury system (Bozrov and Kobyakov, 1996:19–28). The jury system is one of the foreign transplants, which is unfamiliar for the Russian legal system and as such is in danger of not functioning as originally planned. An often-heard opinion from Russian lawyers is that if the ordinary people could decide, then every accused would be found guilty. Such opinions are based on the common inheritance from the Stalinist era and the People's Courts during the civil war. Such an opinion can also be supported by Russian public opinion surveys. According to a survey reported by Mikhailovskaya (1995), the courts are considered as punitive bodies primarily aimed at fighting crime, which is seen as the worst problem of society by 67.2% of the respondents. The majority of the respondents thought that letting a genuine criminal go unpunished poses a greater danger to society than condemning an innocent person. Even more striking is that about one-fifth of the 400-practicing jurist respondents gave priority to the repressive functions of the judicial system.

In his book Stetsovskii (1999:246), however, comments on a legal sociological survey made by the Institute of State and Law in 1988, which claimed that laymen understand justice better than repressive judges. In that survey, only 44% of the judges informed that they would not condemn an accused when the evidence is not complete. A reference group of teachers and scientists understood the basic principles of justice better, since 56% of them would have discharged the accused in the absence of complete evidence. Probably the results would have been different if the reference group had represented ordinary people and not scientists and teachers.

2.2.4.2 Independence of the Judicial System

A separation of powers was unknown in the Soviet Union and the judicial system was not independent from the legislative and the executive power. Actually, it was the Communist Party that also controlled judges and the judicial system. Nowadays, people call the Soviet legal system "telephone law", indicating that a judge could get a telephone call from the party secretary dictating how to decide a case. The constitution emphasizes the independence of judges and the judicial system from the executive and legislative power (article 120). According to the constitution, it is the president of the federation who appoints judges. He is considered to be above the political parties. A panel of judges accepts the candidates prior to the appointment in order to make sure of the independence of the courts and the quality of the judges. Earlier, judges' posts were not permanent and they were elected. Independence has also been guaranteed with regulating that a judge cannot be accused without a legal criminal basis. Charges can be raised only after a panel of judges has approved them.

Judges belonged to the *nomenklatura* and had a lot of privileges during the Soviet era. The high status and respect was ensured with a social and economic position and immunity. The police were not entitled to even impose a fine for a traffic violation or drunken driving. Many economic privileges, such as free apartments, have been preserved in many places. Immunity is still guaranteed by the constitution and in the federal law on the court system (article 122). In practice, however, the working conditions especially in the countryside are often poor without telephones or other equipment and official residences are not available (Country..., 1999). Legislation regulating the court system emphasizes the right for a salary and that it should not be diminished. The state has paid a lot of attention to the salaries of judges compared to others. It is understandable in the present situation, since temptations for accepting bribes increase when the salary is low or not paid on time.

The constitution also emphasizes that financing the judicial system from the federal budget should be sufficient (article 124). Since independence of the judicial system is new in Russia, political leaders especially seem to have mental difficulties in adapting to the new situation. The difference to the earlier role of the judicial system is so big, that the change cannot occur overnight. On the other hand, Russian judges are proud of their newly gained independence. Quoting Nersesyants (1999:358) *"the building of the rule of law depends on the judges because no one else is instead of judges or without the help of judges able to take care of the correct application of law and protect the rule of law"*.

Bribery and harassment of judges is, however, a problem. Organized crime does not hesitate to bribe or threaten or even revenge a judge or an attorney. Judges are given protection on the basis of a law of 20 April 1995. They and their family members are entitled to bodyguards and special protection when needed. The protection system has, however, not been able to prevent the murders of judges every now and then.

Threatening does not always have to come from organized crime. In a case reported by the Lawyers Committee of Human Rights, a judge had discovered that the police had attacked the wrong household in Moscow, killed one person, and then brought charges for hooliganism and resisting lawful arrest against the survivors. After refusing to sentence the accused, the judge started to receive threatening letters and phone calls[29] (Human..., 1993:72).

---

[29] The judge found that the weight of the evidence showed that the policemen had been drunk, unlawfully entered the apartment without cause and used deadly force without justification. Throughout the preliminary investigation, policemen visited the judge to persuade her of the defendants' guilt. A Moscow policeman, a member of the Moscow City Council, also visited the judge regularly. It was then the City Council that elected people's court judges to their terms of office. After the judge handed down the ruling, she received notification from the

Previously, such cases did not see daylight at all. A case like this indicates that there can be pressures to cover-up for the police even by sentencing innocent people. The police still have a Soviet "fulfilling the plan" mentality, which does not exclude framing to maintain Russia's exceptionally high rate of settled crimes. Human rights organizations constantly report about the police framing people by placing narcotics or arms in their belongings or apartments (Country..., 1999). Such stories, which unfortunately do not seem to be rare, show that the police have been able to work for too long without any effective outside control, without publicity or criticism. Such an environment has created cynical attitudes, which do not take the suspect's rights into consideration at all. Misusing the threat, which people feel against organized crime, are attitudes that can even be defended as opinion surveys show (cf., section 2.2.4.1.3).

In spite of all the difficulties in developing the rule of law in a corrupt and economically weak society, the courts have been able to develop the rule of law considerably. The role of the courts is important in Russian transition. Independence has given them both prestige and confidence. The development of a commercial law has given new tasks and more power to the legal system. The rule of law is emphasized in legal education in the Weberian meaning of the concept and the courts have been able to apply formal legal rules emphasizing their importance instead of informal rules. Court cases were previously not an official source of law. Only the law text was emphasized as the starting point of judgments. Nowadays, court cases are increasingly commented upon and criticized in textbooks. In this way, the importance of case law has grown and has also raised the importance of courts and judges.

However, it seems that criminal law and procedure has deep repressive traditions. It is not the development of a trade law but criminal law, which shows the level of the rule of law in any country. Citing Mizulina (1992:52–61), independence (of the judicial system) is not the only guarantee for the rule of law.

---

regional city council that a new apartment, which had been allotted to her as a perquisite of her judgeship, had been denied.

2.2.4.3 The Procuracy

The procuracy is a very old and very Russian institution stemming from the times of Peter the Great. In the original model the procurator was an official, independent of local influence, who acted as the "eye of the tsar" in supervising the conformity of law of the actions of all government departments, officials, and courts, including the Senate itself. After the revolution the procuracy was first abolished but reinstalled within the USSR Supreme Court with powers of constitutional, general, and judicial supervision (Butler, 1999:173).

In the Russian Federation the decision to create a unified Russian procuracy was taken on 15 November 1991. The Procurator General of the RSFSR accepted jurisdiction over all procuracy agencies on Russian territory. In January 1992, the RSFSR Supreme Soviet adopted the Law on Procuracy, which was amended on October 1995 to incorporate the provisions of the constitution of 1993.

According to the constitution and the federal law, the procuracy is a unified and centralized system of procuracy agencies and institutions of the General Procuracy under which the procuracies of the subjects of the federation function. In practice though, procuracy is not completely centralized. In some republics such as Tatarstan, Bashkortostan and Tuva, the procurator works under the supervision of the legislative organ of the republic. Some subjects of the federation also have republican procurators as well as the federal procurator, who are responsible for the republic (Dmitriev and Shapkin, 1995:29). Besides the general procuracy, there are also a number of specialized procuracies, for instance military and transport procuracy. Apart from being the prosecuting authority, the procuracy is also a supervising institution. It has general supervision over the execution of laws by federal ministries and departments and the respective bodies of the subjects of the federation, agencies of local self-government, military administration agencies and officials and over the conformity to the laws of legal acts issued by them. A procurator may react on a violation of law by submitting a recommendation to eliminate the violation, bring a protest against a legal act that is contrary to a law, or apply to a court to demand that a legal act be deemed invalid. The procurator may also initiate civil proceedings for recovery.

Protest does not mean that the agency, which issued the act, must necessarily accept the protest—it can also be rejected. The procuracy cannot protest decrees of the government or laws of the Federal Assembly being inconsistent with the constitution, but the Procurator General has the right to bring inconsistencies to the attention of the president of the federation. The procurator does not have the power to take a case before the constitutional court.

Supervision over human rights is new to the procuracy. The procuracy also supervises the execution of the laws by agencies effectuating operational search activities, inquiry, or preliminary investigation. Inquiry and investigation fall within the field of criminal procedure. Procuracy has jurisdiction over all investigators. The procuracy also supervises prisons and compulsory medical treatment. Conflicts may be raised between different interests of the procuracy. The procurator must act as a prosecutor on behalf of the State and yet initiate objections to procedural or substantive violations by the court. It has been attempted to avoid this conflict by keeping the prosecutor tasks and supervision in a separate department. The huge amount of violations of legal rules and the human rights of citizens suspected of crimes show that the procuracy has probably not been very effective and impartial in its supervising tasks during Soviet times.

Corruption, illegalities and poor control are reflected in the deep distrust in the courts and police. According to an opinion poll, 40% of the respondents declared trust in the courts in 1993, but the rate fell the following year to 17%. The courts have been able to gradually regain at least part of the people's lost trust. In 1998, 24% of the respondents declared trust in the courts. Scandals that were reported in the media may have further decreased the rate of trust among people. Such things were previously not discussed openly. The police are even more distrusted; only 27% of the respondents declared trust in 1993 and 18% in 1998[30] (Rose, 1999:21).[31]

---

[30] Only churches can boast quite a high rate of trust compared to other organizations. 50% of the respondents declared trust in churches in 1994. The rate is, however, declining being only 30% in 1998. A typical Russian phenomenon is that the rate of trust in the army is as high as in churches, 30% in 1998. The trust in the army has also been declining (Rose, 1999:21). According to Rose, the higher rates for the church and the army only indicate

2.2.4.4 Constitutional Court

Judicial control over legislature was introduced to the Soviet Union in 1989 during Gorbachev's era in the form of the Committee for Constitutional Supervision. It was not a real court and its findings had only limited weight, but it proved eager to emphasize human rights norms of the constitution. For instance, it ruled unpublished acts affecting citizens' rights and obligations invalid and found existing procedures on residence permits (*propiska*) unconstitutional (Justice Delayed, 1995). However, unpublished acts are still passed and the residence permit system has not been abolished.

The first Russian constitutional court started on 6 May 1991. The Supreme Soviet decided to establish a genuine court that was separated from the regular court system. The court could also take complaints from individuals. However, it had wide discretion in deciding whether it wished to review human rights complaints. The court concentrated on cases involving the separation of powers and giving the flood of appeals by individuals less attention (Justice Delayed, 1995).

The task of the first constitutional court was not easy. The constitution, which it had to interpret, was the Soviet constitution of 1977 with a lot of amendments hardly responding any more to the needs of a country moving to democracy and the rule of law. The court was often criticized in the press and by legal specialists (Bowring, 1999:266–268) and was later condemned in legal text-books for politicizing cases (Shulzhenko, 1995:127). The involvement of the court in the power struggle between legislature and the president was inevitable but proved to be destructive to the court itself.

---

that these organizations are less mistrusted. Kääriäinen and Furman (2000a:16) explain that trust in the church is ideological. Trust in the army can also be explained as ideological; it is the defender of the Russian Fatherland, which is still important to Russians.

[31] According to another survey made in 1999, trust rates in judges are slightly higher: 3% trust a lot, 31% do trust, 32% do not trust, and 24% absolutely do not trust. Trust in the police is lower: 3% trust very much, 25% trust, 37% do not trust, and 30% absolutely do not trust (Kääriäinen and Furman, 2000a:14).

The first heavily criticized decision was the one finding that presidential decrees banning the activities of the Communist Party were unconstitutional. The final crash came in 1993, when the decision on finding President Eltsin's decree on establishing an extraordinary situation unconstitutional. The decision was open to criticism, since it was made on the basis of the president's televised address and not on the examination of any documentation. "Taking the side of the Supreme Soviet" was, however, legally well grounded since the Soviet constitution of 1977 placed parliament above the executive. The president had no legal right to dismiss the Supreme Soviet. This issue is, however, still largely disputed among Russian lawyers.

Separating law and politics is one of the main principles of legal positivism. Legal decisions should be made only on a legal basis. Even in the United States, where constitutionalism rests implicitly on natural law, the Supreme Court is supposed to make its decisions totally on the basis of legally interpreting the constitution (Alexander, 1998:10). Otherwise the court would not be regarded as an impartial judicial body. Many decisions of the court, however, inevitably have political effects. The fate of the first Russian constitutional court illustrates that without a proper legal basis and in extraordinary situations creating constitutionalism inevitably brings the court in the nexus of a political struggle and damages the reputation of the court as an impartial and purely judicial body. Chief Justice Zorkin's[32] eagerness to give extrajudicial public statements in which he openly took parliament's side in its power struggle with the president were too political not only in terms of Russian legal positivism but also more generally. Even if his opinions were based on a clear legal interpretation of the constitution, the way he expressed them did not increase the credibility in the independence of the legal body he represented.

---

[32] Judge Zorkin was born in 1943, graduated from Moscow State University in 1964, and taught jurisprudence there until 1980. He then became professor in the Department of Constitutional Law and Theory of the State at the Academy of the Interior Ministry of the USSR (Bowring, 1999:267, footnote 49). Nersesyants (1999:319) mentions him among the critics of narrow legal positivism. This critical movement started to publish their opinions in roundtable discussions of the periodical *Sovetskoe gosudarstvo i pravo* in 1979.

The legitimacy of legal rules should be high before a court is able to rule over political matters, and political leadership has to accept legal control. Otherwise, constitutional checks remain a technical tool in the hands of political leaders to legitimize their actions. An authoritarian state does not give a lot of chances to a constitutional court. Constitutionalism and democracy presuppose each other, even though constitutionalism does not have to be democratic. A court does not have to produce democratic decisions, but the decisions must be legal.

President Eltsin solved his dispute with the Constitutional Court with the same kind of methods as with parliament. He did not dissolve the court, as he did with parliament, but he suspended the court. After eliminating both parliament and the constitutional court, Eltsin had free hands to adopt the new constitution, which was also clearly needed to legitimize new power and to end the power struggle.

According to the constitution of 1993, the constitutional court can rule on the constitutionality of federal laws, presidential decrees, constitutions of republics and international treaties that are not yet in force. The court can examine cases on request. The president, the Council of the Federation, the State Duma, one-fifth of the deputies of the Duma or of the members of the Council of the Federation, the government, both Supreme Courts or the executive or the legislative organs of the subjects of the federation have the right for a request. The court can no longer start a case on its own initiative as it did when banning Eltsin's decree on establishing an extraordinary situation. Regular courts can also request to examine the constitutionality of applying law in concrete cases.

According to the previous law on the constitutional court, an individual was allowed to make a petition to the court on the basis of a violation of his or her human rights. The right of an individual to petition to the constitutional court is unclear in the present constitution but, according to the present Law on the Constitutional Court of 1994, the court only examines such cases brought to the court by individuals concerning the constitutionality of laws. It cannot examine the constitutionality of individual decisions of the authorities, say the president, based on those legal norms. Furthermore, citizens cannot challenge the constitutionality of presidential decrees and governmental decrees or lower legal norms. Often, cases brought to the court by individuals have concerned tax or criminal law regulations. The new limitation was grounded with the fear of the court collapsing under the weight of the number of cases to review law application practices (Human..., 1993). In cases containing human rights violations, a citizen can turn to the ordinary courts based on the law on the court system of 27 April 1993. The possibility of turning to the procuracy also exists (see section 2.2.4.3).

The changes made to the draft for a new law on the constitutional court gave President Eltsin a pretext to delay the work of the court. It had to wait first for the new constitution, then the new law and then the fights concerning the appointment of the four new judges. The fact that Eltsin did not dismiss the judges of the Constitutional Court shows that the court might have gained some legitimacy and that the president had to be more cautious towards a court compared to his rudeness towards the Congress. There are 19 judges in the constitutional court instead of 15 in the old one. The Law on the Constitutional Court rules that a judge cannot take part in the work of political parties or give statements to the press concerning questions that are, or might be, brought to the court.

The Constitutional Court has an important role in clarifying obscure rules of the constitution. It is a difficult task since a lot of provisions were left unclear because no political compromise was reached. The court then has to find a legal solution to continue the work of the drafters of the constitution. After the clash with the President, the court seems to have returned to a cautious and narrow legal positivist interpretation.[33] In numerous decisions the court has clarified badly drafted technical rules. One good example is the 14-day rule for the Council of the Federation to consider federal laws (see section 2.2.3.2). The new constitutional court has, however, tried to stay out of political struggles. The court clearly realizes that its rulings may have significant political affects. The result has been that the cases have been decided mostly in favor of the president. The most extreme case was the one finding the secret

---

[33] Ebzeev's (1998:5–12) article on the interpretation of the constitution represents quite an established opinion according to which the interpretation stems from the will of the drafters and gives a lot of attention to the written form.

presidential decrees starting the Chechen War constitutional (see section 2.3.1.3.4).

The court has realized its role as the legitimizer of federal executive power. Also the cases, which have been brought by the subjects against the federation, have mostly been decided in favor of the federal power. However, cases concerning the provisions of constitutions of subjects of the federation have not been taken before the court after 1995 due to political reasons. Treaties between the federation and the subjects have never been taken before the Constitutional Court in spite of their obvious contradictions with the constitution (see section 2.3.1.4.5). There are questions that are politically too dangerous to be left to the mercy of a purely legal decision, as the legal rules in question do not have enough legitimacy. After President Putin strengthened his power and advanced in centralist aspiration, the constitutional court has started to check the consitutionality of the constitutions of the subjects of the federation to make them consistent with the federal constitution (see section 2.3.1.4.2).

The court has had the same problem, which its predecessor already faced. Neither federal nor regional authorities obey the decisions (Shulzhenko, 1995). One good example is the *propiska* practice. Big cities still demand a residence permit to settle in the city. This permit also costs something and requires a lot of time and effort with the city bureaucracy.[34] The new constitution clearly states that everybody can choose where they stay or reside (article 27). In various instances the constitutional court has found the *propiska* practice unconstitutional several times (No. 3, P of 25 April 1995; No. 9-P of 4 April 1996; No. 2, P of 15 January 1998; No. 4-P of 2 February 1998). The mayor of Moscow made a decision concerning one of the rulings. He ordered city officials to begin examining the possibilities of finding alternative fiscal revenues and improve the social situation in the city (Decision of

---

[34] The *propiska* practice is a method of collecting money and is an extremely bureaucratic procedure. This practice has given the police the opportunity of collecting money as "fines" from citizens who do not have the *propiska*. It also enables expelling Caucasians from big cities. They are either not given a *propiska* or are sent back when they do not have one.

the Mayor of Moscow, 29 April 1996, 259-PM). The *propiska* practice still continues because Russian officials do not want to accept human rights principles, which are guaranteed in the constitution, but are not appropriate for them.

Ignoring the decisions of the constitutional court is due to traditions, which know only insider control and has no actual limits of the power of the state organs. The reluctance in implementing the decisions of the Constitutional Court challenges the legitimacy of the court. It also reflects the peculiar asymmetrical federalism in Russia.

2.2.5 Summary

The separation of powers is the most significant change compared to the Soviet constitutions where the Communist Party could rule everything. The balance between the powers was a disputed question, which lead to a power struggle. After having won the struggle, the president introduced a highly presidential constitution. The president of Russia is considered to be the head of both the executive and the organ to check the balances between federal organs as well as between federal and regional organs. Furthermore the president is the main overseer of human rights.

The power given to the president in the constitution is vested on his power to issue decrees in the absence of laws connected with his right to refuse to sign a new law adopted by parliament. In the Russian legal environment with great gaps in legislation, these presidential powers have played an even more significant role in practice. Eltsin's power was only partly based on the constitution. His authoritarian Soviet party leader mentality allowed him to also exceed the constitution.

The Federal Assembly is weak and powerless because of the absence of strong political parties and civil society to control state power. The government is only a tool of the president. Parliamentarism is limited, since the president can dissolve the Duma when disagreeing with its lack of confidence in the government. The corruptness of Russian politics does not encourage democracy to develop. Why should people trust in non-trustworthy organizations?

The Constitutional Court has an important role in interpreting the unclear and inconvenient rules of the constitution. It has concentrated on the questions concerning the separation of powers and was soon drawn into the power struggle. After being defeated and losing its reputation, the renewed Constitutional Court has endeavored to avoid interfering in politics and has concentrated more on clarifying technical regulations and being very cautious with the president.

Russia now has a modern democratic constitution, which was drafted, however, under politically dangerous circumstances. The strong presidency is a result of a bloody power struggle, but also a method for introducing economic and political reforms. Without President Eltsin's stubborn autocratic leadership, reforms would not have been able to be introduced so quickly. It can be disputed whether it was good or bad and whether the changes were too rapid or too slow. President Eltsin's autocratic leadership and rule by decree caused much complaint by the citizens who, however, had no difficulties in coming to the polls and choosing a new tsar, who had already been chosen by the old one.

Introducing democratic values and organizations with an attack has not proved to be efficient. New democratic rules and constitutionalism are not familiar to Russian politicians and state officials. Often, they still seem to think in old Soviet terms relying on previous institutions and personal contacts. The roots of such mentality are not only Soviet, but also reaches back to tsarism and reflect the omnipotence of the unchallengable State power. The Weberian *Rechtsstaat* is not completely understood because of such inheritance. Even if there has been a notable change in the organizations moving in a democratic direction, the informal rules and working habits have, however, not been able to change with equal speed. Institutions, which are inherited from the Soviet past, are not favorable for developing democracy. The changes have also escalated corruptness and the cynical seeking of one's own interests.

Civil society and real democracy grow from the bottom-up. This process has not advanced enough in Russia. The major reason for this is that people have alienated themselves from politics and do not have any trust in political organizations, both due to their unfavorable traditions and constantly learning from increasing cynicism and corruptness. The result is a vicious circle. People do not try to change the situation because they think that they cannot influence it through politics.

Due to the absence of a civil society, courts and lawyers have an important role in establishing the rule of law and constitutionalism in Russia. Determinant reliance on the independence of the court system has already increased the importance of court cases in interpreting new rules. It is a remarkable achievement taking the previous role of the courts in the socialist system into consideration. The courts still face serious problems stemming from corruption and organized crime, which also makes it more difficult to gain the trust of the citizens. There is, however, no doubt that the courts and lawyers would not be able to gradually strengthen the rule of law in Russia.

2.3 Developing Federalism out of Democratic Centralism?

2.3.1 The Federal Structure

2.3.1.1 *Origins of Russian Federalism*

The RSFSR was already a formal federation within the Soviet Union. The Soviet Union consisted of republics, which according to the Soviet constitution were sovereign republics with all the formal symbols and signs of independence. The Soviet constitution emphasized the voluntary nature of the union allowing the republics to withdraw from it. In practice, however, even increasing the possibility to withdraw would have been dangerous. As soon as the first winds of reforms started to blow, the forced basis of the union began to shake. In the Federal Treaty that Gorbachev tried to make the republics sign, the possibility to withdraw was already abolished.

It was paradoxical that Russia was the final initiator of the Minsk Treaty, which terminated the Soviet Union, since the Soviet Union was the successor of the Russian Empire. Secession from the Soviet Union was, however, considered to be necessary in order to begin the economic and political reforms, for which the reformers and the president of Russia, Boris Eltsin had actively propagated. Secession from the Soviet Union was explained to mean independence from the socialist system of the Soviet Union. At that time, there were complaints about other republics gaining more from the union than Russia.

President Eltsin and the leadership of the Russian Republic have later been criticized for "sacrificing" the union to obtain the power to rule Russia. With the independence of the Baltic States, President Eltsin has been explained as having bought the support of the United States and Germany. He has been accused of diminishing the original Russia—the Russian Empire of the Tsars—because of a short-term political power struggle. In a textbook of the history of the state administration for university students, the authors express their astonishment of "the wrong kind of patriotism" of the reformers, "who should have understood that their true fatherland Russia is actually the historical Russian Empire" (Istoriya..., 1999). For centuries, Russian "patriotism" has exceeded the areas populated by ethnic Russians. There is even widespread opinion that the Russians, as a more developed people, have both the right and an obligation to rule "underdeveloped" Caucasian and Central Asian peoples. According to opinion surveys, a great majority of Russians did not approve of the Minsk Treaty and blamed the collapse of the Soviet Union for the economic difficulties of Russia (see section 2.2.1.1).

Russian federalism stems from different origins than American federalism, which is usually regarded as the most advanced model. While American federalism rests on an agreement between former colonies, Russia developed as an empire enlarging its territory to protect and strengthen the center. The Bolsheviks promised to turn "the prison of the peoples" into a voluntary union and give autonomy to national minorities.[35] The same slogan was used again during the collapse of the Soviet Union.

In spite of the official concepts of federalism and autonomy, the Soviet Union developed into a centrally governed state with regions submitted to the center. The Communist Party and its politburo directed the so-called democratic centralism. It was probably the most centrally governed system in Russian history. The union was, however, too large to be centrally directed. The regions, especially

---

[35] The self-determination of peoples was a political principle, which for Lenin was only a weapon in changing the society into the trail of socialism. He explained socialism to automatically guarantee self-determination (Lenin, 1967).

the republics dominated by non-Russians, soon developed a kind of a "feudal" relationship with Moscow similar to the earlier Russian Empire. The orders from Moscow were obeyed and the plans fulfilled or at least were pretended to be. The local party leaders, who had to be approved by the politburo, tried to keep good relations with the center and their own region under their own authoritarian control. The party leader was the representative of the regions to the faraway center, which did not play a significant role in ordinary peoples' lives.[36] A significant difference to American federalism was that there were no limitations of the authority of the government, which was the sovereign to be obeyed. Although the center officially ruled the whole union, the regions were able to decentralize in practice. In most cases after the collapse of the union the new independent republics continued under the leadership of the same regional elite, the party bureaucrats and the *nomenklatura* (cf., section 2.2.1.1).

2.3.1.2 The New Constitution and Demands for Decentralization

President Eltsin had to discover that centrifugal tendencies in the Russian Federation only escalated because of the collapse of the Soviet Union. Also in the Russian Federation there are people who were annexed to the Russian Empire against their will. The most extreme example are the Chechens, who have clearly pointed out that they—like other North Caucasian people—were annexed to Russia by force and would prefer to withdraw from the federation.

Not only the multiethnic but also the regions populated almost totally by ethnic Russians have demanded more power to the regions. Moscow-oriented specialists of federalism like to point out that the regional elites, which have always been complaining and demanding more power, are actually greatly dependent on Moscow (Stelmakh, 1997). The Soviet system was built in such a way that

---

[36] As examples of semi-autonomous policies, Hosking (1985:427–439) mentions Akhundov in Azerbaijan, Mzhavanadze in Georgia, Johannes Käbin in Estonia and Anton Snieckus in Lithuania, all of whom were more or less successful in protecting their own language and culture. For Shelest, in Ukraine, a similar policy cost him his position and V.V. Shcherbitskii, who was Brezhnev's man and followed more Muscovite policy, replaced him.

the decisions were made in Moscow and the delivery of the revenues of the budget was decided in Moscow. Even one of the richest regions Sakha-Yakutia, which produces diamonds, is dependent on the delivery of food products during the winter period. Even if their own region has been more important for them than the union, the regional elites have, however, been used to obey or at least pretend to obey every order coming from Moscow. Excluding Chechnya, the same quite narrow circle of communist *nomenklatura* stayed in power in the regions, which explains a lot about the mentality of the regional elites.[37] The problem from the regions' point of view is that they were left alone without the support of the center, which was occupied with the hectic power struggle on the federal level. In this power struggle the regions tried to gain more power, while the fighting rivals of the center promised them more power in return for their support.

Traditionally, the Moscow elite has regarded itself as the leading *intelligentsia* and the best specialists of the country and has drawn a parallel between regionalism and backwardness. Therefore, even the Moscow elite thinks that decentralization should be developed at the center and then "given to the peasants". It is indeed true that new ideas take time to reach the periphery. Regions are more conservative than the center, which in Russia means that communism still rules in the countryside. Decentralization is also regarded as a threat for the unity of Russia. This opinion is also found in history textbooks, which equate decentralization and the weakness of the country explaining that Russia has been the strongest (and most expansive!) when it has been centralized under a strong leader. However, during the few years before and after the collapse of the Soviet Union also the Russian republican leaders spoke for self-determination and decentralization. Such messages from Moscow found fertile soil in many regions, but the regional

---

[37] The leaders in Moscow have always been afraid of national movements, because they tend to be separatist. Therefore, the Chechen leadership was labeled as criminal and the opposition (read: former *nomenklatura*) was given political and economic support including arms. Moscow has assisted even the worst old communist leaders to crush nationalist movements in former Soviet republics.

elites have gradually returned to the old trail after Moscow leaders started to govern the regions again.[38]

There is much truth in the belief that there is a danger in decentralization from the point of view of the center. If such a huge country as Russia is going to be decentralized, the regions might develop their economic and political relations to other more natural directions than Moscow and might be able to manage without Moscow. Even if economic dependency has been planned and developed for a long time, it can still be broken. The Russian Empire was anyhow an attempt to increase the security of the center by spreading its influence even further. Such politics does not have much to give to the faraway regions. In the most favorable cases, the faraway regions are left alone to get on independently if they, at the same time, officially submit themselves to the authority of the center. The starting point in discussing "federalism" at the center still seems to be that orders always come from above and that the regions are for the center not vice-versa. According to opinion surveys in 1993, both centralism and decentralism in governing the regions were equally supported (Rose *et al.*, 1993:45). Opinion polls cannot, however, illustrate how people actually understand these concepts.

There is a lot of economic potential in the regions and the federation, as a whole, would benefit from their economic growth. Without decentralization the regions are not going to develop. President Eltsin agreed that decentralization is necessary and he negotiated with political leaders of the regions during the drafting process of the constitution to gain their support in his power struggle with the legislative power (Stelmakh, 1997:10). However, it can be read in the constitution that many of the disputed issues were not solved but diluted into unclear compromises. The main reason for leaving the most important question such as the division of powers between the federal and the regional level and the principles of fiscal federalism open was that President Eltsin quickly needed a new constitution to legitimize his leadership and the reforms. Other issues were of minor importance.

---

[38] There is, however, a difference between the Great Russian regions and regions with ethnically more mixed population. Especially Tatarstan and Bashkortostan have difficulties to give away their newly gained "sovereignty".

On the other hand, President Eltsin already started to establish firm presidential control on the regions from the beginning. The first step was to appoint the presidential representatives in the regions to serve as the "eye" of the president and to monitor and report to the presidential administration. In November 1991, Congress gave the president freedom to appoint the regional leaders for a year in advance. The next year, the president informed them that the next elections were going to be only in 1994 and that the leaders that were appointed by him had to continue until those elections. In this way the president managed to change many leaders of the regions. In the elections, however, regionalist candidates were more successful, which gave a new headache to the president who started to plan on how to replace them with his own men. The regionalist candidates were often also "conservative" old communists who were not interested in President Eltsin's reforms.

The quasi-federal and extremely presidential constitution of 1993 was not received with enthusiasm in the regions. According to the region-by-region results of the referendum on the constitution published by the Central Election Committee, the constitution received more than 50% of the votes in 59 subjects of the federation. In Dagestan, only 20.9% voted in favor of the constitution (Grigoriev *et al.*, 1994). The neighboring republic Chechnya refused to arrange the referendum at all. It was not even possible to participate in the referendum because Chechnya had previously—in September 1991—proclaimed independence, and had arranged new parliamentary and presidential elections in October 1991. The national movement won the elections and the new president, Dzhokhar Dudaev, immediately issued a Decree on State Sovereignty (1 November 1991). Also Tatarstan protested the referendum but made it possible for the citizens to participate in it, however, only 13.43% of those entitled to vote bothered to do so in the referendum. Connecting the resistance of economic reforms and the wish to return to the old system with low voting rates undermines the fact that many of these regions are poor and remote areas where nationalist feelings and their own different culture alienate people from the federal center.[39] Voting reflects the relationship of

---

[39] This connection is drawn in a report by Grigoriev *et al.* (1994).

the regional and federal leadership. Regional leaders are able both to affect the voting in their region and trade with votes with the federal center.

Tatarstan and Chechnya had also refused to sign the Federal Treaty in March 1992. There were three different treaties, the idea of which was to keep the regions in the federation until the new constitution was signed. The treaty, which was made between the federation and the republics, give the republics the ownership of their natural resources as well as sovereignty. Another treaty was signed with the territories and regions and a third with the autonomous regions and areas. Also, they gained the ownership of their natural resources but did not get sovereignty. With these treaties, autonomous regions received the same rights as the regions and territories within which they are situated.

Especially the republics, which were proclaimed sovereign, insisted that the Federal Treaty should be incorporated into the constitution. The treaties are incorporated into the constitution, but are given a lower status than the constitution (part 2 of the constitution). It is the rules of the constitution that count when rules contradict each other. Those, who wanted the treaty to be included in the constitution, however, saw that Russia is primarily a contractual federation.

2.3.1.3 *Status of the Subject of the Federation*

2.3.1.3.1 *The Notion "Subject of the Federation"*

According to article 65 of the constitution of 1993, the Russian Federation consists of 89 so-called subjects of the federation. The concept "subject of the federation" dates back to Soviet times and was invented to cover all kinds of different regions of the federation. There are 21 republics (*respublika*), 6 territories (*krai*), 49 regions (*oblast*), 2 cities of federal importance, namely Moscow and St. Petersburg, one autonomous region (*avtonomnaya oblast*), and 10 autonomous areas (*avtonomnyi okrug*). The borders of the areas of these different subjects of the federation are the same as in the former Soviet Russian Federation. The three different groups of regions were preserved as such, which they were in the Federal Treaty of 1992.

Russia inherited a complicated structure from the Soviet past, a structure that was originally created with the first constitution of Soviet Russia in 1918 to solve the national question by giving national minorities self-determination in the form of territorial autonomy. Even if autonomy was of quasi-autonomous character, it for example guaranteed the indigenous peoples or national minorities of the area quotas to universities or jobs in the local administration. In this way, the Soviet power maintained otherwise forbidden nationalism in quasi-autonomous structures.

2.3.1.3.2   Equality with Two Different Statuses

All of the different regions have the status subject of the federation and the constitution declares that they are all equal (article 5.1). The constitution further specifies that in relations with the federation all subjects are equal (article 5.4). This equality permits every subject two seats in the Council of the Federation (article 95.2) in spite of the different sizes in area and population of each subject. For example, the area of the Republic of Adygeya is 7,600 square meters, which is 0.04% of the area of the whole federation, while the area of the Republic of Sakha-Yakutia is 3,103,200 square meters, which is 18.7% of the total area of the federation. The City of Moscow has the largest population with about 9 million in the smallest area of the federation—1,500 square meters. While the population living in the area of the Evensk Autonomous Region with 7,657,600 square meters is about 20,800 (Shulzhenko, 1995).

The equal amount of seats in the Federal Council has the same solution that was made in the United States, where each state sends two senators to the Senate. In Germany, however, the number of the seats in the *Bundesrat* depends on the number of inhabitants in the *Bundesland*. The equal number of seats was chosen in Russia, because it would have been too difficult to negotiate a more cumbersome system that depended upon the size of the population or the size of the area or a mixture of both.

Even if the constitution clearly declares in article 5.1 that all the subjects of the federation are equal, it defines the status of the republics in a different way to the status of the other subjects in Article 5.2. This is one of the reasons why Russian constitutional lawyers call Russia an "asymmetrical" federation (Shulzhenko, 1995; Lebedev, 1999). A republic has its own constitution (*Konstitutsiya*) and legislation while the other subjects have a charter (*ustav*) and their own legislation. The constitution also uses the notion "state" as a bracketed synonym for a republic. This difference has lead to a disputed interpretation of the status of the subjects. The supporters of the disputed theory explain that republics are sovereign states within the sovereign state of Russia, while the other subjects of the federation are governmental formations either on territorial (territories, regions and the two cities) or national basis (autonomous region and autonomous areas) without sovereignty.

This quite widespread opinion is not based on the constitution alone, but on the three different Federal Treaties of 1992, which were incorporated into the constitution. The treaty between the republics and the federation gave the republics a higher status than the other subjects. The definition of a republic reflected the official Soviet doctrine of sovereign republics. The original Soviet doctrine was actually more confederal than federal.[40] In practice, however, the Soviet Union soon started to function as a unified highly centralized state, where the regions were only centrally governed areas. The republics would have liked to return to the original confederal idea, which never materialized in the Soviet Union. The republics also wanted to preserve their higher status compared to the other subjects of the federation. The Federal Treaty was incorporated into the constitution of 1993 as a political compromise (The Constitution, Second Section: Concluding Provisions) (Lebedev, 1999).

Some law scholars praised the treaties for legitimizing decentralization (Polenina, 1993). As time has passed, the advocates of a more centrally governed federation have denied the legal force of the Federal Treaty. They argue that the treaty was signed before the

---

[40] The reason for such a doctrine was a struggle between centralist and decentralist ideas among the Bolsheviks themselves. In addition to that the demands of national minorities had to be satisfied at least formally in that political situation. Russia was a unitary state before the Bolsheviks took power.

constitution, which is now the basic legal document with the highest legal power in the whole area of the Federation (article 15.1). Furthermore, they argue that in the course of time the treaty has proved to be unnecessary and old-fashioned and has been completely replaced by the new constitution (Lebedev, 1999). The political compromise was not properly secured on the legal level, which has made it possible for Moscow-based constitutional lawyers to explain in a typical formal legal positivist manner that it was "only a necessary political compromise" without any legal foundation.

The legal doctrine giving the republics a better status has encouraged territories, regions, autonomous regions and areas to demand a change in their status to republics. According to the constitution, the status of a subject can be changed by common consent with the federation and the subject by a federal constitutional law (article 66.5). This means that, apart from the consent between the federation and the subject, such a change would require a three-quarter majority in the Federal Council and a two-third majority in the State Duma. There is even a disputed draft under preparation specifying the procedure to change the status of a subject (Kozlov *et al.*, 1996). The dispute is about the length of the draft. This law would also allow uniting or separating subjects from one another, changing borders between them and almost all the possible changes within the federation. According to the critics, such a law would require the constitution to be changed as well (Lebedev, 1999).

Autonomous areas are situated inside a region, territory or republic. The constitution does not specify their status clearly enough. They exist in the territory of another region with which they are equal. The constitution provides that their relationship is organized with a mutual treaty or by a federal law. The Constitutional Court ruled in a case (14 July 1997, No. 12 P), where the Khanti-Mansi and Yamalo-Nenetsk autonomous areas and the region of Tyumen did not have a contract, that the autonomous area is equal to the region. The region is not allowed to interfere in the administration of the autonomous area but the population of the autonomous areas is entitled to take part in the elections of the Tyumen region. Such an interpretation actually makes the autonomous area in principle "more equal" than the region. In practice, however, an autonomous area usually constitutes such a minor part of the population of the region that their representation in the legislative organ of the region does not have any real significance.[41]

2.3.1.3.3   Federal and Regional Laws Conflicting with Each Other

Other sources of "asymmetry" are the constitutions and charters of the subjects of the federation. According to the Federal Constitution they should not contradict it. Also the legislation of the federation takes precedence over that of the subjects. It is a well-known fact that almost all the constitutions and charters of the subjects of the federation more or less contradict the federal constitution (Lebedev, 1999:99).

The federal constitutional court is the judicial organ that decides whether the constitutions or legislation of the subjects of the federation contradict the federal constitution. There have been only a few of these cases before the present constitutional court (1994–). After 1995 and until the end of President Eltsin's period there were no longer any cases. The earlier constitutional court (1991–1993) had to decide on more of these cases, which were usually initiated by the deputies of the parliament.[42] Quite often the constitutional court found that the constitution of the subject contradicted the federal constitution.

However, the subjects of the federation have often ignored the decisions of the federal constitutional court. This has been the case for example, in Tatarstan and Udmurtia, not to mention Chechnya. The subjects of the federation have also elevated their status to resemble that of a state by adopting their own constitutional court where the constitutionality of the legislature and executive power can be challenged. The federal organs have been reluctant to further

---

[41] The disputed question in the Tyumen region concerns oil and gas incomes. Oil is produced in the Khanti-Mansi autonomous area and gas in the Yamalo-Nenetsk autonomous area. The Tyumen region would also like to decide how the oil and gas incomes are used. The Tyumen region was originally created in 1944 around the autonomous areas to control their oil and gas resources. The autonomous areas were already created in 1930 (Dobrynin, 1998:46).

[42] Nowadays, individual deputies cannot bring a case before the Constitutional Court. It has to be one-fifth of the deputies of the Duma or members of the Federal Council who have the right for a request (see section 2.2.4.4).

challenge the constitutionality of the constitutions and charters of the subjects since such cases might be politically dangerous (Lebedev, 1999:100).

The presidential administration has, however, tried to use executive power and the power to give decrees to implement federal laws in the regions. In June 1996, Eltsin issued a Decree (No. 810) "On Order and Responsibility in Governmental Positions". This decree made the head of the subject of the federation responsible to the federation for failing to implement federal legislation. Lebedev (1999) comments on this decree by stating that it was necessary due to the constant negligence by the subjects of the federation and because there was no obligation imposed on the subjects in the constitution.

After President Putin managed to establish his power and the centralist tendencies with his own party 'Unity' in the Duma, the constitutional court has started to check the constitutions of the subjects of the federation to make them consistent with the federal constitution (27 June 2000, No. 92 – O; Adygeiya, Bashkortostan, Ingushetia, Komi, North Ossetia, etc.). The initiative came from the deputies of the Duma.

2.3.1.3.4   Chechnya—Constitutionalism Sacrificed for the Sake of Federal Unity

The most extreme case in which the Constitutional Court decided to put the unity of the federation before the rule of law concerns the constitutionality of the presidential decrees on restoring order in Chechnya using armed forces (2 November 1993, No. 1833; 9 December 1994, No. 2166).[43] The court found (31 June 1995, No. 10-P) the decrees consistent with the constitution even if they were confidential, which clearly contradicts the constitution (article 15.3) and even if the decrees allowed violation of basic human rights that are guaranteed in the constitution and in the international human rights treaties that Russia has ratified. The court actually found the decrees justified on political grounds in order to secure the unity of the federation.

---

[43] These are confidential presidential decrees and not available.

However, the decision was not unanimous—8 out of 19 judges gave a dissenting opinion. Justice Vitruk claimed that the confidentiality of the decrees already made them unconstitutional. His opinion emphasizes formal legal positivism. The strongest opinion was given by Justice Zorkin who saw that in accepting to resort to arms on the grounds of the unity of the federation paves the way for also using extreme methods in the future. His opinion reflects a conception of law according to which there are principles of justice above the legal positivist hierarchy of norms. Justice Luchin pointed out that when the president, who is supposed to be the guarantor of human rights, uses armed forces against the people the constitution loses its meaning of serving individuals. Furthermore, he points out that it is not the president without any control to solve the conflict by armed force with a secret decree. According to Justice Luchin, even if something needed to be done with the situation in Chechnya, the measures should have been legal. The warning of the dissenting Justices has proved to hit the nail on the head. The decision by the Constitutional Court denied Chechens the right for legal protection and accepted that law can be overruled for higher political purposes.

The situation strikingly resembles that in the Weimar Republic, where the *Staatsgerichtshof* made a similar decision (25 October 1932) and issued the Decree on the State of Emergency (14 June 1932), which Papen had squeezed out of President Hindenburg; consistent with the article 48 of the Weimar Constitution. Leaning on this decree, Papen removed the Prussian Government from office and became commissioner for Prussia (20 June 1932). The excuse was found in "the communist rebellion" of Altona, one of the suburbs of Hamburg. The decision to accept the *coup d'état* of the Nazis was based on article 48 of the constitution that clearly authorized the president to ensure that the duties of a *Land* are performed even with the help of armed force. Compared to the Russian attack on Chechnya, the formal authority of the president was much clearer in Germany. Another question was that the reason for the state of emergency was not adequate. The decision of the *Staatsgerichtshof* was, however, based on formally correct reasoning. In the decision of the Russian Constitutional Court, the rule of law did not materialize even in the formal legal positivist meaning. The decision simply legalized political purposes.

Chechen separatism has indeed been a difficult question, which actually cannot be solved by legal methods only. Chechnya-Ichkerya gave her Declaration of Independence as early as 6 September 1991, grounding it on the principle of self-determination of peoples and regarding the Chechens as a colonialized people. Such wordings were not rare in Russia at that time. Colonialism was how Lenin described the tsarist enlargement policy and rule, and colonialism was how the regions in Russia explained the relations with the center during the collapse of the Soviet Union. Even if Chechnya, according to contemporary international law, would have a legal right to independence, as the author of this book holds, gaining independence always depends on politics. Independence *de lege* cannot be reached without the recognition of other independent states, which Chechnya will not get without the consent of Russia (Nystén-Haarala, 1994; 1999).

The textbooks of constitutional law argue that the Chechen Republic is one of the subjects of the federation simply because it is included in the list of the subjects of Article 65 of the constitution (Konstitutsiya..., 1994). According to the constitution there is no escape from the federation. The territory of the federation cannot be diminished in any way.[44] A constitutional law (article 66.5) can change the status of a subject of the federation, but there is no provision for withdrawal. However, Chechnya consented to be excluded from article 66, and the whole federal constitution. Subordinating her under the federal constitution against her will is against the principle of self-determination of peoples and the voluntary basis, which the federal constitution officially rests on. Chechnya did not participate in the referendum on the constitution declaring that she is not subordinated to the federal constitution. Chechnya also did not send representatives to the Council of the Federation, which

---

[44] The present interpretation of the constitution of not allowing the territory of the federation to diminish also means that neither the president of Russia nor any other state organ can decide to return, e.g., the Kuril Islands to Japan, Karelia to Finland, or Kaliningrad to Germany. On the other hand, the constitution would not prevent in agreeing with Ukraine to give Crimea to Russia.

federal constitutional lawyers regard as a breach of the constitution (Lebedev, 1999:121).

Chechnya has also been *de facto* independent since her Declaration of Independence. Dzhokhar Dudaev refused to act as "a vassal" of the federation. In the Russian Federation he could have maintained control over Chechnya with a lot of informal autonomy, but on the condition that he would have leaned towards being a vassal under the President of the Federation. President Dudaev and the national movement, however, required full independence. The federal power in the area has only been temporary and then effectuated with extreme violence. However, the 1994–1996 war ruined Chechnya so badly that the former commander-in-chief of the Chechen forces, Aslan Maskhadov, who was elected president of Chechnya in 1996 after the war as a war hero and a peace negotiator, was not able to restore governmental power and protect the population from armed terrorists.[45] Terrorism is a direct result of the cruel war against the Chechens.

In the autumn of 1999, the leaders of the federation decided to solve the Chechen problem once and for all with the most extreme methods. Exactly as in the Weimar Republic, mysterious bombs exploded in the capital. Even if those, who were responsible for the attacks were not found, the Chechens were declared guilty in the mass media. The government supported the propaganda. Such allegations were considered to be a sufficient reason to attack Chechnya with armed forces.

The war, which is a logical result of the decision of the Constitutional Court finding the earlier Chechen War constitutional, has even been popular in Russia. It was well prepared and journalists have not been allowed to enter the area except for propaganda purposes. Fighting against terrorism has been the official explanation from the beginning, and the legal basis of the operation is the Law on Fighting Terrorism.[46] It is,

---

[45] For more information about the situation in Chechnya between the two wars, see Altamirova's (1999) article.

[46] Statement by the president of the Russian Federation, Boris N. Eltsin, regarding the situation in the Northern Caucasus; press release on 3 December 1999. Since the Federal Law on Fighting against Terrorism is applied to the situation in Chechnya, no interviews or statements of the representatives of the

however, quite clear that no law in a rule of law country can legitimize a full-scale civil war to catch a few terrorists. Russian legal mentality, which can accept innocent victims in the more important task of punishing criminals, seems to accept even huge violations of human rights.[47] In 1996, the Russian population or actually the intellectuals were against the war in Chechnya. President Putin has, however, been able to use the fear of the population for personal safety and connect it with the need to be a great nation.[48] At the moment there are no legal limits in the power of the federal executive when it can only be justified with the unity of the federation. Legal specialists have also started to emphasize that the most important principle of the constitution is the unity of the federation.[49]

The war is cruel punishment for those who insist in leaving the federation and Russian predominance and a good weapon to threaten those who might want to "steal" too much power from the State, which is considered to be the federal center. The war has caused a lot of damage to the attempts of developing sustainable and genuine federalism in Russia. The Peace Treaty between the belligerent parties[50]defined Chechnya as a sovereign State within the Russian Federation. There were also plans to develop self-determination of the Chechen people and perhaps even arrange a

---

Chechen party can be published, because it is considered to be promoting terrorism and breaking the afore-mentioned law.

[47] See the survey presented by Mikhailovskaya (1995) mentioned in section 2.2.4.1.3.

[48] President Putin explained in an interview of Kommersant (10 March 2000) that the war was "his mission" and that "the enemy has to be hit before he hits and do it so well that the enemy does not rise up again". The fact that a person with such KGB mentality can be elected as the President of Russia because of his good leadership capabilities, indicates that the fear of personal safety connected with the need to be a great nation is a powerful weapon to replace the principle of the rule of law for the unity of Russia.

[49] Professor Aleksandr Malyi's lectures: 19 September 2000 in Rovaniemi (University of Lapland) and 3 October 2000 in Helsinki (University of Helsinki).

[50] Published in Izvestiya 13 July 1997. In the Nazran Protocol of 10 July 1996 for cease-fire, signed by Aleksandr Lebed and Aslan Maskhadov, both parties acknowledge the other as belligerent parties. The protocol was, however, never brought to the State Duma.

referendum on independence after a five-year period.[51] The new war blocked any development of Chechen self-determination. Chechnya was taken under direct presidential control, which has no legal basis at all.[52] The actions of the army in Chechnya are also likely to escalate terrorism in the future. There are Muslim terrorist organizations in other countries, which will take care of cultivating hatred, which the Russian army has seeded among the growing generation of Chechens.

2.3.1.4 Division of Powers between the Federation and Its Subjects

2.3.1.4.1 Contradicting Legal Sources

One of the most confusing parts of the constitution is the division of legislative, executive and judicial powers between the federation and its subjects, which is regulated in articles 71–73. Article 71 lists the powers of the federation, while article 72 lists the joint powers, which the federation and the subjects use together. The constitution does not define how the joint powers are used. It has later been specified with federal laws often overriding the power of the subjects of the federation. Article 73 states that everything that is not included either in the powers of the federation or in joint powers belong to the powers of the subjects of the federation alone. The idea of such division of powers was taken from the federal treaties of 1992 as such. The precise definition of these powers and especially the joint powers was made neither in those treaties nor in the constitution.

---

[51] Tadevosyan (1997) refers to those plans and sees that a confereral or association treaty would not satisfy the Chechen party and that, therefore, even independence after a transitory period should be considered.

[52] Direct presidential control means that there is a representative of the president of the federation in Chechnya responsible for the republic. Russian legal specialists have discussed how the legal basis should be arranged. According to them the possibilities are a federal law on Chechnya or a presidential decree on the emergency situation in Chechnya or the nomination of a representative of the president in Chechnya under the existing legislation. In any case, according to Russian sources the direct federal control of Chechnya is going to last years, perhaps a decade (Kommersant, 11 April 2000).

The division of powers between the federation and its subjects is also regulated by the so-called federal treaties, which are allowed in article 11.3 of the constitution. These treaties, which are nowadays a rule and not an exception, are the main source of "asymmetry" of Russian federalism. Russian federalism is being developed under political pressures. There are two contradicting tendencies, with no common plan or commonly accepted idea on how to reach a consensus on sustainable federalism. On the one hand, new federal laws tend to strengthen the powers of the federation over the subjects and, on the other hand, federal treaties between a subject and the federation allow the subjects more powers than federal laws or even the federal constitution permits.

2.3.1.4.2 Division of Legislative Powers According to the Federal Constitution

Lobbying through the Council of the Federation. There is legislative power on the level of the federation as well as on the level of the subjects. Each of the subjects has its own system of legal norms that is based on its own constitution or charter, which according to the federal constitution should not contradict it. The subjects of the federation have the right to initiate the drafting of a bill for federal legislation in both chambers of the Federal Assembly. They also have the right to challenge the constitutionality of federal laws in the Federal Constitutional Court or to turn to the president of the federation when federal and regional laws contradict one another. The subjects of the federation can also initiate a change into the federal constitution.

Since the Supreme Soviet received so much support from the regions in the battle between the president and parliament, President Eltsin offered more power to the regions and promised to take their interests into consideration in the drafting process of the Federal Constitution. The regions managed to lobby the Council of the Federation to become the power center of the local leaders. Actually, their lobbying concentrated on this very issue (Stelmakh, 1997). The constitution rules that the two representatives of each region in the "upper chamber" represent the legislative and the executive power of the subject (article 95). This arrangement means that the federal elite occupies the Council of the Federation. In this way, the representatives of the regions can control the legislative process on the federal level (cf., sections 2.2.4.2 and 2.2.4.3).

The regional influence on the legislative process was, however, later weakened when a new law was passed on 5 December 1995 ordering that the representatives of the subject in the Federal Council have to be the heads of the executive and legislative organs. It is not likely that the heads of the subjects would have time to work effectively on both the federal and the regional levels. This new law makes the Federal Council more of a ceremonial body, which does not have the possibility to affect effectively on the legislative process. Especially the 14-day rule would require that members could concentrate only on parliamentary work. On the other hand, the Council of the Federation is now an organization where the regional leaders can exchange their opinions on a regular basis. In a country with traditions of leader-oriented rule it is a logical solution. This also means that the representatives of the Council of the Federation concentrate on taking care of regional interests on the federal level. For this reason the Council of the Federation is politically more powerful than earlier. The change also elevated the status of the governors. President Putin's attempts to move the governors from the Council of the Federation have caused a lot of resistance. He has initiated a proposal for a new federal law, which would give the representation of the executive power of the subjects of the federation to a representative appointed by the governor or other head of the executive power of the subject. The governors see that losing their parliamentary immunity would submit them too effectively under the federal president. Decentralization in Russia does not necessarily bring more democracy to the regional level. In practice, decentralization diminishes authoritarian rule of the federal center but strengthens authoritarian rule of the governors instead.

The problem of regional lobbying is the lack of coordination. In passing laws there is no real coordination between the two chambers. They even physically exist in different places, because the constitution wanted to ensure the independence of both chambers, but did not take coordination enough into account (Parlamentskoe..., 1999). Eltsin wanted to make sure that the chambers would not be able to unite their forces against the President. Yet, the Council of the Federation is the federal organ, which can in principle coordinate regional interests. It seems, however, that the interests of the regions seldom meet and that the president of the federation can therefore quite easily use the old Roman principle of *divide et impera* in leading the federation.

Regional Parliaments. Every subject of the federation has its own legislative organ, which functions by being regulated by their own constitution or charter (*ustav*). According to the federal constitution (articles 10; 77.2; 95.2), each subject of the federation has chosen the model for their parliament independently from the center.

Since the issue was disputed it has taken a long time before the federal law, coordinating and unifying the structures of the legislative bodies of the subjects, was passed. It has been debated how far a federal law can go to regulate the structure of the governmental bodies of the subjects. Finally, the Law on the General Principles of the Organization of Legislative and Executive Power of the Subjects of the Federation was issued on 6 October 1999. The rules regulating the structure of the legislative body are quite flexible. It is only necessary that the principle of the separation of powers be followed. There are still regional legislative bodies that follow the Soviet principle of executive power subjected under the parliament. The Constitutional Court, however, formulated a principle in 1996 according to which the organization of the legislative and executive power on the level of the subject of the federation should reflect the one on the federal level to the extent that is needed to ensure a unified system.[53] Otherwise the parliament may consist of either one or two chambers and the number of deputies has to be decided in the regional constitution. Regional parliamentary elections are regulated and detailed in the law.

Branches of Federal legislation or coordination. Legislative power on certain branches of jurisdiction belongs completely to the federation. Financial, currency and customs legislation can be passed only on the federal level, which means that economic policy is almost totally in the control of the federation. The

---

[53] Ruling of the Constitutional Court No. 2-P of 18 January 1996. The case concerned the charter of the Republic of Altai.

constitution declares that the legal basis of "the single market" of Russia is regulated by federal legislation. According to the constitution, international economic relations are regulated on the federal level. This is often interpreted in legal literature that the federation coordinates these relations. Such an interpretation takes the Federal Treaty into consideration. Russian lawyers complain that legal rules are obscure and inadequate in this respect (Pustogarov, 1994).

The idea is to keep a common market in Russia under the same regulations and legal framework. Separate markets could, in practice, add pressure also to separate statehood. When economic policy and foreign trade issues belong completely to the federation, the regions lack real possibilities to develop direct economic relations with cross-border areas. This is the case especially in Russia, where the federation controls international economic relations with strict and often contradictory or even absurd norms. Such policy blocks the economic development of the regions. Their entry into the world market could give the Russian economy a boost. The old centralist mentality is a serious constraint to the development of the regions. It can be claimed that the institutions are still built on a centralist foundation. The idea of a Moscow-centered economic entity with fulfilling plans has not disappeared either from the center or from the regions.[54]

In the United States, there was also a debate over foreign trade when the foundations of the federation were established. The result was that foreign policy and a lot of economic policy is concentrated on the federal level. There is, however, competition between the states on who is able to give better opportunities for business. In Russia, it should also be understood that the question is not so much about whether it is the federation or the subjects that guide

---

[54] Aleksandr Kirilichev's statement to the Financial Times (27 April 2000) is a typical example. He is the president of the Primorsk Shipping Corporation, who stood against Evgenii Nadratenko in the governor's elections in Vladivostok. He stated: "*I prefer to believe in the dictatorship of law as advocated by the new president Putin. Without a change in the system of power Russia does not have a future. Putin's program will create a new legal base for the country and we will be able to change people who do not fulfill federal laws.*"

economic policy, but that it is the economic activity and business, which should be thought about.

However, according to federal treaties a region may have powers to conclude treaties with foreign countries in spite of the regulations of the constitution (see section 2.3.1.4.5). For example, Tatarstan, Sakha and Bashkortostan do conclude treaties with other states. The complicated legal situation, however, makes foreign countries less reluctant to conclude treaties with the regions. Treaties, which have been concluded, are more cere-monial in that they express mutual interests. Most constitutional lawyers, who represent the interests of the federation, consider that federal treaties on the division of power are on a lower level in the hierarchy of norms than the constitution or even the federal laws (Lebedev, 1999). In legal terms this means that such treaties of the subjects with foreign states might be declared as unconstitutional.

This question reflects the power political nature of the dispute. In Russia, the federation is still largely involved in foreign trade. It can be claimed that centralized exports are reviving the state monopoly of foreign trade (Kirkow, 1996). This fact is clearly visible in the federal budget. In the 1997 budget, 1.6% of the revenues came from foreign economic operations and 3.8% of the revenues were collected by taxing foreign trade (Byudzhetnaya..., 1999). The subjects of the federation do not have such incomes. Liberalization would inevitably abolish export duties and reduce export tariffs. In a free market economy, it is anyhow the enterprises that conduct foreign trade. The question is about whether the state gives them an adequate legal framework for foreign trade, be it the federation or its subjects.

Quite a few branches of jurisdiction are only regulated on the federal level. Legislation in both criminal and civil (private) law including the corresponding procedural laws is completely federal. Also, intellectual property law and private international law (conflict of laws) are regulated only on the federal level. Employment, family and tenancy laws are not included in the civil law in Russia but are regulated both on the federal and regional levels. In the United States, each State has its own legal structure including private international law. Economic development has, however, harmonized the different legal systems especially in trade law. In Russia, the need for preserving the common market is used for explaining why the subjects of the federation are not given legislative power. While the development in the United States has occurred from bottom-up, the drafters of the Russian federal constitution decided that there is no time to wait for an evolutionary development, but that it is better to keep the legal systems of the subjects as harmonized and unified as possible.

Joint powers between the federation and its subjects. Tax and administrative laws are branches of joint powers as well as environmental law, regulation of health care and education. The tax system would need coordination, since there are taxes on all the three possible levels; federal, regional and municipal. The General Part of the Federal Tax Code of 31 July 1998 representing new federal tax legislation, however, regulates merely general principles of taxation concerning the relationship between the taxpayer and the tax collector. The General Part of the Tax Code, however, gives an exhaustive list of the possible sources of taxation, which means that it is not lawful to invent new sources of taxation on any level. It was decided that these provisions would enter into force with the second part of the tax code. However, the second part of the tax code, which entered into force on 29 December 2000, again introduced new sources of taxation.

There are also contradicting environmental regulations on both federal and regional levels. The responsibility for pollution is a disputed issue, which neither the federation nor the regions would like to take over. The regulation and organization of expensive health care is a burden in the present economic situation. Local demands for financing a hospital from the federal budget can be answered that such social political questions belong more naturally to the sphere of local self-government (see section 2.4).

Fiscal federalism, which is an important part of the German constitution or any real federal constitution, is completely absent in the Russian constitution. Again, the reason was the need to quickly produce a new constitution to legalize the political bodies. The principles of fiscal federalism were so open at that time that it was impossible to agree about them. Later, such principles have been introduced with federal laws (see section 2.4). The system of dual subordination has remained in Russia. Tax authorities have continued to share revenues upward from the local to the regional and then to the federal budget. This takes place on a non-transparent, bargained *ad hoc* basis and creates open-ended commitments for the Russian government. 71% of the budgetary expenditure is spent on the regional level, but about half of the total sum consists of central subsidies mainly for housing, agriculture and transport. High dependence on central subsidies, which are divided arbitrarily, has lead to the low efficiency of local tax collection and weak responsiveness by regional governments to local demand (Kirkow, 1996).

The power to regulate the use of land and natural resources as well as the property rights question was a disputed issue after the collapse of the Soviet Union. The possibility of reprivatization has, however, not been seriously discussed in Russia. The strongest rivals in the struggle for natural resources have been the federation and its subjects. The question is not so much about ownership but about who has the right to economic benefit. For an outsider, the situation can be quite confusing. For the economic development of a transitional country, it is vitally important to know at whose disposal the natural resources are and who is able to dominate them. Do the fish in a river belong to the federation, or to the subject of the federation, to the local community or might they actually belong to the indigenous people living in the area? For example, in the Kola Peninsula the federal government has sold fishing rights to foreign tourists and prohibited the Sami, whose traditional source of livelihood is fishery, from fishing in the same river. According to the Federal constitution (article 67.1) inland waters, as well as territorial seas, and air space belong to the territory of Russia. The above-mentioned article separates those areas from the territory of the subjects of the federation.

When the constitution was being drafted, the dispute over natural resources was lively. So, the constitution left this dispute unsolved and regulated that the power to regulate the use of natural resources is to be used jointly both on the federal and the regional levels (article 72.1, c, d). Deciding over the status of air space, territorial seas and the continental shelf are reserved for the federation (article 71, m). The constitution states that land and other natural resources are under the special protection of the federation (article 9.1) and further that they can be in private possession, state or municipally owned or within some other system of ownership (article 9.2). Alternative property rights systems were kept open.

Constitutions of the republics may, however, have regulations contradicting the Federal constitution. The constitution of the Permsk Region regulates that air space, waters and below ground resources belongs to the Permsk Region. The constitution of the Republic of Sakha-Yakutia also adds the continental shelf to the territory of the republic (Lebedev, 1999:112). The constitution of Tatarstan goes even further since it regards Tatarstan as a sovereign state, which has been associated with the Russian Federation. The former speaker of the Tatarstan Parliament, Mukhametshin, explained that the wording of the constitution and the treaty between Tatarstan and Russia means that the federation is a union of sovereign states, which have delegated other powers. He sees the possibility of building a new type of federalism there (Mukhametshin, 1994). Such a genuine federalist point of view is, however, strange to soviet centralist mentality, which the bureaucrats and specialists serving the federal executive power represent.

The idea of divided sovereignty, which can be found in the Federal Treaty between the republics and the federation, is of Soviet origin. It did not have any practical value then. Now, sovereignty seems to be understood in a new way, which reflects more the practice of Soviet times with the idea of a unified state. There can only be one sovereign, which cannot be divided (Kondrashev, 2000:10–15). The discussion about sovereignty and the dangers of confederalism seems to be an either/or dispute, which cannot descend on the level of division of powers between the center and the regions and developing genuine federalism.

Tendencies to strengthen federal power within joint powers. There is a strong tendency to strengthen federal powers within the joint legislative powers by promulgating new federal laws. The constitution does not define at all, what joint legislation actually means and how far the federation can go in determining the framework on the federal level. Sometimes the federal law goes so far that it actually usurps the whole legislative regulation to the federal level. This has happened with both the Federal Law on Below Ground Resources of 1995 and the Federal Forest Code of 1997.

In the federal constitution, legislative powers on oil, gas and minerals are regulated to occur jointly between the federation and its subjects (article 72.1, c). The Federal Law on Below Ground Resources ('*o nedrakh*'), however, usurped them to the property of the federation (1995, No. 10). Lebedev (1999:111) explains in his study of the status of the subjects of the federation that it is clear and commonly accepted that these kinds of property should be in common ownership of the whole nation even if it is not mentioned in article 67.1. Lebedev's opinion reflects the traditional Soviet centralist mentality. The article states that the territory of Russia includes the territory of the subjects, inland waters, territorial sea, and air space. The constitution separates waters and air space from the territory of the subjects. Inland waters are, however, under joint powers of regulation (article 72.1, c) along with land, minerals, gas, oil and other natural resources.

The Federal Forest Code of 1997 regulated that the forests form a so-called federal forest fund (*lesnyi fond*), which is included in the property of the federation.[55] Before the Federal Forest Code, several codes had been passed on the regional level regulating the use of forests, which included forests in the property of the subject of the federation. Some of them even allowed private ownership. The former federal law of 1993 on the Principles of Forest Legislation regulated that forest resources were in joint ownership of the Russian Federation and its subject. The Federal Council actually delayed the legislative process, but finally had to concede.

The Republic of Karelia and the Khabarovsk Territory took the issue before the Constitutional Court claiming that the Federal Code contradicts the constitution, which includes both natural resources generally (article 72.1, c), and the administration and legislation of forests (article 72.1, j) into joint jurisdiction. They also regarded the code as unconstitutional because the Code made forests completely federally state-owned even if the constitution regulates that land

---

[55] The structure of the Russian forest sector is presented in IIASA's Forestry Project reports. For example, see Efremov *et al*. (1999), which also presents the structure of the forest sector in Khabarovsk krai. The structure of the Karelian forest sector is presented in Piipponen (1999). For information about forest legislation before the federal forest code, see Sheingauz *et al*. (1995).

property could also be in private or municipal ownership. The Constitutional Court, however, held that the Federal Forest Code does not contradict the constitution (No. 1-P of 9 January 1998). Joint jurisdiction in this case means that even if the forests are included in the "federal forest fund" the use and profit of this property can be regulated on a contractual basis between the federation and the subject. This means, in practice, that the subject of the federation, for example, the Karelian Republic, is entitled to a share of the income from harvesting the forests on its territory. According to the Forest Code (article 106), the share of the subject is 60%, while the federation receives 40% of the income from harvesting. A different share can be agreed upon between the federation and the subject. It is actually the subject of the federation that decides about the use of the federal forest fund, not the owner. The subject decides on renting or leasing plots of forest land for harvesting purposes. In these decisions they should implement federal forest policy. Such an arrangement is one of the odd compromises of the Russian federal structure. However, transfer of ownership is not allowed by means of an agreement between the federal state and a subject. The Forest Code rules that only parts of the forest fund may be transferred to the possession of a subject, by virtue of a federal law.

In the case that Karelia and Khabarovsk took before the Constitutional Court, the court held that the forests also belong to the whole Russian nation, and form a special kind of property, about which there is specific legislation. Forests were not regarded as ordinary land property. Even after the privatization of forest enterprises, the administrative structure of the forest sector has remained mainly in the same form that was established in the 1930s (cf., footnote 55). Forest legislation has changed and now includes, for example, different alternatives of ownership but only on a regional level. The decision of the Constitutional Court indicates that acts issued by some of the subjects regulating private ownership of forests are unconstitutional even though the constitution clearly declares (article 9.2) that land can be in private ownership.

The Federal Land Code has been under preparation for a long time, mainly due to the dispute on what forms of property rights can be accepted. Many subjects of the federation already have their own property law legislation, which will probably turn out to contradict the forthcoming federal code. Some subjects of the federation allow private ownership of land while others do not. In such cases, the subjects of the federation might decide not to change their property law legislation to correspond to the federal code.

The ongoing struggle over legislative authority between the federation and the subjects makes the legal framework blurred and shaky. As long as the federal structure remains disputed, economic activity does not have a secure basis. Investments on a long-term basis are especially risky. Centralized decision power may be advocated both with more clearance and with legal traditions, but it will prevent the development of genuine federalism. Since decentralization is common practice, it should be accepted also on the legal level and developed to an acceptable balance. Federalism is, of course, a continuous process not an eternal structure laid down on a written document. However, a continuous dispute between the federal center and the regions does not make Russian federalism either democratic or effective. What the Americans call a 'due process of law' is missing. There is no real undisputed legal basis where to look for legal solutions and no rule of law to lean on.

2.3.1.4.3 *Division of Executive Powers between the Federation and its Subjects*

The struggle on the federal model has been hectic on the sphere of executive power. Every subject of the federation has its own government and usually a huge local administration with a lot of ministries and committees. The head of the subject is usually called a president in the republics and a governor in the other subjects. In most cases the executive power is presidential just like on the federal level. However, the executive power is far from a unified structure.

The president of the federation, as head of the executive power, has tried to unify the executive power, solve the problem of "asymmetry" and take the executive power of the federal subjects under his control with presidential decrees. In October 1994, President Eltsin issued a Decree "On the Measures to Strengthen the Unified System of Executive Power in the Russian Federation (No. 1969), according to which the appointment of the heads of subjects other than republics is submitted to the president of the federation. The president is also entitled to dismiss them. The Constitutional Court found the decree consistent with the constitution (31 April 1996, No. 11-P) accepting the explanation of the presidential administration that these measures were only temporarily functioning in the absence of a proper federal law. The court also held that the decree does not deprive the subjects of the federation the right to independently arrange elections for the governors. President Eltsin's original purpose was to change regionalist governors into his own men. The congress gave Eltsin the right to appoint governors in 1991 and he was able to keep them in power until the election of 1994, in which the regionalist candidates were more successful.

The other means to control the executive of the subjects is the system of representatives of the president. They are federal civil servants under the presidential administration. President Eltsin started the institution when he obtained power from congress to nominate governors in 1991. In the beginning, he presented them as observers with no power to control the governors. In many regions, the relation between the representative of the president and the governor were not good at all (Lysenko and Lysenko, 1998:14). President Putin has tried to intensify the control of the federal president by issuing a decree on establishing new "super regions" above the subjects of the federation for his representatives to control the implementation of federal legislation and report to the president about the situation in the area (No. 849 of 13 May 2000). His plan seems to be to gradually give more tasks to his representatives in the administrative super regions and more power over the subjects of the federation. He makes these changes with his own decrees diluting the division of power stipulated in the constitution.[56]

There was a draft law in 1995, which would have given the center the power to order the structure and the powers of the

---

[56] There is another centralist reform of administration prepared under President Putin. He has informed the governors that their membership in the Council of the Federation may be cancelled. Like his predecessor, President Putin has also tried to affect the elections of the governors.

executive of the subjects. The Council of the Federation, however, did not accept the draft. A new law, which subordinates the executive of the subjects under the control of the presidential administration, came into force in September 1999. This law, however, gives the subjects the power to decide about their own state structure. This is already guaranteed in the constitution (article 77). The powers of the head of the subject do not have to be similar with the powers of the federal president, but the separation of powers is required. There are still several subjects of the federation where the executive has been subjected to be under the parliament according to Soviet principles. The Constitutional Court has emphasized the need for a unified system in its ruling from 1996 concerning the Altai region (cf., section 2.3.1.4.2).

Participation in local elections has been so low that it is difficult to tell how much the people support regionalism. Opinion surveys show that centralism and decentralization are supported equally (see section 2.3.1.2). It may also be that the regional level is considered to be so unimportant that people do not bother to vote (Stelmakh, 1997). Low participation in all the elections also reflects the low interest of the people towards politics. Since regional difficulties are nearer to the people, regional misconduct and corruption may also alienate people from politics more on the regional level and even increase the popularity of centralism. In Russia, regional leaders traditionally tend to govern their regions like feudal vassals. Since their management skills usually stem back to communism, decentralization has not lead to increased democracy, but are a reflection of the authoritarian rule of the center with corruption and "friendship" relations. The misconduct of power and corruption on the regional level has made it easier for the federal center to get support from the population for intensified centralism. It is a general phenomenon everywhere that people tend to react more to corruption the nearer the decision-maker is to them. This is also why it is important to start building a civil society from below.

Regionalist leaders have tried to get more power from the center, while the center has been weak. However, as soon as the center started to strengthen again, it has tried to "put the regions back in order". At least the center has had difficulties in regaining the powers that had already been given to the regions. The centralist mentality regards the situation as such that the center gives power to the regions and the regions try to rob it. According to Kondrashev (2000:11), who sees that there can be only sovereignty, it is only the sovereign itself (read: the federal center), which can limit its sovereignty. While the point of view of the regionalists is that the federation consists of its regions, which delegate powers to the center (Mukhametshin, 1994). However, with the help of federal legislation and with the consent of the Constitutional Court, the central power is gradually strengthening its sphere usurping away what the regions were able to negotiate in exchange of support for the president of the federation.[57]

The regionalist leaders have not been successful in coordinating and lobbying regional interests. Nowadays, the Council of the Federation is an organ where the regional leaders can meet regularly, and where their interests can sometimes meet in spite of the constant *divide et impera* policy of the federal center. There have also been attempts to establish unofficial organizations of some regions. One example is the association of the regions producing oil and gas, which was founded in 1994. The aims of the association are to take part in the state energy policy and coordinate the activity of the regions. This means that the regions try to lobby together to affect the price of oil and gas in the inner markets of Russia. Such lobbying is, however, not consistent with the federal competition law prohibiting monopolies or pools.

There was also an attempt to stop the Chechen War (1994–96) by establishing a lobbying group of the heads of those republics with large ethnic minorities. President Eltsin, however, responded by gathering another group of Great Russian regional leaders to fight against the group lobbying against the war. The different interests of the Great Russian regions were used against the interests of the regions with ethnic minorities. The Chechen War did not raise a unified front of the regions against the center to defend the separatist republic. Actually, the Great Russian regions managed to lobby for

---

[57] After the elections of the State Duma of 1999, the center will be able to strengthen itself even more on condition that the deputies of the Unity Party will stay under the control of President Putin. The president has also been able to strengthen the center by issuing decrees on administrative changes. It will remain to be seen whether these changes only increase bureaucracy and how long they will last.

their own interests against the earlier budgetary politics favoring poor Caucasian regions in order to keep them peaceful (Stelmakh, 1997). In a federation with no firm and transparent rules of fiscal federalism, regionalist leaders cannot afford to resist the federal president, who can take budgetary measures to force the regions to obey the center.

It should, however, be borne in mind that the regional leaders traditionally have some freedom in governing their own regions. Even if the federal president tries to affect the nomination of candidates of the regional elections to ensure obedient regional leadership and even if he has a lot of executive power to make an affect on the regional level, he cannot control the huge federation completely. The centralization tendencies are now strong. President Putin's ideal of a unified state seems to be in clear conflict with federalism. Decentralization tendencies advance more silently, but may be able to succeed in the long run simply because governing such a huge multicultural and multinational country like a unified state is a pure impossibility in practice. Authoritarian rule on both the federal and regional levels is likely to continue because of the absence of a civil society and effective control of state power from the grass-root level.

2.3.1.4.4 Judicial Power of the Federation

Judicial power exercised by independent courts is almost completely federal (article 71.1, n). All of the court instances are governed by federal legislation and financed from the federal budget. The subjects have, however, the right to establish courts of the first instance (*mirovye sudi*), which are also regulated in regional legislation. These courts are so new that it is difficult to say what their role is going to be in the future. There is reason to fear that because of the different sources of financing the activity, regional courts may become the bone of political contention (Malyi, 1999). The Procurator's Office is also a large federal organization controlling the court system and implementing legal rules on both federal and regional levels. In many regions, however, procurators are also under regional control or there is a regional procuracy competing with the federal system existing (see section 2.2.4.3).

Even if there are no competing courts on the regional level, most of the republics have their own constitutional court where constitutionality of regional laws can be challenged as well as the decisions of regional executive power. Such courts are independent and do not belong to the federal system of courts. There is no right to appeal to the federal constitutional court. They are also quite different in the different subjects. Some of them are only administrative quasi courts. In Irkutsk, for instance, the constitutional tribunal can only give a recommendation in disputes between state organs. The members are chosen in many different ways. In Adygeya, Dagestan and Sakha, the judges are elected. In Tatarstan, parliament has to accept the appointment of the judges taken by the court itself. In Tuva, parliament appoints the judges on the nomination of the court and after acceptance by the president (Malyi, 1999).

Many subjects of the federation have also established a regional ombudsman system. According to the Federal constitution, the protection of human rights and the rights of national minorities both belong to the federal powers (article 71) and to joint powers of the federation and the subject. Establishing such organs as constitutional courts and ombudsman adds more signs of statehood to the status of the subjects of the federation. However, their efficiency is often low and their role often seems to be more ceremonial than actually taking care of constitutionality and human rights in the region.

2.3.1.4.5   Federal Treaties—The Other Legal Source of Federalism

The Federal constitution did not solve the dispute concerning the division of power between the federation and its subject. Articles 71–73 are unclear and leave a lot to be specified with future federal legislation. Such important questions are the specification of joint powers and fiscal federalism. Even if the regions got the control of federal legislation through the Council of the Federation, they have not been able to effectively prevent the strengthening of federal power through controlling the legislative process on the federal level. Unclear rules of the constitution also give the Constitutional Court a lot of power to interpret it. The court has quite clearly favored central power in cases where usually the subjects of the federation have challenged it. It has also not paid attention to the Federal Treaty, which legalized decentralization and which the subjects of the federation wanted to be incorporated in the constitution.

There is, however, another additional way for the regions to gain more power from the federation. According to the constitution, it is possible to conclude treaties between the organs of executive power of the subject and the federal executive power on transferring powers to the other party, on the condition that such treaties do not contradict the constitution (article 11.3).

The first of such a treaty was signed between the Presidents of the Federation and the Republic of Tatarstan at the beginning of 1994 (*Ross. gaz.*, 14 February 1994). Tatarstan refused to sign the Federal Treaty in 1992 and did not participate in the Referendum on the constitution of 1993 although the citizens were allowed to go to the ballots. Like Chechnya, Tatarstan referred to President Eltsin's famous utterance in Kazan, in which he urged the regions to take as much power themselves as they could manage. Since Chechnya was even more separatist and would have agreed to negotiate only on independence, the president wanted to show that he was able to decentralize power to the regions as long as the region stays within the federation. In this political environment, the president of Tatarstan was able to make a treaty, which actually acknowledges the sovereignty of the republic. Tatarstan even received powers for direct foreign relations. The treaty is an association treaty with the federation and Tatarstan. The constitution of Tatarstan is often described as being more confederal than federal (Pustogarov, 1994). It regards the republic as a sovereign state, which has been associated with the Russian Federation.

Those in power in Tatarstan at that time belonged to the former Communist *nomenklatura*. They were probably only interested in keeping the republic in their own control. There was, however, a strong nationalist opposition, which claimed Tatarstan independence or at least a lot more power. President Shaimiev felt that he was forced to listen to the nationalists. Later, however, the nationalist movement split and weakened. The *nomenklatura* managed to maintain control and slow down privatization in Tatarstan (McAuley, 1997).

The treaty between Tatarstan and the Federation quite clearly contradicts the Federal constitution since many of the powers given to Tatarstan would belong to the powers of the federation according to the constitution. This fact has openly been admitted and accepted by federal constitutional lawyers as a political necessity (Lebedev, 1999). Quite a few specialists do not consider the situation to be ideal, but see the treaties as an acceptable and practical means to develop Russian asymmetric federalism (Tadevosyan, 1997). For some scholars, federal treaties reflect the break down of the Soviet centralist principles and represent decentralization, which can also develop from below, not only from above (Polenina, 1993). Some critics of the treaties emphasize their temporary nature, since the president had explained that the treaties were made in the absence of federal legislation (Eliseev, 1999). Karapetyan (1996), who sees equality of the subjects of the federation as the only acceptable foundation for a federation, expressed the most severe criticism.

The treaty method is not as safe as taking the same powers into the constitution but politically it was the only possibility of introducing a more decentralized federalism through the back door. This is felt as pressure at the federal level. Constitutional lawyers ironically comment that it will soon be the subjects who demand that the federal constitution should not contradict their own constitutions (Lebedev, 1999). Such a step would actually make Russia a more genuine federation, since it would mean an acceptance of the idea that it is the subjects forming the federation and that the federation exists for the subjects not *vice versa*.

Several other regions followed Tatarstan's example. President Eltsin made these treaties to gain more support before the presidential elections. In 1995, 4 treaties were made and 11 in 1996. By the beginning of 1999, 46 treaties already existed on the division of power between the federation and a subject. These treaties were made either between the presidents or the prime ministers. Federal treaties became more a rule than an exception. These treaties were initially made with republics, but from 1996 to 1998 there was a wave of treaties with subjects other than republics (Lebedev, 1999).

These treaties contradict the federal constitution also because they are often partly confidential. The treaties contain a basic agreement with special agreements attached. Special agreements are more detailed and usually focus on a specific problem of the subject of the federation. It is these special agreements, which are often confidential. Other subjects of the federation are not supposed to know what benefits were gained by the agreements.

Many of these treaties do not clarify the division of powers between the federation and the subject. From the point of view of the federation, the aim of the treaties seems to have been to keep the subjects of the federation content and ensure that the subjects of the federation do not have separatist objectives. The practice of secret treaties totally undermines the whole idea of federalism and shows how weak and undemocratic the foundation of the federation actually is. The inequality these treaties create can cause more contradictions between the subjects of federation. This may even be the aim of the center relying on the principle of *divide et impera.* When regions envy each other, they are less likely to unite their forces to put pressure on the federal center.

When most of the subjects of the federation had already concluded treaties with the federation on the division of powers, a federal law clarifying the practice and the contents of such treaties was finally passed. The law "On the Principles of Dividing Power between the Russian Federal Government and the Subjects of the Federation" came into force in July 1999 and, if implemented correctly, should also end the practice of secret treaties. None of these treaties, which are part of the policy of taming the dissatisfied regions, have been taken before the Constitutional Court. In the case concerning the constitutionality of the Federal Forest Code, the court did not deal with the contradictions between the treaties on the division of powers and the constitution. The whole practice is a political necessity, and clearly contradicts not only the constitution, but also the principles of democracy. The Constitutional Court would be in a difficult situation, if the constitutionality of one of these treaties were taken before it. A decision, which would be in line with the earlier rulings of the constitutional court that emphasized the superiority of the constitution, would be politically dangerous.

From the point of view of the regions, decentralization is not based on a legally secure foundation. It is always possible that if the federation gains so much power over the subjects that splitting into parts would no longer be a great threat, the constitutionality of these treaties might be challenged. Then the law could be used as a weapon in power politics. The unconstitutional and undemocratic way to make the federation more "asymmetric" to prevent it from splitting or shifting into a confederal basis, shows that the center may regard the situation as temporary and has only decided to use the old strategy of *divide et impera*. It is, however, also a development towards shifting the decentralized practice from an informal level to one of formal legal rules. The uneven and asymmetric development does not look good in the eyes of a lawyer, who would prefer a clear system. It is, however, a development towards accepting the existing system. It has moved the gap between decentralized practice and centralist legal rules to the level of official legal rules.

2.3.1.5 Summary—Is There Any Future for Russian Constitutional Federalism?

Developing sustainable federalism is one of the most important challenges among the other political, economic and social problems of the new transforming federation. There are at least two competing models of Russian federalism. The first is a centrally governed pretended federalism with some decentralization to silence the regions. It is based on the idea that only the federation is a state and the subjects are parts governed from above. The federal center and its legal specialists support this model. The second model is based on the idea that the subjects of the federation are states, which together can form a federation to gain more economic and political power. The more genuinely federal model stems from the early decentralizing ideas of the Soviet Union, according to which Russia could have been developed into a Confederation of Sovereign States. The latter model, essentially supported by the regional elites, is more or less functioning in practice. Between these two models, a compromise model might be found. Apart from federalism and confederalism, there is also separatism, fighting against which is used for strengthening the center.

The centralist constitutional lawyers, however, seem to think that a confederation would be as destructive to the unity of Russia as actually separating. Confederation is regarded as a long step ahead towards finally splitting up. Calling the regionalist model confederal actually reflects this fear of the centralists. To prevent such a destiny they have established legal solutions for developing Russian federalism under the existing constitution. One suggestion is that the federal treaties should be replaced with a new Federal Treaty between the federation and all its subjects (Lebedev, 1999). In this way, asymmetry would be replaced with an equal status. If the treaty would be consistent with the present constitution, Russia would stay on quite a centralist type course of federalism. It would of course, be a clearer model but also less democratic since democracy requires decentralization and not strict and clear central control. It is, however, not presumable that the subjects of the federation would accept such a treaty and return to the center powers, which some of them have gained by virtue of separate treaties with the federation.

If, however, federalism is going to be developed to a more decentralized direction, the constitution has to be changed. Changing the constitution is complicated, because it would require a three-quarter majority of the Federal Council and a two-third majority of the State Duma of the Federal Assembly (article 134). Furthermore, changes in chapters 1, 2 and 9 that define the constitutional structure of the federation, cannot be made unless a three-fifth majority of all the members of both chambers supports the proposition and a Constitutional Assembly is appointed. The Constitutional Assembly can either accept the amendment or revision or draft a new constitution and accept it with a two-third majority of all its members. It can also submit the draft to a referendum, in which case the constitution is considered adopted if over half of the voters support it (article 135). Changing the constitution towards a more federal and decentralized basis would require a more complicated procedure. There are, however, gaps in the constitution, which have allowed the President to intensify and centralize administration through decrees and administrative decisions.

As long as no mutual political consensus has been reached, there are no legal methods to develop Russian federalism. The centralists seem to prefer a legally vague situation, which is based on administrative treaties and increases the asymmetry of the federation at the cost of clarity and constitutionality. They hope that the situation is only temporary and that sooner or later the federation is going to be unified and the legal foundation purified from obscurities. This seems to be the strategy of the federal presidential administration. The regionalists, on the other hand, regard the administrative treaties as their only available possibility to increase pressure on the federal center, which tries to strengthen its own powers relying on the constitution and its centralist interpretations. As the regionalists have now been able to make the practice appear also on the legal level, it is highly unlikely that they will forfeit their power. They can always use passive resistance and wait until the bureaucracy at the federal center gets tired. In practice, pure centralism is impossible in such a huge and inefficient federation.

The Chechen War (1994–96) was destructive to the development of federalism. It showed that the center is apt to use violence against a disobedient region. Disobedient subjects are forced to sign "a social contract", which happens to be the constitution prepared by federalist lawyers and reflecting mostly centralist ideas. The support of the Great Russian regions offered Eltsin the weapons to punish separatist ethnical movements, and blame the Chechens for all kinds of misery. Since also the Constitutional Court accepted violations of human rights in protecting the unity of the federation, it is quite clear that it is now acceptable that the federal center does not have any limits to its power, when it considers that the unity of the federation is at stake.

The war has been able to channel the frustration of not only the political leaders of the country and the military but also the disappointment of the people on the misery caused by unsuccessful economic reforms, corrupt politics and increased insecurity because of organized crime. Especially the citizens' feelings of insecurity were cynically connected with Great Russian patriotism and channeled against an ethnic group inside the federation. History shows that such frustrations can easily be projected on an ethnic group but with serious consequences. Finding a common enemy is an easier way to unite people than finding a democratic consensus. Finding consensus in such a multicultural and multinational country as Russia is extremely difficult even in normal circumstances, without Soviet and tsarist traditions. From the point of view of historical development, the balance seems to be blurred but such a situation is more "ordinary" in Russian history. Strict centralist rules have always been circumvented or ignored until they finally wither away.

Transition increases the difficulties in keeping the asymmetric, inefficient and bureaucratic federation in existence. A state, which should exist to protect its citizens, finds it more justified to protect its own existence at the cost of the citizens. Such politics is a return to Tsarist Russia, with constant wars in peripheral areas. Unfortunately, Russia has not been able to find a new democratic ideological basis for its existence but has turned to the old imperialist ideology. Such a development does not indicate a triumph of voluntary, efficient and democratic federalism in the near future. Those regions, which have been able to gain an exceptionally independent status, may be the next targets of the unifiers. Recent demagogy indicates that Russia may try to "take the lost empire back". Great Russian expansion has fertile soil to grow, since the Russians seem to be sure to blame the collapse of the Soviet Union for their economic problems. A Great Russian centralized state is regarded as a normal and eligible situation in Russia. Anything deviating from the traditional model is abnormal and unfavorable to the mentality of Russian centralist bureaucracy, which can effectively hinder democratic federalism from developing.

Compared to American federalism, Russian federalism is something deeply contrary to American ideology. Limited authority of the government, based on a due process of law, is quite contrary to Russian authoritarian struggle and demand for unqualified submission to a sovereign, which however, is circumvented in practice. Authoritarianism, lack of transparency, and arbitrary unequal treatment of the regions stem from the "feudal" system of the Russian Empire where remote provinces were given to vassals. The Russian asymmetric development, however, shows creativity. Unfortunately, the development is not in anyone's control, because it is not based on a mutual convention. The situation and the relations inside the federation are so different than in the United States that Russia should be able to find its own democratic and decentralized model of federalism. The centralist aspirations of the presidential administration are doomed to fail in the long run and separation is not out of the question either.

2.4 Local Self-Governance

Municipal self-governance was introduced to Russia by the constitution of 1993. The constitution only contains four articles concerning municipal self-governance (articles 130–134), but afterwards two laws were passed—one on Self-Governance (1996) and the other on the Financial Basis of Self-Governance (1997).

The model for municipal self-governance in Russia is the European Charter of Self-Governance, the implementation of which was one condition for the membership of the Russian Federation in the Council of Europe. Municipal self-governance is, however, something totally new in Russia. During the Soviet era, the state took care of all the administration, also at the local level. Russian textbooks of municipal law mention the *zemstvo* institute before the revolution as a historical predecessor. The *zemstvo* institute did not, however, fulfill the requirements of modern democracy (Ovchinnikov, 1999). It was more an organization of arranging local leadership for the villages. Referring to the *zemstvo* institute, Russian scholars want to emphasize that they also have their own traditions of local self-governance in spite of its total absence during the Soviet period.

According to the Law on Municipal Self-Governance (1996), the local population elects representatives to the local council, which is responsible for local affairs such as public transportation, health care, education, planning and deciding on building and using land. The division of municipalities and the number of representatives of each unit are decided by legislation of the subject of the federation.

The law of 10 September 1997 arranged the financial basis of self-governance. According to this law the income of the local budget consists of local taxes and payments, shares of both federal taxes and taxes of the subject of the federation. On this financial basis, the local council decides on its budget independently from the state. It also accepts a municipal ordinance independently. The local level is, however, totally dependent on subsidies from the federal level, the distribution of which is arbitrary and not transparent (cf., section 2.3.1.4.2).

The first part of the Federal Tax Code lists all the possible local taxes. The second part of the tax code again changed the sources available for taxation. Local authorities have been creative in inventing new local taxes, which are not all legal. The authority to complain to is the procuracy, which has the duty of supervising that the law is followed on the municipal sector. Inventing new municipal taxes is due to the fact that most tax revenues are collected for the federal and regional budgets, while most of the costs remain at the local level. The local level is forced to rely on subsidies and shares, which they receive from the federal and regional budgets if the federal and regional decision makers are willing to give them anything.

The law of 1997 stipulates that the income of privatized munici-pal property goes completely to the municipal budget. Also 10% of the income of privatized state property on the territory of the municipality is paid to the local budget. The most important income is 50% of the property tax from enterprises and 50% of the income tax from physical persons. The total income of private entre-preneurs goes to the municipal budget. The municipality also receives at least 10% of the value-added tax on below ground resources that have been excavated in the municipality. The municipality is also entitled to at least 5% of the tax on alcohol and 10% of the excise tax. All these percentages are the minimum that the law allows the municipalities. The shares that the municipalities received from the budgets of the subjects of the federation in 1996 were considerably higher than the minimum that the law of 1997 requires (Feigin, 1998:47). This is logical, since most of the costs of health care and social services rest on the municipal level. The new law actually gave the subjects of the federation the power to diminish the shares given to the municipalities (Feigin, 1998:47). Besides these percentages of tax income, the municipality is also entitled to income from renting its property, fines, and so on.

The problem for organizing self-governance, which has not existed before, is that its regular sources of income are unsure. The local level has to negotiate with both the federal and regional levels about its share of the federal and regional budget revenues. The Budgetary Code of 1998 even gave more power to state authorities. The local level receives what the regional and federal levels are prepared to give them. The law of 1997 only stipulates the minimum shares. The local level also has to negotiate on the responsibility of its share of the costs of its vital investments. For instance, in implementing federal complex programs, which are obligatory at all levels, the municipalities have to accept the share of responsibility that the federal level puts on them.

In the present "virtual economy", the problem is not only the arbitrary division of subsidies but also the taxpayers. The enterprises do pay taxes but mostly on the barter basis. In practice, this means that the local self-governmental bodies have to be satisfied with such municipal technology that can be offered by the local enterprises in exchange for taxes. Obtaining tax payments *in natura* may even weaken the possibilities to get a better share from the regional budget because the regional level may decide to give a better share to those who are in an even worse situation. The lack of cash limits the possibilities to plan and develop the infrastructure of municipalities. The social infrastructure was transferred to the municipalities with the income from privatizing municipal or state enterprises. The income of privatization has, however, not been very high. The income tax of physical persons is very low in Russia. Taxes were minimal in the Soviet Union and in its successor's virtual economy it is impossible to pay higher wages to increase the share of taxes. Even the existing low wages are not always paid on time. Gradually the municipal sector should, however, be able to take over the social tasks, which enterprises earlier offered to its workers, family members, and pensioners.

In many big cities, municipal enterprises and banks as well as municipal stockholdings in companies can constitute a good asset for the municipal economy. Many municipalities have indeed noticed the possibilities of security trading (Uvarov, 1998:II, 41). Restrictions and obscurities in the regulation of the sale of real estate are a hindrance for the municipalities. Federal Land Law has been prepared for a long time. In the meantime, many subjects of the federation have passed their own laws, which contradict the present and presumably also the future federal legislation. In such an environment municipalities take a risk in operating in the land market (Uvarov, 1998:II, 41).

Apart from the lack of money another significant hindrance for developing municipal self-governance is the Russian centralist mentality. There is a lot of high quality theoretical discussion in Russian periodicals of jurisprudence. Specialists of municipal law seem to understand the idea of municipal self-governance.[58] There are, however, also a lot of voices against local self-governance, criticizing it as being unsuitable for Russia. Many critics do not see any reason to change the earlier practice, where local administration belonged to the state administration. These legal specialists, as well as a lot of politicians, are afraid of competing power for state power (e.g., Krasnov, 1990:10; Eliseev, 1999:12). The president, on the other hand, has supported local self-governance to weaken the

---

[58] See for example, roundtable discussions in *Gosudarstvo...*, (1993; 1997).

regional governments and the power of the governors (Lysenko and Lysenko, 1998:14). With increasing his presidential power, the president has "forgotten" to develop local self-governance. During President Putin's regime, legislation has made the local level even more dependent on the arbitrary decisions of the state power. It can be claimed that local self-governance is, in practice, treated as part of the state administration.

The local leaders, on the other hand, are often the same communist bosses that were appointed by the Communist Party during Soviet times. There are only a few newcomers to take care of local questions. In practice, this means that the same old methods are used and the same old relations count. Newcomers may actually have difficulties in obtaining subsidies from the regional and federal levels, if they do not have good personal relations with the state authorities. The level of legal knowledge is also quite poor at the local level.[59] In introducing decentralism local self-governance is crucial. This is exactly where civil society would start to affect political power. Alienation of the people from political power and their deep distrust in political institutions tends to keep politics in the hands of those who are used to govern on Soviet terms.

2.5 Summary and Discussion

Russian inheritance of legal positivism in a distorted communist version and a concept of unlimited state authority controlled by the infallible Communist Party is not a favorable starting point for developing democracy and the rule of law. The people, who should be able to transform society into a new democratic and constitutional

---

[59] There are also local cultural differences. In cultures other than Russian, there are pressures to decide local matters according to their own old traditions. Such double standards existed through the Soviet period. For example, in North Caucasus village elders were, in practice, much more influential in peoples' lives than local "communist" bosses, who represented the foreign state power. Traditions from below are therefore opposing local self-governance, which is understood at the local level as a model given from above. See, e.g., Shakhmanaev's (1999) article describing difficulties in introducing local self-governance in Dagestan.

trail, are mostly the same former communists who were used to obey party rules and think on centralist soviet terms. If we suppose that people are not totally imprisoned by their previous attitudes and mentality, but are able to learn new things, the unfavorable starting point could be regarded only as a temporary hindrance for development. The hindrance is, however, even stronger because the dominant institutional setup forces people to adapt only with the institutions. Those acting ahead of the times will definitely suffer.

Technically the preconditions for modern constitutionalism exist in Russia, because there is a written constitution and a formally independent judicial body supervising it. The separation of powers led to a severe power struggle that ended with the president's victory. The separation of powers was not understood as providing limits to state power, but it caused a constant power struggle of who has the ultimate power of the sovereign. As a result, the highly presidential system with a weak parliament and a party structure has proved to support autocratic leadership. For the introduction of reforms a strong leadership might, however, have been more favorable than an open democracy that would soon have blocked all the reforms, which are economically heavy on the people. However, autocratic rule has not solved economic problems either.

In Russia, the minimum requirements for constitutionalism to function have not yet materialized. Rules are not transparent. Even a civil war can be started with secret presidential decrees. In the absence of new laws, the country has largely been ruled by presidential decrees on a temporary basis. Sometimes even laws enacted by the parliament have been superseded by presidential decrees. Decentralization is not regarded as an important objective. Actually there is a tendency to strengthen the power of the federal executive—tendency that has not been turned down in the interpretations of the constitution by the constitutional court. Decentralization, which does not find enough support from the constitution, is developed through the back door with the help of treaties between federal and regional state authorities. These treaties, unfortunately, rest on a vague legal foundation since they often contradict the constitution and contain secret provisions. Therefore federalism is not developed openly. The presidential administration seems to have a centralist rule as an objective. The superiority of centralism is argued with clearness, order and the unity of the federation. The presidential administration is full of bureaucrats for whom authoritarian centralist rule seems to be a good option. Constant strengthening of this agency gives more weight to centralist mentality.

The constitution has served well as a formal legitimizer of the federal executive power. After being defeated in the power struggle between the legislature and the executive the Constitutional Court has offered legal support for the president. It has interpreted the powers of the president quite widely and often found some exceptions such as the temporary nature of the presidential decree. Its decisions have had a significant role in closing the gaps in the constitution and trying to clarify obscurities. However, the state authorities neither on the regional nor on the federal level have not always obeyed the decisions of the court. In the extraordinary environment in Russia, the Constitutional Court is inevitably drawn into the political battle, which it should settle in legal terms preserving its reputation as a purely legal body. The absence of a commonly accepted convention, a social contract of society, makes the role of legal checks difficult. Politically, the most dangerous issues such as federal treaties on the division of power have not been brought before the Constitutional Court.

Federalism can definitely be called virtual in Russia. It is not democratic and transparent federalism but contains an inner conflict. Centralist mentality regards federalism as an authoritarian system where the federal center should have the last word to say and the president ultimate authority. However, the existence of competing power centers is a practice that has to be tolerated. Setting limits for state power may develop in this process.

"Constitutionalism", allowing serious violations of human rights in the name of the unity of the federation, can be only called a pretended or a fallacy of constitutionalism. Even reaching the *Rechtsstaat* in the classical Weberian meaning of strictly following legal norms that are set for those who represent state power, seems to be too difficult for Russian leadership and state officials. The rule of law is not as President Putin regards "dictatorship of law"— obedience to the non-erroneous sovereign. The rule of law does not function from above but requires democracy and a well-established civil society to control it.

It seems that Russia has not been able to simultaneously develop democracy, the rule of law and a market economy to a satisfactory level. This situation has lead to dubious attempts to restore order with bloodshed. There are alarming similarities with the failed democracy of the Weimar Republic and Russia today. As Carl Schmitt predicted, people wanted order and Adolf Hitler answered their needs with sad consequences. Hans Kelsen, the other influential lawyer in the Weimar Republic, considered that every society has to be based on positive law and that democracy can be built only on a proper legal foundation. According to Tolonen (1996), Kelsen's approach functions only in a normal situation, while Carl Schmitt was right in claiming that the rule of law cannot be developed through positive law in an unstable situation (*Ausnahmezustand*) without first restoring order.

"Restoring order" has already caused a lot of damage for developing the rule of law in Russia. Human rights are deprived. Fighting against crime demands a lot of innocent victims in Chechnya, but does not include investigating illegal business and corruption in the Kremlin itself. Rebellious governors are more likely to be punished for their corruptness than those working within the presidential administration. The development is going to lead to more punitive and arbitrary law, like in the Soviet Union. Restoring order to the regions means increasing centralism. The total abolishment of democracy and the rule of law in the name of restoring order may, in Russian circumstances, not lead to a well functioning market economy either. Corruption takes care of that.

As an instrument, law has been used a lot in transforming Russia into a rule of law country. The flood of contradicting legislation has, however, led to an inflation of the law. Unclear rules only confuse people who do not even know what laws are in force and what they regulate. Circumventing law and unofficial rules becomes more important in such an environment. Predictability is the most important feature of a functioning law. In a Weberian traditional *Rechtsstaat*, predictability is reached with exact rules that are applied strictly in the same way in all similar situations. In the Russian environment such predictability unfortunately does not exist.

Legitimacy does not stem from the state, as Russian legal positivist mentality supposes. Legitimacy is gained with the voluntary acceptance of the people and with the respect they show to law. True rule of law, therefore, has to be connected with democracy. Developing a market economy may be more effective in the absence of democracy but not developing the rule of law. On the one hand, reforms are possible only when there is order and an adequate legal framework. On the other, only when there is the rule of law can the framework be transparent and respected by the people. In Russian circumstances, the absence of trust and abundant corruption hinders any kind of reform. Dictatorship of the present corrupt elite might push economic reforms ahead but cannot produce a stable economy. The only solution in Russia is to try "to rebuild the ship at sea" (cf., Elster *et al.*, 1998). Restoring order in the Russian meaning of the word only means a return to the centralist, harsh and arbitrary state power with a corrupt elite leading the country.

Civil society does not develop easily and rapidly. In the absence of a civil society, lawyers and courts have an important role in establishing the rule of law. Even if opinion surveys do not show high trust in courts, they have been able to raise their significance with the help of their newly gained independence. Specialists are able to show that something can be done to restore trust and a well functioning rule of law. In this way, a civil society might be able to have better soil to grow.

However, the rule of law and democracy are difficult to develop when the economy is a disaster. The economic failure in Russia is therefore the crucial key for the misery and the vicious circle also hindering democracy and the rule of law to develop. Therefore, a clear vision for economic development is desperately needed, not an illusion on the greatness of Russia. A functioning economy does not develop from above either. The state should offer a predictable framework for the economy to grow from below. Successful regions with successful companies would gradually diminish the need for superpower mentality. Perhaps Russia is too big to be effectively developed from the center above. Unity should not be preserved only for itself, if it does not produce any real advantages.

References

Books and Articles

Alekseev, S.S. (1999). Pravo. Azbuka, teoriya, filosofiya. Opyt kompleksnogo issledovanya (Law, the Elements, Theory, Philosophy. Experience of Comprehensive Research). Statut. Moscow (in Russian).

Alexander, Larry (1998). Introduction. In: Larry Alexander (ed.) *Constitutionalism. Philosophical Foundations.* Cambridge University Press, United Kingdom, pp. 1–15.

Altamirova, Zura (1999). Zhizn v poslevoennoi Chechne (Life in Post-war Chechnya). In: D. Furman (ed.) *Chechnya i Rossiya: Obshchestva i gosudarstva (Chechnya and Russia: Societies and States).* Publications of the Andrei Sakharov Centre, Moscow (in Russian).

Berman, Harold J. (1983). *Law and Revolution. The Formation of the Western Legal Tradition.* Harvard University Press.

Berman, Harold J. (1996). The Struggle for Law in Post-Soviet Russia. In: A. Sajo (ed.) *Western Rights? Post-Communist Application.* Kluwer, pp. 41–55.

Bowring, Bill (1999). Politics Versus the Rule of Law in the Work of the Russian Constitutional Court. In: Jiri Priban and James Young (eds.) *The Rule of Law in Central Europe. The Reconstruction of Legality, Constitutionalism and Civil Society in the Post-Communist Countries.* Ashgate, Dartmouth, pp. 257–277.

Bozrov, V.M. and V.M. Kobyakov (1996). Nekotorye protsessualnye aspekty naznacheniya sudebnogo zasedaniya i poryadka predvaritelnogo slushaniya v sude prisyazhnyh (Some procedural aspects in nominating the composition of a court session and pretrial procedure in jury courts). *Gosudarstvo i pravo*, No. 6, pp. 19–29 (in Russian).

Butler, William E. (1999). *Russian Law.* Oxford University Press.

Byudzhetnaya sistema Rossii (1999). *Uchebnik dlya vuzov (The Russian Budgetary System. A Textbook for Universities).* G.B. Polyak (ed.), Yuniti, Moscow (in Russian).

Chesnov, Ya. (1999). Byt chechentsem: lichnost i etnicheskie identifikatsii naroda (Being a Chechen: Identity and Ethnical Identification of the People). In: D. Furman (ed.) *Chechnya i Rossiya: Obshchestvo i gosudarstva (Chechnya and Russia: Societies and States).* Publications of the Andrei Sakharov Center, No. 3, pp. 63–101 (in Russian).

Country Reports on Human Rights Practices. Russia (1999). Released by the Bureau of Democracy, Human Rights, and Labor, US Department of State, 25 February 2000.

Dmitriev, Yu.A. and M.A. Shapkin (1995). Problemy tsentralizatsii v rukovodstve organami prokuratury (Problems of centralization in the management of the organs of procuracy). *Gosudarstvo i pravo*, No. 7, pp. 29–34 (in Russian).

Dobrynin, N.M. (1998). Problemy pravovogo regulirovaniya otnoshenii kraya (oblasti) s vhodyashchimi v ih sostav avtonomnymi okrugami (Problems of legal regulation of the relations of territories and regions with autonomous areas, which are situated in the territory of the latter). *Gosudarstvo i pravo*, No. 7, pp. 46–50 (in Russian).

Dyzenhaus, David (1997). *Legality and Legitimacy*. Carl Schmitt, Hans Kelsen and Hermann Heller in Weimar. Clarendon Press, Oxford.

Ebzeev, B.S. (1998). Tolkovanie konstitutsii konstitutsionnym sudom Rossiiskoi Federatsii: Teoreticheskie i prakticheskie problemy (Interpretation of the Constitution of the Constitutional Court of the Russian Federation). *Gosudarstvo i pravo*, No. 5, pp. 5–12 (in Russian).

Efremov, Dmitry F., Lars Carlsson, Mats-Olov Olsson and Alexander S. Sheingauz (1999). Institutional Change and Transition in the Forest Sector of Khabarovsk Krai. Interim Report IR-99-068. International Institute for Applied Systems Analysis, Laxenburg, Austria.

Eliseev, B.P. (1999). Dogovory i soglasheniya mezhdu Rossiiskoi Federatsiei i subektami Rossiiskoi Federatsii: Reshenie ili porozhdenie problem? (Treaties and agreements between the Russian Federation and the subjects of the Russian Federation: Solving or Raising Problems?) *Gosudarstvo i pravo*, No. 4, pp. 5–13 (in Russian).

Elster, Jon (1993). The Necessity and Impossibility of Simultaneous Economic and Political Reform. In: D. Greenberg and S.N. Katz (eds.) *Constitutionalism and Democracy. Transitions in the Contemporary World*. Oxford University Press, New York, pp. 267–274.

Elster, Jon, Claus Offe and Ulrich K. Preuss (1998). *Institutional Design in Post-communist Societies. Rebuilding the Ship at Sea.* Cambridge University Press.

Feigin, U. (1998). Federalnoe zakonodatelstvo o finansovyh osnovakh mestnogo samoupravleniya (Federal legislation on the financial basis of local self-government). *Khozyaistvo i pravo*, No. 11, pp. 44–51 (in Russian).

Gorobets, V.D. (1998). Sistema komitetov i komissii palat federalnogo sobraniya (The system of committees and commissions of the houses of the federal assembly). *Gosudarstvo i pravo*, No. 8, pp. 33–38 (in Russian).

Gosudarstvo i pravo (1993). Roundtable Discussion. No. 6, pp. 141–147 (in Russian).

Gosudarstvo i pravo (1997). Roundtable Discussion. No. 5, pp. 24–45 (in Russian).

Grigoriev, Serguei E., Serguei A. Nagaev and Andreas Wörgötter (1994). Regional Economic Development and Political Attitudes of the Population of Russia: Results for the December 1993 Federal Elections. No. 15, Institute for Advanced Studies, Vienna, Austria.

Hosking, Geoffrey (1985). *A History of the Soviet Union*. Fontana Press/Collins, Glasgow.

Human Rights and Legal Reform in the Russian Federation (1993). Lawyers Committee for Human Rights. New York, March.

Istoriya gosudarstvennogo upravleniya Rossii dlya studentov vuzov (1999). (History of Russian State Administration for University Students). V.G. Ignatov (ed.). Feniks, Rostov-na-Donu (in Russian).

Justice Delayed (1995). The Russian Constitutional Court and Human Rights. A Report of the Lawyers Committee of Human Rights, March.

Kääriäinen, K. and D. Furman (2000a). Religioznost v Rossii v 90-e gody (Religiousness in Russia in the 1990s). In: K. Kääriäinen and D. Furman (eds.) *Starye tserkvi, novye veruyschie. Religiya v massovom soznanii postsovetskoj Rossii (Old Churches, New Believers. Religion in the Public Knowledge of Post-soviet Russia)*. Letnii sad, Moscow, pp. 7–48 (in Russian).

Kääriäinen, K. and D. Furman (2000b). Religiya i politika v massovom russkom soznanii (Religion and Politics in the Russian Public Knowledge). In: K. Kääriäinen and D. Furman (eds.) *Starye tserkvi, novye veruyushchie. Religiya v massovom soznanii postsovetskoj Rossii (Old Churches, New Believers. Religion in the Public Knowledge of Post-soviet Russia)*. Letnii sad, Moscow, pp. 49–78 (in Russian).

Kagarlitskii, Boris (1999). Interview with Boris Kagarlitskii. *Liberation*, 18 December (in French).

Karapetyan, L.M. (1996). K voprosu o "modelyakh" federalisma (Kriticheskii obzor nekotorykh publikatsii) (The question of the "models" of federalism (A critical survey of some publications)). *Gosudarstvo i pravo*, No. 12 (in Russian).

Kay, Richard D. (1998). American Constitutionalism. In: Larry Alexander (ed.) *Constitutionalism. Philosophical Foundations*. Cambridge University Press, United Kingdom, pp. 16–63.

Kirkow, Peter (1996). Distributional Coalitions, Budgetary Problems and Fiscal Federalism in Russia. *Communist Economies and Economic Transformation*, Vol. 8, No. 3, September, pp. 277–298.

Kondrashev, A.A. (2000). Konstitutsionno-pravovye sposoby federalnogo prinuzhdeniya: Problemy teorii i realizatsii v konstitutsii Rossiiskoi Federatsii (Legal means of federal coercion: Problems of theory and practice of the constitution of the Russian Federation). *Gosudarstvo i pravo*, No. 2, pp. 10–15 (in Russian).

Konstitutsiya Rossiiskoi Federatsii (1994). Kommentarii (Constitution of the Russian Federation. A Commentary). B.N. Topornin, Yu.M. Baturin and R.G. Orehov (eds.). Yuridicheskaya literatura, Moscow (in Russian).

Kozlov, A.E, T.S. Rumyantseva and V.I. Chekharina (1996). Initsiativnyi proekt federalnogo konstitutsionnogo zakona Rossiiskoi Federatsii "O poryadke izmeneniya konstitutsionno-pravovogo statusa subekta Rossiiskoi Federatsii, obrazovaniya v ee sostave novogo subekta i prinyatiya v Rossiiskuyu Federatsiyu novogo subekta" (A Proposal to introduce a federal constitutional law "On the procedure to change the legal status of a subject of the Russian federation, to form a new subject within the federation and to take a new subject into the federation"). *Gosudarstvo i Pravo*, No. 3, p. 110–117 (in Russian).

Krasnov, M.A. (1990). Mestnoe samoupravlenie: gosudarstvennoe ili obshchestvennoe (Governmental or social local self-governance). *Sovetskoe gosudarstvo i pravo*, No. 10 (in Russian).

Krestyaninov, E.V. (1995). Osobennosti poryadka prinyatiya federalnykh konstitutsionnyh zakonov (Special features of passing federal constitutional laws). *Gosudarstvo i pravo,* No. 5, pp. 3–14 (in Russian).

Kulyabin, A.I. (1992). Prezidentstvo—luchshaya li eto forma ispolnitelnoi vlasti? (Presidency—the best form of executive power?). *Gosudarstvo i pravo*, No. 8, pp. 20–21 (in Russian).

Kuznetsov, E.L. (1996). Iz istorii sozdaniya instituta Prezidenta SSSR (The history of founding the institution of presidency in the Soviet Union). *Gosudarstvo i pravo*, No. 5, pp. 95–104 (in Russian).

Lebedev, A.N. (1999). Status subekta Rossiiskoi Federatsii. Osnovy kontseptsii, konstitutsionnaya model, praktika (The Status of a subject of the Russian Federation. The foundations of the concept, the constitutional model, practice). Institut gosudarstva i prava, Moscow (in Russian).

Lenin, V.I. (1967). Thesis of the Socialist Revolution and the Right of Nations to Self-Determination. Selected Works.

Lukyanov, A.I. (1999). Interview with A.I. Lukyanov, Head of the Committee of the State Duma for Legislation and Legal Reform. A.I. Kovler, *Gosudarstvo i pravo*, No. 12, pp. 6–11 (In Russian).

Lysenko, V.N. and L.M. Lysenko (1998). Institut gubernatorstva v istorii i sovremennoi Rossii: Nekotorye obshchie i otlichitelnye cherty (The institution of governorship in modern history of Russia: Some general and distinctive features). *Gosudarstvo i pravo*, No. 5, pp. 13–16 (in Russian).

Malyi, A.F. (1999). Organy gosudarstvennoi vlasti oblasti: problemy organizatsii (Organs of state power of the regions: Problems of organizing). Arkhangelsk. Izdatelstvo Pomorskogo gosudarstvennogo universiteta imeni M.V. Lomonosova (in Russian).

Mateikovich, M.S. (1998). Problemy pravogogo regulirovaniya vyborov v zakonodatelnye i ispolnitelnye organy gosudarsvennoi vlasti subektov Rossiiskoi Federatsii (Problems of legal regulation of elections of legislative and executive organs of state power of the subjects of the federation). *Gosudarstvo i pravo,* No. 7, pp. 51–56 (in Russian).

McAuley, Mary (1997). *Russia's Politics of Uncertainty.* Cambridge University Press.

Mikhailovskaya, I. (1995). Constitutional Rights in Russian Public Opinion. *East European Constitutional Review,* Vol. 4, No. 1 (winter).

Mishler, William and Richard Rose (1995). Trust, Distrust and Skepticism about Institutions of Civil Society. Studies in Public Policy 252, Center for the Study of Public Policy, University of Strathclyde, United Kingdom.

Mizulina, E.B. (1992). Nezavisimost suda eshche ne est garantiya pravosudiya (Independency of the court does not yet guarantee justice). *Gosudarstvo i pravo*, No. 4, pp. 52–61 (in Russian).

Mukhametshin, F.H. (1994). Rossiiskii federalizm: problemy formirovaniya otnoshenii novogo tipa (Russian federalism: Problems in formulating relations of a new type). *Gosudarstvo i pravo*, No. 3, pp. 49–59 (in Russian).

Nersesyants, V.S. (1999). *Filosofiya prava. Uchebnik dlya vuzov (Philosophy of Law. Textbook for Universities)*. Izdatelskaya gruppa Norma–Infra, Moscow (in Russian).

Nystén-Haarala, Soili (1994). Does the Russian Constitution Justify an Offensive Against Chechnya. *Humanitäres Völkerrecht*, No. 2, pp. 104–107.

Nystén-Haarala, Soili (1999). Rossiisko-chechenskii konflikt— mezhdunarodnoe pravo i politika (The Russian-Chechen conflict— international law and politics). In: D. Furman (ed.) *Chechnya i Rossiya: Obshchestvo i gosudarstva (Chechnya and Russia: Societies and States)*. Publications of the Andrei Sakharov Center, No. 3, Moscow, pp. 360–371 (in Russian).

Ostrom, Vincent (1987). *The Political Theory of a Compound Republic. Designing the American Experiment.* Second revised and enlarged edition. University of Nebraska Press, Lincoln and London.

Ovchinnikov, I.I. (1999). Mestnoe samoupravlenie v sisteme narodovlastiya (Local self-governance in democracy). Institut gosudarstvo i pravo, Moscow (in Russian).

Parlamentskoe pravo Rossii (1999). (Russian parliamentary law). I.M. Stepanov and T.Ya. Habrieva (eds.). Institut gosudarstvo i pravo, Moscow (in Russian).

Piipponen, Minna (1999). Transition in the Forest Sector of the Republic of Karelia. Interim Report IR-99-070. International Institute for Applied Systems Analysis, Laxenburg, Austria. Also published in: *Fennia*, 177:2, 196.

Polenina, S.V. (1993). Federativnye dogovory i struktura zakonodatelstvo Rossii (Federal treaties and the structure of Russian legislation). *Gosudarstvo i pravo*, No. 1, pp. 3–12 (in Russian).

Pustogarov, V.V. (1994). Mezhdunarodnye svyazi subektov Rossiiskoi Federatsii i ih pravovoe regulirovanie (International relations of the subjects of the Russian Federation and their legal regulation). *Gosudarstvo i pravo*, No. 7, pp. 131–138 (in Russian).

Putnam, Robert D. (1993). *Making Democracy Work*. With Robert Leonardi and Raffaella Y. Nanetti. Princeton University Press.

Remington, Thomas F., Steven S. Smith and Moshe Haspel (1998). Decrees, Law and Inter-Branch Relations in the Russian Federation. *Post-Soviet Affairs*, Vol. 14, 4, pp. 287–322.

Roeder, Philip G. (1994). Varieties of Post-Soviet Authoritarian Regimes. *Post-Soviet Affairs*, 10, 1, pp. 61–101.

Rose, Richard (1996). New Russia Barometer VI: After the Presidential Election. Studies in Public Policy 272, Center for the Study of Public Policy, University of Strathclyde, United Kingdom.

Rose, Richard (1998). Getting Things Done with Social Capital: New Russia Barometer VII. Studies in Public Policy 303, Center for the Study of Public Policy, University of Strathclyde, United Kingdom.

Rose, Richard (1999). New Russia Barometer Trends Since 1992. Studies in Public Policy 320, Center for the Study of Public Policy, University of Strathclyde, United Kingdom.

Rose, Richard and Christian Haerpher (1994). New Russia Barometer III: The Results. Studies in Public Policy 228, Center for the Study of Public Policy, University of Strathclyde, United Kingdom.

Rose, Richard and Dop Chull Shin (1998). Qualities of Incomplete Democracies. Russia, the Czech Republic and Korea Compared. Studies in Public Policy 302, Center for the Study of Public Policy, University of Strathclyde, United Kingdom.

Rose, Richard, Irina Boeva and Viacheslav Shironin (1993). How Russians are Coping with Transition: New Russia Barometer II. Studies in Public Policy 216, Center for the Study of Public Policy, University of Strathclyde, United Kingdom.

Russia Today (2000a). 19 January.

Russia Today (2000b). 20 January.

Satarov and Krasnov (1999). *Nezavisimaya gazeta*, 19 August.

Shakhmanaev, U.Sh. (1999). Sovershenstvovanie izbiratelnoi sistemy i reformirovanie mestnogo samoupravleniya v respublike Dagestan (Improving the electoral system and the reformation of local self-governance in the Republic of Dagestan). *Gosudarstvo i pravo*, No. 1, pp. 5–10 (in Russian).

Sheingauz, Alexander, Sten Nilsson and Anatoly Shvidenko (1995). Russian Forest Legislation. Working Paper WP-95-045. International Institute for Applied Systems Analysis, Laxenburg, Austria.

Sheinis, V.L. (1997). Ternistyi put rossiiskoi konstitutsii (The thorny path of the Russian constitution). *Gosudarstvo i pravo*, No. 12, pp. 62–73 (in Russian).

Shulzhenko, Yu.L. (1995). Konstitutsionnyi kontrol v Rossii (Constitutional control in Russia). Rossiiskaya akademiya nauk. Institut gosudarstvo i prava, Moscow (in Russian).

Skapska, Grazyna (1999a). Between "Civil Society" and "Europe". Post-Classical Constitutionalism After the Collapse of Communism in a Socio-Legal Perspective. In: Jiri Priban and James Young (eds.) *The Rule of Law in Central Europe. The Reconstruction of Legality, Constitutionalism and Civil Society in the Post-Communist Countries*. Ashgate, Dartmouth.

Skapska, Grazyna (1999b). Paradigm Lost? The Constitutional Process in Poland and the Hope of a "Grass Roots Constitutionalism". In: Martin Krygier and Adam Czarnota (eds.) *The Rule of Law After Communism*. Ashgate, Dartmouth.

Stelmakh, Vladimir (1997). Velikorusskie regiony v kontekste vnutrennykh otnoshenii v Rossii (Great Russian regions and intra-Russian relations). *Novoe Pokolenie*, Moscow, No. 1, Vol. 2, Autumn (in Russian).

Stetsovskii, Yu.I. (1999). *Sudebnaya vlast. Uchebnoe posobie (The Judicial Power. A Textbook)*. Delo, Moscow (in Russian).

Tadevosyan, Ye.V. (1997). O modelirovanii i teorii federalizma i problema asimmetrichnykh federatsii (On formulating and the theory of federalism and the problem of asymmetric federations). *Gosudarstvo i pravo*, No. 8, pp. 58–68 (in Russian).

Tolonen, Juha (1996). Legal Aspects of Transformation. A General View. Proceedings of the International Symposium on Law, Economics and Business in the Melting Pot, 11–12 March 1996. Copenhagen Business School, Law Department and Tokai University, Research Institute of Social Sciences, pp. 127–141.

Uvarov, A. (1998). O pravovykh osnovakh sozdaniya i upravleniya munitsipalnoi sobstvennostyu (On the legal basis of founding and managing municipal property). *Khozyaistvo i pravo*, No. 11, pp. 40–44 (in Russian).

Vedeneev, Yu.A. (1995). Politicheskie partii v izbiratelnom protsesse (Political parties in the electoral process). *Gosudarstvo i pravo*, No. 7, pp. 19–28 (in Russian).

Weber, Max (1978). *Economy and Society*. Guenther Roth and Claus Wittich (eds.), The University of California Press, USA.

Official Sources

Treaties

The Minsk Treaty of 8 December 1991 (Soglashenie mezhdu Respublikoi Belorusyu, Rossiiskoi Federatstiei (RSFSR) i Ukrainoi o sozdanii Sodruzhestva Nizavisimyh Gosudarstv, nodpisannoe v g. Minske 8 dekabrya 1991 goda).

The Federal Treaty between the Republics and the Russian Federation, spring 1992 (Dogovor o razgranichenii predmetov vedeniya i polnomochii mezhdu federalnymi organami gosudarstvennoj vlasti Rossiiskoi Federatsii i organami vlasti suverennyh respublik v sostave Rossiiskoi Federatsii).

The Federal Treaty between the Federation and its Territories and Regions as well as the Cities of Moscow and St. Petersburg, Spring 1992 (Dogovor o razgranichenii predmetov vedeniya i polnomochii mezhdu federalnymi organami gosudarstvennoj vlasti Rossiiskoi Federatsii i organami vlasti krayev, oblastej, gorodov Moskvy i Sankt-Peterburga Rossiiskoi Federatsii).

The Federal Treaty between the Federation and its Autonomous Regions and Territories, spring 1992 (Dogovor o razgranichenii predmetov vedeniya i polnomochii mezhdu federalnymi organami gosudarstvennoj vlasti Rossiiskoi Federatsii i organami vlasti avtonomnyh oblastej, avtonomnyh okrugov v sostave Rossiiskoi Federatsii).

The Treaty between the Governments of the Russian Federation and the
Republic of Tatarstan of 15 February 1994 (Soglashenie mezhdu
Pravitelstvom Rossiiskoi Federatsii i Pravitelstvom Respubliki Tatarstan
o razgranichenii polnomochii v oblasti mezhdunarodnykh i
vneshneekonomicheskikh svyazei ot 15 fevralya 1994 goda, Rossiiskaya
gazeta 14 fevralya 1994 goda).

Laws, Decrees and Other Legislative Sources

Constitution of the Russian Federation of 12 December 1993 (Konstitutsiya
Rossiiskoi Federatsii).

Federal Law on Presidential Elections of 31 December 1999, No. 228
(Federalnyi zakon o vyborakh prezidenta RF).

Federal Law on the Election of Deputies of the State Duma of 24 June 1999
(O vyborakh deputatov Gosudarstvennoi Dumy Federalnogo Sobraniya).

Federal Law on the Composition of the Council of the Federation of the
Federal Assembly of the Russian Federation of 5 December 1995, No. 192
(O poryadke formirovaniya Soveta Federatsii Federalnogo Sobraniya
Rossiiskoi Federatsii).

Federal Law on the General Principles of the Organization of the Legislative
and Executive Power of the State Organs of the Subjects of the Russian
Federation of 6 October 1999 (Ob obshchikh printsipakh organizatsii
zakonodatelnykh (predstavitelnykh) i ispolnitelnykh organov gosudarstvennoi vlasti subektov Rossiiskoi Federatsii).

Federal Law on the Principles of the Division of Power between the State
Organs of the Russian Federation and the State Organs of the Subjects of
the Federation of 24 June 1999, No. 119 (O printsipakh i poryadke
razgranicheniya predmetov vedeniya i polnomochii mezhdu organami
gosudarstvennoi vlasti Rossiiskoi Federatsii i organami gosudarstvennoi
vlasti subektov Rossiiskoi Federatsii).

Federal Constitutional Law on the Constitutional Court of the Russian
Federation of 21 July 1994, N 1 (Federalnyi konstitutsionnyi zakon o
konstitutsionnom sude Rossiiskoi Federatsii).

Federal Law on Arbitration Courts (Special Commercial Courts) of 28 April
1995, No. 1 (Ob arbitrazhnykh sudakh v Rossiiskoi Federatsii, Ross. Gaz.,
No. 93; 16.05.95).

Federal Law on the Courts of the Russian Federation of 31 December 1996, No.
1 (O sudebnoi sisteme Rossiiskoi Federatsii, Ross. Gaz., No. 3, 06.01.97).

Federal Law on the Legal Status of Judges of 26 July 1992, changed 20 June
2000 (O statuse sudei v RSFSR, No. 3132-1).

Federal Law on Procuracy of 17 October 1995, No. 47 (O prokurature).

Federal Law on Protecting Judges and Civil Servants of the Organs of Legality
Control of 20 April 1995, No. 45, changes from 6 January 1999 (O
gosudarstvennoi zashchite sudei, dolzhnostnykh lits pravoohranitelnykh i
kontroliruyushchikh organov).

Federal Law on Fighting Against Terrorism of 27 July 1998, No. 130 (Federalnyi zakon o borbe s terrorizmom, Ross. Gaz., No. 146, 4.8.98).

The Budgetary Code of 31 July 1998, No. 145 (Byudzhetnyi kodeks Rossiskoi Federatsii).

Federal Tax Code, Part 1 of 31 July 1998 and Part 2 of 5 August 2000 (Nalogovyi kodeks RF chast pervaya No. 146, 147 i chast vtoraya No. 117 and 118).

Law on the General Principles of Organizing Local Self-Governance of the Russian Federation of 28 August 1995, No. 154 with changes of 17 March 1997 (Ob obshchikh printsipakh organizatsii mestnogo samoupravleniya v Rossiiskoi Federatsii).

Federal Law on the Financial Basis of Municipal (Local) Self-Governance of the Russian Federation of 27 September 1997, No. 126 (O finansovykh osnovakh mestnogo samoupravleniya v Rossiiskoi Federatsii).

Civil Code of the Russian Federation, Part 1, 30 November 1994 (Grazhdanskii kodeks RF, chast pervaya ot 30 noyabrya 1994 g.).

Federal Law on Changes and Amendments to the Law of the Russian Federation "On Below Ground Natural Resources (Federalnyi zakon ot 3 marta 1995 g. "O vneshenii izmenenii i dopolnenii v Zakon Rossiiskoi Federatsii "O nedrakh").

The Forest Code of the Russian Federation of 29 January 1997 (Lesnoi kodeks RF).

Decree of the President of the Russian Federation on Referendum No. 1633 of 15 October 1993 (O referendume).

Decree of the President of the Russian Federation on the Measures to Strengthen the Uniform System of Executive Power of the Russian Federation of 3 October 1994, No. 1969 (Ukaz Prezidenta RF o merakh po ukrepleniyu edinoi sistemy ispolnitelnoi vlasti v Rossisskoi Federatsii).

Decree of the President of the Russian Federation on the Order and Responsibility of the Governmental Position of June 1996, No. 810, changed on 27 June 2000 (O merakh po ukrepleniyu distsipliny v sistemy gosudartvennoi sluzhby).

Decree of the President of the Russian Federation on the Guarantees to the Former President of the Russian Federation and his Family Members of 31 December 1999, No. 1763 (O garantiyakh prezidentu Rossiiskoi Federatsii, prekrativshchemu ispolnenie svoih polnomochii, i chlenam ego semi).

Decree of the President of the Russian Federation on a Representative Authorized by the President of the Russian Federation on Federal Regions of 13 May 2000, No. 849 (O polnomochnom predstavitele prezidenta Rossiiskoi Federatsii v federalnom okruge).

Decisions of the Constitutional Court of the Russian Federation

Postanovlenie No. 3-P ot 25/04/1995 Po delu o proverke konstitutsionnosti chastei pervoi i vtoroi stati 54 Zhilishchnogo kodeksa RSFSR s vyazi s zhaloboi grazhdanki L.P. Sitalovoi (A propiska case).

Postanovlenie No. 10-P ot 31/07/1995. Po delu a proverke konstitutsionnosti Ukaza Prezidenta RF ot 30.11.94 N2137 "O meropriyatiyakh vosstanovleniyu konstitutsionnoi zakonnosti i pravoporyadka na territorii Chechenskoi Respubliki" i Ukaza Prezidenta RF 09.12.94 goda N2166 "O merakh po..." (The presidential decrees on returning constitutional order to Chechnya).

Postanovlenie No. 10-P ot 22/04/1996 Po delu o proverke konstitutsionnosti ryada normativnykh aktov goroda Moskvy i Moskovskoi oblasti, Stavropolskogo kraya, Voronezhkoi oblasti i goroda Voronezha, reglamentiryushchikh poryadok registratsii grazhdan, pribyvayushchikh na postoyannoe zhitelstvo... (A propiska case).

In consequence of the decision above: Regulation of the Mayor of Moscow. Rasporyazhenie Mera Moskvy ot 29 aprelya 1996 g. 259-PM "O postanovlenii konstitutsionnogo suda Rossiiskoi Federatsii ot 04.04.96 N 9-P".

Postanovlenie No. 11-P ot 30/04/1996 Po delu o proverke konstitutsionnosti punkta 2 Ukaza Prezidenta Rossiiskoi Federatsii om 3 oktyabrya 1994 goda N 1969 "O merakh po ukrepleniyu edinoi sistemy ispolnitelnoi vlasti v Rossiiskoi Federatsii" i punkta 2.3 Polozheniya o glave administratsii... (On the presidential decree submitting appointment of the heads of administration of the subjects of the federation temporarily to the president of the federation).

Postanovlenie No. 2-P ot 18/01/1996 Po delu o proverke konstitutsionnosti ryada polozhenii Ustava (Osnovnogo Zakona) Altaiskoga kraya (The Constitution of the Altai Territory).

Postanovlenie 12-P ot 14/07/1997 po delu o tolkovanii soderzhashchegosya v chasti 4 stati 66 Konstitutsii Rossiiskoi Federatsii polozheniya o vhozhdenii avtonomnogo okruga v sostav kraya, oblasti... (Tyumen region v. Khanti-Mansi and Yamalo-Nenetsk autonomous areas).

Postanovlenie No. 1-P ot 9/01/1998 Po delu o proverke konstitutsionnosti Lesnogo kodeksa Rossiiskoi Federatsii (The Forest Code).

Postanovlenie No. 2-P ot 15/01/1998 Po dely o proverke konstitutsionnosti polozhenii chastei pervoi i tretei stati 8 Federalnogo zakona ot 15 avgusta 1996 goda "O poryadke vyezda iz Rossiiskoi Federatsii i vezda v Rossiiskuyu Federatsiyu" v svyazi s zhaloboi Grazhdanina A.Ya. Avanova (Freedom of Movement).

Postanovlenie No. 11-P ot 6/04/1998 Po delu o razreshenii spora Gosudarstvennoi Dumoi i Prezidentom Rossiiskoi Federatsii ob obyazannosti Prezidenta Rossiiskoi Federatsii podpisat prinyatii Federalnyi zakon "O kulturnykh tsennosyakhi..." (The duty of the president to sign a federal law when the veto of the president has been broken in the federal assembly).

Postanovlenie No. 17 ot 1/12/1999 No 17/P Po sporu o kompetentsii mezhdu Sovetom Federatsii i Prezidentom RF otnositelno prinadlezhnosti po izdaniyu akta o vremennoi otstaranenii Generalnogo prokurora RF ot dolzhnosti... (Dispute on the temporary dismissal of the procurator general).

Postanovlenie No. 92-O ot 27/06/2000 Po zaprosu gruppy deputatov Gosudarstvennoi Dumy o proverke sootvetstviya Konstitutsii Rossiiskoi Federatsii otdelnykh polozhenii konstitutsii Respublika Adygeya, Respubliki Bashkortostan, Respubliki Ingushetiya, Respubliki Komi,... (Constitutions of several subjects of the federation).

3

RUSSIAN PROPERTY RIGHTS IN TRANSITION

3.1 Introduction

3.1.1 Property Rights in Legal Studies and Institutional Economics

Property rights have a great influence on the economy. The political nature of property rights is clearly visible in transforming economies. They are one of the most significant political issues in Russian transition, and unclear property rights are an obstacle for sustainable economic growth in Russia. However, neoclassical economics takes property rights as a given ready-made system. Property law is built on the assumption of the existence of a ready-made clear and precise system of property rights as well. Law is supposed to be neutral. Different property rights, such as ownership, leasing, possession or use, lead to a different set of legal rights and duties that do not depend on who is the holder of the right.

The Russian environment constitutes a problem for such a standpoint because the property rights structure is not yet clear. It is vague and in a constant stage of transition. The socialist planned economy excluded private ownership of natural resources, industry and commerce. It is now disputed to what extent private ownership should be returned and for what kind of property. This struggle is escorted by informal privatization. Those, who are in a good position to do it, privatize "loose" state property either informally or formally for themselves. The lack of order in privatization has serious negative effects on the development of the Russian economy and society. The developing property rights system lacks credibility. It is therefore necessary to go beyond the legal system of property rights to understand property rights in transition.

According to Hohfeld (1919) rights can be understood as a combination of duties and claims, the content of which is what a right-holder can claim and what a duty-bearer should respect. It is not the resource itself that is owned it is a portion of the rights to use a resource that is owned (Alchian and Demsetz, 1973). Modern property law regards property rights as relations between the different right holders and analyzes the legal positions and consequences in these relations.[60] The concept of property rights is wider in new institutional economics than in law because it attempts to go beyond the legal system. Property rights are relations among people concerning the use of things (Furubotn and Pejovich, 1972). Property rights specify relations among those who have various rights and duties to honor the rights, as well as mechanisms that are available to make the duty bearers comply with the rules. The property rights system includes the rights themselves, the formal and informal institutions that create the structure, and economic transactions including decisions concerning the exchange and accumulation.

Law and the legal system of property rights are the formal institutions. Even if modern property law sees property rights as relations, it concentrates on the formal legal effects of regulating these relations (Zitting, 1951; Aarnio, 1989). Informal institutions are excluded from legal studies, limiting law to neutral legal analysis.[61] Laws are important on the condition that people expect

---

[60] Especially in Nordic legal studies, property law is seen as dynamic relations not just as stable absolute rights vested on things, as property law used to be according to the German Roman law-based tradition. Modern property law focuses on the protection of third parties in dynamic transactions with the help of analyzing the relations between different right holders and duty bearers. In Finland, the analytic tradition to cut legal relations into different pieces of rights and duties was started by Zitting (1951).

[61] In Nordic countries with a strong influence of legal realism, the courts are allowed to use obvious real facts in their legal analysis ("reella övervägande")

that they are followed. When legal institutions are weak or incomplete, property rights are informal. Rights that have been enforced informally, for example, through self-help can, however, become legal in the course of time.

Leblang's (1996) statistical study of 106 countries showed a correlation between strong economic growth and strong property rights. The study was made using the measure of economic freedom, which Raymond Gastil and Lindsay M. Wright developed, as a proxy for strength. Leblang's study proves that countries with a strong property rights system seem to have growth rates almost twice those of countries with weak property rights. Whether a country has a democratic regime does not seem to have an effect on economic growth once its property rights system is taken into account. According to Leblang, it is the commitment of the political regime to property rights that count and indirectly influences economic growth.[62]

According to Riker and Weimer (1993; 1995) four character-istics of property rights systems seem to be especially relevant to economic behavior:
- clarity of allocation,
- cost of alienation,
- security from trespass, and
- credibility of persistence.

These characteristics affect the efficiency with which an economy uses its available assets. The credibility of persistence is also impor-tant for dynamic efficiency and political stability (Weimer, 1997).

De jure allocation of rights to commodities and assets is typically precise. However, it is very seldom complete. *De facto*

---

but cannot, however, ground their decision completely on such facts without the support of other more official legal sources (see Aarnio, 1989).

[62] The linkages between strong property rights and economic growth have been studied a lot. Arbitrary seizure of property rights has always had serious effects on declining economic growth (Torstensson, 1994), but the effect of the choice between state or private property is difficult to show even though countries with private property rights have shown better economic growth rates. The connection between democracy and economic growth is also complicated and it can only be shown that the most successful countries are democratic and that they are the richest (Hellivell, 1994).

patterns of use complete the allocation, sometimes superseding *de jure* allocations. Since *de facto* alienation is typically imprecise, it prevents alienation and diminishes the security from trespass and credibility of persistence. Therefore, neoclassical economics assumes a clear and precise allocation of private property rights to all commodities and productive assets. It is a precondition for Pareto efficiency of competitive equilibrium within a market economy. Markets fail to achieve Pareto efficiency when private property rights are not clearly defined. A typical example of failure is the so-called tragedy of the commons, when open access to natural resources causes inefficient over-consumption and under-investment follows. The use of private assets is generally more clearly allocated and therefore more efficient in terms of neoclassical economics. The reason is that it is assumed that principals using state-owned property have weaker incentives to specialize in monitoring than private principals (De Alessi, 1983; Lott, 1987; Vining and Weimer, 1990). There is also a considerable amount of empirical literature supporting this assumption (see Vining and Boardman, 1992).

In socialist economies, with large amounts of state and common property, less clear allocations of use rights than in market economies is typical. This fact is usually interpreted as causing inefficiency (Kornai, 1990; Moore, 1981). In post-communist countries, the collapse of the central political and economic planning institutions makes the allocations of use even less clear. This fact can provide an explanation for the immediate economic decline of post-communist countries (Olson, 1992).

In a market economy, changes in technology, the distribution of wealth and consumer tastes require the reallocation of commodities and assets. The less costly it is to alienate property, the more effectively market forces can move commodities and assets to their most valuable uses. The costs of alienation are likely to be high for transferring *de facto* use rights. Black markets quickly develop for illicit commodities. Legal restrictions on the transfer of formal property rights may also hinder alienation and lead to inefficiency. Government policies can raise the cost of alienation in different ways. Several post-communist countries have placed restrictions on the sale of assets to foreign investors. Price controls, a lingering legacy of selected commodities in post-communist countries, raise the cost of alienation by pushing exchanges to black markets (Weimer, 1997).

The efficient use of assets depends on their security from trespass. Both formal and informal institutions affect security from trespass. Criminal and tort laws belong to formal institutions, but also social norms regarding respect for people, property and the rule of law support the efficiency of criminal and tort laws. Self-protection substitutes for effective institutional support for security from trespass. Security systems, hired guards, and violence against intruders make the assets more difficult and expensive to use.

Economic legality has not yet developed in post-communist countries. There are no traditions of independent courts. Judicial as well as enforcement capabilities are still inadequate to provide effective security from trespass through formal institutions. Networks of relationships, which developed during the communist regime, existed to exploit black-market opportunities. Such a situation facilitates the development of criminal organizations, which seek to corrupt public officials. This vicious circle already existed in the former Soviet Union, and after the collapse of the communist system the mafia burst out thereby increasing corruption.[63]

Uncertainty about the persistence of property rights for natural resources encourages too rapid exploitation and discourages their preservation (Libecap and Wiggins, 1989). The greater the risk of losing existing property rights, the less likely the holders of those rights will be to consume the property as soon as possible. Investments are not made and economic growth does not appear. Governments play an especially important role in the credibility of the persistence of property rights. Economic historians have shown the importance of credible property rights for understanding the rates of growth in different time periods and regions (North and Thomas, 1973). Torstensson (1994), who studied 68 developed and developing countries, found a strong statistical and negative relationship between the rates of growth per capita and the index of

---

[63] According to opinion polls, Russians seem to think that either most officials (53% of the respondents) or almost all (36% of the respondents) are corrupt. They also think that compared to Soviet times corruption has increased a lot (52% of the respondents) (Rose, 1998:37).

risk of arbitrary governmental seizure of private property. According to his study the degree of state ownership, however, does not have a statistically significant effect on growth rates after controlling the risk of seizure. It is obvious that weak property rights contribute to weak economic growth. Weak property rights also seem to have a negative impact on the development of political democracy.

3.1.2 Aim, Method and Structure of this Chapter

This chapter focuses on a holistic view of the transformation of the Russian property rights system. Development of the formal legal system is dependent on the political and economic situation and especially on the interests of those who can affect the development. Positive law in itself cannot guarantee an efficient transformation to a market economy, if informal institutions do not support it. Formal legal rules and independent courts to implement them are, however, important to make the new property rights strong and effective. Their role should, however, not be exaggerated, because it is both formal and informal rules that constitute the level of the rule of law. This level is dependent on the values of society, on which both political and economic circumstances affect.

The aim of this chapter is to explain how the Russian property rights system is developing and why it is still weak and does not contribute positively to economic growth.

Since law is supposed to be neutral and only systematize a ready-made formal system of property rights, no theory from legal studies can be used to study property rights in transition. There are a lot of institutional theories, which can be used for explaining the transformation of property rights in post-communist countries. The influential groups of society are of great importance. Interest groups continuously struggle for power and influence (Olson, 1992). Institutionalists also emphasize path-dependency, which is due to the interests and mentality vested in institutions (North, 1992).

If the government is assumed to be passive and only providing the framework for bargaining among affected parties, institutional change results from the realization of opportunities for changes in rules that are Pareto improving (North and Thomas, 1973). Changes are, in principle, Pareto improving but transaction costs may prevent parties from reaching an agreement, which could improve

Pareto efficiency. The state may also be an important actor pursuing goals such as revenue maximization or electoral success through changes in formal rules. Then, changes in property rights follow to a great extent from changes in government interests (North and Thomas, 1973).

The distribution theories see institutional change as the byproduct of conflicts among interest-seeking distribution gains (Knight, 1992; North, 1993). Bargaining among interested parties establishes rules that have distributional consequences. The rules reflect bargaining power among the participants. Knight uses the asymmetric power concept.

No theory can, however, encompass the whole situation of transformation. Institutional theories, however, can be tools in explaining the transformation of property rights. Unfortunately theories, which have developed in fairly stable market economies, are not able to explain all the special aspects that are connected with transition. The strength of institutional theories lies in their ability to explain broader cultural features, which are vested in institutions and can be strong elements in path-dependency.

The first part of this chapter focuses on the privatization of former state enterprises, which constituted the foundation for the current Russian economy. The privatization of enterprises thrust private property rights into the Russian economy. Since ownership and the running of companies is an important form of property rights, a brief analysis of the results of privatization on Russian companies and the framework in which they operate is included. The analysis focuses on the results, especially economic efficiency of the change in the property rights system. This chapter focuses on the development of the framework of the system of property rights. Company law and rules governing the management of companies is the subject of chapter 4.

The second part of this chapter analyzes the development of property rights concerning immovable property. It touches on the problems of ownership and use of natural resources and the methods in developing them in Russian circumstances.

3.2 Socialist Property Rights and Reforms under Socialism

3.2.1 Socialist "Command Economy" and its Shadow Economy

Transition cannot be understood without knowing anything about its starting point. The socialist planned economy was an attempt to abolish both private property rights in production and distribution and the markets. Production was organized by a plan, which was prepared by Gosplan. Consumption then had to follow the plan, which was based on production. The economy had to fulfill 1-year, 5-year, 10-year and 15-year plans, which were all mixed together. Every level of the system demanded fulfilling the plan from the lower level and reported its own fulfillment to the upper level.

The fulfillment of the plans was assured with a system of administrative contracts. This system was created in the 1960s to bring in the civil law system beside the administrative system (Tolonen, 1976). During Khrushchev's era, a movement started among Soviet law scholars of bringing contract issues on a civil law basis and developing civil law. Socialist organizations (firms) started to conclude contracts according to the requirements given by the economic plan. These contracts could not be modified or adjusted. They were written in standard form that had to be followed. There was no freedom of contract. If an economic organization, for example, a factory could not fulfill the contract, its contracting party, which was also tied up in the net of inflexible administrative contracts, could take the case to an arbitration court. The court then gave a decision forcing the factory to fulfill the contract or pay damages instead. It was a contractual system in name only, and the arbitration courts were courts also in name only. This change towards using contracts did not abolish the administrative system; it only gave a slight flavor of civil law. Actually enterprises committed themselves to the system instead of only acting according to commands. The idea of development towards civil law, however, continued its life in the minds of the next generation of lawyers.

Socialist enterprises were organized in a hierarchical way. There were tens of ministries governing tens of industry branches. Some organizations were subjected to be under a state committee. There was no competition, but both production and distribution were based on forced relations. Some branches of the economy were organized as "all Soviet", some as republican and some as "all Soviet"-republican. The most important branches of industry were administered as "all Soviet", which means that they were lead from Moscow. Enterprises were all socialist enterprises. The state was the owner of these enterprises, but the managers administered them. The enterprise itself had the right to control and use the property of the enterprise including the land on which it stood (cf., chapter 4).

Besides socialist state ownership there were also the collective farms (*kolkhozes*), which were cooperatives but were run like state enterprises. They were cooperatives in name only (Mozolin, 1992). The *kolkhoz* had no real independence in an economic system where the seeds had to be bought from a certain deliverer at a fixed price, and the state officials gave the machinery. All production property was mainly state property. Land and natural resources were exclusively state property.

According to Wiles (1977), the whole economy operated like a huge enterprise. The soviet system was a good example of an extreme hierarchy (e.g., Eggertsson, 1990; Williamson, 1985). The original idea was to rationalize the economy and avoid profits going to capitalists. In principle, such a system could save transaction costs. In reality, the "enterprise" was too big and clumsy. Transaction costs were not taken into consideration. It was only the volume of production that counted. There were also problems with agency relations. In principle, the next upper level could have controlled the agency relations but, in practice, the loss of goods was significant on each level. The control on behalf of the state as the principal was inefficient and arbitrary. There were so many levels between the top and the grass-root levels that information from the production and consumption level had definitely disappeared on its way upward. The long principal–agent chain effectively blocked all of the important feedback, which would have been needed to correct the plans (e.g., Nove, 1977). Stealing state property was not considered as a dangerous crime, even if the criminal code sanctioned many economic crimes with the death penalty. On the other hand, enterprises were explained as belonging to the workers.

The economy was based on false assumptions and created an atmosphere of getting what was given from above. It also created a huge shadow economy correcting the defects of the inflexible planned economy. There were underground factories, which could exist by relying on bribery (Hosking, 1985). The falsified economy explains why corruption was so widespread. It also explains the nature of criminality in the Soviet Union and Russia, her successor. Production of goods or services to gain profit by using the labor force or in the form of a company or an organization was a crime according to the RSFSR criminal code. Since private economic activity was criminal, those who took part in the activity were criminals according to the Soviet law and therefore had to find "protection" either from the criminal gangs or the corrupted state and party officials or usually a combination of both. The economically important and profitable shadow economy was based on bribery and protection money.

Organized crime did not emerge because of *perestroika* or the collapse of the Soviet Union. The collapse only revealed the mechanism of criminality and made the criminal organizations struggle for their future in the new society. They also successfully took part in the competition for economic resources and political influence. Some members of the criminal sector could transfer their activities into the legal sector. Some preferred to stay illegal. A lot of Russian enterprises still operate on the gray sector of the economy. Private enterprises, which are not privatized former state enterprises, do not always register in order to avoid taxation. Registered enterprises often produce partly unofficially to the gray market using double book keeping. There are no reliable statistics concerning the volume of the shadow economy. It is a well-known fact that those who had capital for business were either members of the old *nomenklatura* or former "criminal" businessmen or even simply criminals. For these reasons, a considerable number of Russian businessmen and politicians are not used to doing business governed by official legal rules. This fact has had profound effects on Russian business culture. Knowing this casts a totally different light on the textbook assumption of rational behavior.

The history of the Soviet shadow economy also explains the difficulties of introducing private entrepreneurship in Russia. Earlier, people were taught that private property and private enterprises were capitalist exploitation. Since economic equality was a socialist moral principle, the sudden enrichment of some people caused a lot of envy and bitterness among the less fortunate fellow-citizens. It is also a commonly known fact that those, who could make profit in the new situation usually, either had a more or less criminal background or could make use of their connections within the Communist *nomenklatura*. Even honest businessmen were labeled dishonest because the common opinion is that business simply cannot be an honest activity. These kinds of sentiments and values of the people are easy to use for political purposes against private ownership and private enterprises.[64] Socialist values are the reason why the idea of private property is so difficult to extend to immovable property and especially to natural resources. The other reason, besides the values, is the fear that Russian natural resources would end up in the hands of a small circle of private persons who already control Russian industry.

3.2.2 Reforms under Perestroika

Mikhail Gorbachev, who was a younger leader than his predecessors, became the first agent of change. He and many others of his generation of Russian communists realized that something had to be done to modernize the Soviet Union. However, the pressures inside the Soviet Union were so heavy that when the transformation process started it also swept away Mikhail Gorbachev. Soviet society could not face new openness (*glasnost*), which revealed its rotten nature. The corruption and the privileges of the *nomenklatura* were too much, when it was finally possible to discuss it openly. Gorbachev would have preferred to direct the country smoothly towards a market economy in the guidance of the Communist Party. But it was the Party, which was not tolerated any more. Even the party members themselves seemed not to believe what they said. Many adherents of gradual transition still think that Gorbachev's gradual reforms would have led to a better result than the shock

---

[64] Jones and Moskoff's (1991) book about the cooperatives during *perestroika* describes the clash of moral values, mixture of feelings and how they were used in politics.

therapy, which was chosen after the collapse of the Soviet Union.[65] In principle, they might be right but reality was against Gorbachev. His reforms came too late and the Communist Party no longer enjoyed respect or trust.

Gorbachev's reforms aimed at introducing the private sector and decentralizing the control of state enterprises. A new law on state enterprises was passed in 1987. Before then, state enterprises had been regulated only by administrative regulations of the government. A state enterprise was determined as a juristic person. In practice, they remained part of the state administrative bureaucracy (Mozolin, 1992). As there were no companies in the Soviet Union but there were cooperatives, it was these that started to be used as the first form of economic activity allowing private ownership. The Soviet Law on Cooperatives from 1988 allowed private property to be used beside state property.

Cooperatives became extremely popular in the Soviet Union. Managers of state enterprises channeled economic activity to new cooperatives, which could sell at higher prices than the state enterprises whose prices were centrally controlled. Cooperatives, small businesses and leased assets were also allowed, according to the new laws to undertake economic activities, which were forbidden to state enterprises. The directors established parasitic cooperatives, collectively owned entities, lease agreements and joint ventures, which became profit centers feeding off the assets of large state enterprises. In this way, cooperatives started the spontaneous privatization of state property. Partly because of these activities, cooperatives became targets of those who resisted changes. They were labeled in the media as exploitation. Some

---

[65] Gradual transition could have taken into account the fact that it is almost impossible to manage both economic and political reforms simultaneously (Elster, 1993). It has not been proved that economic growth would need democracy (see footnote 62). It can therefore be argued that democracy can be developed after economic growth has made the situation easier for changes. Tolonen (1996) pays attention to the danger of chaos because order is absent in the society, where simultaneous changes easily lead. Without legal order changes cannot be introduced. The Austrian economy argues that gradual change is possible with the help of creating small businesses (Kregel *et al.*, 1992).

cooperatives even had to face the anger of rioting masses (McFaul and Perlmutter, 1995:43; Jones and Moskoff, 1991).

Gorbachev also tried to persuade foreign investors to enter Soviet markets in cooperation with Soviet enterprises. *Joint venture* became a special form of company regulated by a decree of the Soviet Council of Ministers No. 49 from 1987. Foreign enterprises were allowed to form a joint enterprise together with Soviet organizations. The economy was still strictly state controlled at this stage of development. A new Soviet Law on Enterprises and a Decree of the Council of Ministers on Joint Stock Companies and Limited Liability Companies was introduced in 1990 but, because Russia announced the declaration of independence on 12 June 1990, this new regulation did not enter into force. The Decree of the Russian Federation on Joint Stock Companies of 25 December 1990 was adopted instead.

When the Soviet Union collapsed, reformers or adherents of revolutionary transition (shock therapy) came into power in Russia with President Boris Eltsin. Egor Gaidar and many other economists had studied neoclassical economics in the United States in the neo-liberal form (Milton Friedman, James Buchanan and Friedrich Hayek), and were sure that the liberalization of prices and privatization of enterprises would lead to rapid economic growth and spontaneous generation of markets and market institutions. It was a considerable change in the ideology of transition from state controlled gradual transition to liberalization and passive government theory. The main argument for shock therapy was that the bureaucratic state interference blocked reforms (Sachs, 1993; Åslund, 1997:454). The earlier experience of market socialism in Hungary, for instance, gives weight to such arguments. According to Kornai (1990:131), market socialist countries maintained the fundamental attributes of the socialist system. The state-owned sector still dominated the economy and the main coordinator of economic activities was the centralized bureaucracy. Shock therapy and liberalization, however, produced a shock with long-lasting and unexpected effects without being able to rapidly turn Russia into a market economy.

3.3 Privatization of Enterprises

3.3.1 Mass Privatization without a Proper Legal Framework

3.3.1.1   *Rapid Privatization as the Goal*

Privatization of state enterprises was immediately launched after the collapse of the Soviet Union and the victory of the reformers in the new Russian Federation made it impossible to reverse the development. Private property rights were seen as being necessary for a market economy and economic efficiency. This was a clear fact for the reformers who had a lot of experience from an inefficient planned economy and socialist property rights. The common explanation of the inefficiency of the socialist economy was that people did not want to take care of property, when they did not have access to decide on its fruits (cf., Vining and Weimer, 1990; Lott, 1987).

The role of the government was important in Russian privatization, even if the choice was officially a liberalist passive government ideology. Relying on market forces had long-term effects on the Russian economy. The choice was political since it aimed at preventing any attempts to reverse the trail.

Fast privatization should not be an objective in itself. The results are more important. The rapid privatization process in Russia was described both as a success story (Åslund, 1995) and a huge theft of state property (Stiglitz, 1999). Especially in the beginning of the process, the fast enforcement was praised (Frye, 1997; Åslund, 1995). From the official beginning of the program in 1992 until 1 September 1993 one third of the state enterprises were already privatized (Radygin, 1995:5). Between 1991 and 1994, 75% of the state enterprises were privatized. Stiglitz (1999), chief economist of the World Bank, belongs to those who use the notion *"robber baron"* privatization. According to him, the alternatives of privatization for the government in countries of transition were the sale of national assets abroad, voucher privatization or taming "spontaneous" or illegitimate privatization as in Russia's case.

Illegal privatization, which had started with the emergence of new cooperatives during the *perestroika* period, was one reason for a rapid start of the official privatization program (Radygin, 1995).[66] It has also been claimed that the government actually attempted to restore central control over the economy with a legal framework under which enterprises could be subjected to instruments of governmental economic, financial and monetary policy (Clarke and Kabalina, 1995). Especially foreign advisers emphasized the need to break the monopolistic structure of the Russian economy as well as separate management from ownership (Lipton and Sachs, 1990; McFaul and Perlmutter, 1995).

Since communist *nomenklatura*—managers of socialist enterprises and businessmen, who had participated in the shadow economy—were those who had access to capital and the knowledge required in the privatization process, they were those who benefited most from privatization and who started to run the privatized companies. Since the old system was falling apart and a new one had not been created yet, these people acted quite rationally and path-dependently in that situation considering their social capital. Even if the formal structures collapsed, the informal networks remained and increased the opportunities of the *nomenklatura* as an interest group. *Homo sovieticus* can also be described as Simon's (1985) institutional man, whose rationality is tied with the opportunities that the existing environment can provide.

3.3.1.2 *Structure of the Legal Framework of Privatization*

The official legal framework is now relatively clear, when most of the state enterprises have already been privatized. The problem was that the legal framework was created while privatization was going on and the methods and the extensiveness of it were largely debated. Several interest groups tried to influence the drafting of the new legislation, and the power struggle between the president and parliament made the legislative process chaotic. Privatization

---

[66] As soon as joint stock companies were introduced in Russia, many directors made the workers' collective decide to change the enterprise into a closed joint-stock company with insider ownership. Such privatization occurred both with and without the consent of the state authorities (Krüssmann, 1998).

was started before any constitutional foundation existed.[67] Thus, privatization was carried out almost completely leaning on presidential decrees.

The Supreme Soviet passed a decree on 27 December 1990 concerning the limitations of privatization. In this early decree, the defense industry, railroads and natural resources such as forests, for example, were excluded from the privatization program.[68] The energy sector, however, was included, probably because privatizing the continuously profitable oil and gas industry appeared lucrative to many. Abolishing the monopoly of the state in the energy sector can also be reasoned with competition arguments. Leading western advisers emphasized at least this argument (Lipton and Sachs, 1990; Åslund, 1995).

The decree on the limitations of privatization, which is not legally relevant any more, shows on the one hand, quite a radical interest in privatization in the Supreme Soviet, which, however, had been elected during the communist period. On the other hand, the limitations of privatization in the decree probably reflected not only the opinions of the deputies of the Supreme Soviet but also the general opinion of the people, the well-established attitudes and values of Russian society.

The Law on Privatization of State and Municipal Enterprises was passed on 3 June 1991 and amended on 5 June 1992 and 24 December 1993. This law was inadequate because it was quite general in character and was actually largely superseded by subsequent presidential decrees. According to the law, the government should present a privatization program that includes the aims, priorities and the limitations of privatization. The program is then accepted by parliament. In practice, however, presidential decrees played the most important role in the privatization process. Privatization programs were given through presidential decrees

---

[67] The constitutional basis of private property was laid out in the new constitution of 1993, which acknowledged private, state, municipal and other types of property (article 9).

[68] Enterprises of the defense industry were also privatized with the permission of the State Committee of Privatization. Private railroads also exist. In some subjects of the federation, natural resources have also been privatized to some extent.

and the choice of the methods of privatization was decided upon at the governmental level. The president had a good reason to press forward legal regulations of privatization, since illegal spontaneous privatization[69] was going on while the Supreme Soviet disputed the legal contents of privatization. On the other hand, privatization would have required a lot of preparatory work to find buyers, ensure restructuring of the enterprises, ensure profitability, and arrange proper monitoring of the program. In studies of the failures and successes of privatization in the Americas, it was found that in successful privatization the commitment of institutions is important as well as political stability and adequate preparation (Spiller, 1995). In Russian privatization of state enterprises all these preconditions of successful performance were missing.

Privatization was officially launched with the first privatization program of the government already in the fall of 1991, before the Law on Privatization was passed. The Gaidar government pre-pared plans for privatization as part of a reform package and issued "The Fundamental Provisions of Privatization" on 27 December 1991. The first privatization program would have given 25% of a company's stocks free of charge to the workers' collectives. These stocks would, however, have lacked the right to vote in the shareholders' meeting. Managers would have received only 5% of the stocks with voting rights. The remaining shares would have been sold at public auction, when the working collective could have bought 10% of the shares with a 30% discount. This was the only method of privatization in the proposal. With this privatization program, President Eltsin wanted to force the enterprise insiders to accept outside ownership (Radygin, 1995). The program also prohibited closed joint stock companies for the same reason.

---

[69] It is difficult to know how common illegal privatization was. There were dozens of cases reported every month in the media. The scandal effect of them, however, diminished because of their abundance and the media lost immediate interest in them (Krüssman, 1998).

3.3.1.3 Interest Groups of Privatization

Managers, who preferred insider privatization, largely opposed the first model of the government. Industrial managers became the most influential lobby and were led by the Russian Union of Industrialists and Entrepreneurs. They found support both in the Supreme Soviet and in the government. Their position became even better when Mr. Chernomyrdin[70] became head of the government in December 1992 (Frye, 1997).

The employees were also a lobby group. They had a vast number of votes and they could benefit from the attitudes and ideals of worker ownership, which were inherited from socialism. Because their union was weak and had always been dominated by managers, they decided to ally themselves with the latter to protect their interests against outsiders. Unemployment was the greatest threat to them. Employees were also under tight control of the managers because of Soviet authoritarian management. Soviet enterprises, especially in remote districts, took care of their employees including their social life and entertainment. The employees were actually not independent or ready to resist management taking over the property of the enterprises. The managers also knew how to propagate their own takeover in the name of the "labor collective" (Clarke and Kabalina, 1995; Krüssmann, 1998).

This combined lobby group of managers and employees compromised a second option that allowed enterprise insiders to buy 51% of the shares at a closed auction prior to public sale. 29% of the shares had to be left for voucher privatization and 20% for the government to be sold through cash auction or investment tenders (Frye, 1997; Gurkov, 1998; Radygin, 1995).

The organ responsible for privatization was the State Committee of Property (Gosudarstvennyi komitet RF po upravleniyu gosudarstvennym imushchestvom—GKI). It could greatly influence the actual process and the chosen methods. The GKI was occupied

---

[70] Victor Chernomyrdin was the former director of Gazprom, the giant state enterprise producing and selling natural gas. He is said to be a prominent shareholder of the new privatized Gazprom. Russian joint stock companies, however, hold information about stockowners as a business secret.

by neo-liberalists who were at least as radical as the Gaidar government, which started privatization. While the GKI governed the privatization process, the practical work for preparing the state enterprises to be privatized was handed to the Foundation of State Property (Rossiiskii fond federalnogo imushchestvo). Financial responsibility for privatization belonged to the foundation.

There were regional State Committees of Property established in all the subjects of the federation either by the federal president, or the president or governor of the subject of the federation. The regional GKIs were supposed to form a uniform administration under the federal GKI. In many areas, the regional *nomenklatura,* however, took care of its own interests setting limits of ownership for citizens outside the subject itself. Some regional GKIs worked quite independently from the federal administration. Federal and regional interests were often contradictory (Krüssmann, 1998).

An antimonopoly committee was also established to work together with the GKI. It was supposed to control the markets so that they would not become too monopolistic.

Since circumstances were chaotic and the government had to persuade both the insiders of state enterprises and the public to support the program, firm and steady lobbying had immense effects on shaping legislation and the actual process. Managers had a lot of bargaining power, which they were able to use to secure their positions in a changing environment. There were also other motives such as simple rent seeking and transferring earlier illegally privatized enterprises within the legally privatized property. Restructuring could also appear among the objectives of the managers, which in the long run was connected with ensuring their own positions.

3.3.1.4 *Corporatizing and Voucher Privatization*

The most important legal sources governing privatization activity were the Presidential Decree on Corporatizing State Enterprises (1 July 1992, No. 721) and the Decree on Reforming State Enterprises (23 May 1994, No. 1003). The presidential decree on corporatizing accelerated privatization giving state enterprises only 60 days to corporatize and submit their privatization plan. In practice, corporatizing means that a state enterprise changes into an open joint stock company. Sixty days is an extremely short period taking into consideration that corporatizing requires an evaluation of the property of the enterprise. A short time period increased the opportunities for those who had both access to the information and the required knowledge. In this case, it was the managers who were in the best positions.

The so-called second way was chosen by 74% of the state enterprises, which let the insiders buy 51%. Many managers also tried to get the 29% voucher share from the employees or circles around the enterprise (Gurkov, 1998). Only 24.2% of the enterprises chose the original model of the privatization program. The so-called third option was chosen by 1.6% (Radygin, 1995), although the third option was included to satisfy the industrial lobby. According to this option, managers and employees of small and medium-sized enterprises could each buy 40%, if they agreed to restructure (Frye, 1997:90).

Most Russian state enterprises were privatized through vouchers in the mass privatization in 1992–1994. Eltsin introduced a Decree on Voucher Privatization on 14 August 1992. He accelerated voucher privatization in a situation where the Duma had postponed the Law on Voucher Privatization for 1993 and had left for summer vacation.

Vouchers are a claim against the equity of an enterprise undergoing privatization. Vouchers were distributed free to all citizens and had a nominal value of 10,000 rubles, which was an average monthly salary in November 1992. Like all ruble-denominated assets, vouchers lost much of their value in 1992 and 1993 because of the high rate of inflation.

Vouchers were a substitute for capital markets, which were to create a new class of owners in Russia. Vouchers could be exchanged for shares in an enterprise, traded for cash, or sold to a voucher investment fund. Making vouchers transferable was a decision, which shaped the privatization process considerably in Russia. In Czechoslovakia, where voucher privatization was put into effect before Russia, vouchers were not as freely transferable.[71,72] The Russian voucher program did not make the

---

[71] Voucher privatization was officially adopted from Czechoslovakia, because of the idea of making all of the citizens stock owners and acquaint them with a

majority of the people shareholders as was the original official idea, but escalated a market of vouchers (Frye, 1997). However, after the program ended Russia had more shareholders than Germany or the United States (Krüssmann, 1998).

The GKI registered the first voucher fund in 1992 and within a year there were more than 600 voucher funds operating in Russia. The reform oriented GKI allied with the voucher funds and conducted a vast public campaign for mass privatization. The GKI was, in principle, against insider privatization and therefore wanted to promote mass privatization. Conservative state officials occupied ministries, but the bargaining power of earlier powerful ministries had decreased considerably after the collapse of the planning system. Once the GKI had started the process, all attempts to reverse or alter it failed (Frye, 1997).

By the end of voucher privatization in July 1994, the public had invested 139 million of 148 million vouchers in enterprises. A fortunate investment could bring great returns. Shares in the communications giant *Rostelkom* were issued at 80 cents but traded at US$6.50 by August 1994. The vast majority of funds experienced severe financial difficulties and were relatively inactive. Promises to pay high dividends attracted many investors but reduced the credibility of the funds. The scope of abuse was also great due to little monitoring and the lack of accounting skills. Several scandals involving organizations that collected vouchers also reduced the credibility of the funds (Frye, 1997; Gurkov, 1998). The worst scandal was the MMM pyramid; the collapse caused one million people to lose their savings in 1994.

Voucher privatization was the first large-scale attempt to introduce the principles of a market economy to the citizens, to draw them in and let the market decide. The GKI tried to govern the

---

market economy. There was, however, another reason to choose voucher privatization in Czechoslovakia. The managers of state enterprises were not cooperative with the non-communist government. They were drawn by voucher privatization, which enabled insider privatization. In the Czech Republic, most of the vouchers finally ended up in the hands of state-owned banks (Tomass, 1999).

[72] Voucher privatization was presented to the Polish Minister of Privatization in a report by Frydman and Rapacinsky (Tomass, 1999).

process to a market-oriented result hoping that the market would do the rest. However, the results largely differed from the original ideas because powerful interest groups managed to turn the trail to a more favorable direction for them.

3.3.1.5 Insider Privatization as a Result

The insiders were too strong a lobby group with all the knowledge, information and social capital to be able to privatize the enterprises themselves. The government also needed the support of this important interest group, which could have blocked the rapid privatization and thus enabled the communists to prevent the whole process. The result was not Pareto optimal but, however, path-dependent.

According to the Law on Privatization, the methods of privati-zation were bidding competition, auction, selling shares or other property of the enterprise. The State Committee of Property had the power to choose among these different methods. The GKI leader-ship favored auctions and tenders to direct bargaining by arguing that competition facilitates fair prices, simplifies the evaluation of enterprises and guarantees the highest prices (Radygin, 1995:11).[73] However, auctions and tenders were often arranged and settled beforehand. Corruption and good relations among the *nomenklatura* people made arrangements not only possible but even easy.

Counting on auctions and tenders as a method and the markets to take care of the optimal competitive result is not realistic in the Russian environment. There is not necessarily a lot of competition when a big amount of unprofitable state enterprises are for sale. The situation cannot be compared to privatizing British enterprises during the Thatcher government. Monitoring and control is easier to arrange in an organized society with well-functioning stock markets like Britain. It can also be claimed that in direct bargaining, issues of restructuring could have been taken more easily on the negotiation agenda. In direct bargaining, foreign investors could have played an important role with their restructuring programs. Restructuring is much more important for the Russian economy in

---

[73] Mr. Radygin was one of the main advisers of the GKI.

the long run than the amount of money that privatizing produces for the state. It is quite obvious that the GKI also knew this, but was helpless under the pressure and desperately tried to count on competition, even when it could not find enough buyers for a competition.

The methods of payment are an issue, which the law on privatization allows the seller and the buyer to agree between them. The payment method can also be part of the bidding process or the auction. Payment can be decided to happen at one time or gradually. Also leasing can be a method of payment. Through leasing, both insiders and outsiders could have tried entrepreneurship without any large investments. There was a leasing movement, which however, was crushed by the mass voucher privatization (Gurkov, 1998). There was also a presidential decree on leasing companies from 14 October 1992.

The choice was political. Privatization had to advance rapidly. It was not so important that people would have had time to become acquainted with running businesses and obtain the required information and knowledge. Paradoxically, rapid voucher privatization favored the managers of state enterprises, which was quite contrary to the original ideas of the GKI. If the government tried to obtain control or at least regain part of its soviet time control, it did not succeed in that either (Clarke and Kabalina, 1995).

The employees and other insiders were given such privileges that their involvement in privatization was quite well supported. According to the law on privatization, members of the working collective and pensioners of the privatized company could buy at a 30% discount, but had to pay the whole sum within three years from the registration of the company. If there were people in this insider group who either had money or had friends in the newly emerged banking sector, insider privatization could take place easily. The problem for ordinary employees was that it was very difficult to obtain credits in Russia. Ordinary people had lost their savings with the introduction of the shock therapy. It was the managers who had friends in the banking sector. They also had access to dividend policy, since they made it themselves. On the other hand, insiders took care that also many less profitable enterprises could be privatized because they had their own interests to protect in the process.

In most enterprises, managers took over more than 70% of the shares.[74] Besides the 51% of official insider shares, managers managed to make use of the 29% of the shares that were distributed as vouchers. They encouraged the employees to buy shares and use their vouchers with their family members. Later on they offered to buy the shares from the employees (Bim, 1995; Krüssmann, 1998).

3.3.2 Robber Barons Build up a New Empire

3.3.2.1 Examples of Misconduct

There was already misconduct in bidding practices and the rules on the maximum amount of insider shares were circumvented with intermediaries. Auctions were often not officially announced and some bidders were even prevented from taking part. Attempts were made to exclude foreigners from the game. Law, lagging behind the actual privatization process, had only little effect in taming spontaneous privatization. A good example of misconduct was the privatization of *Yukos*, the second largest oil company. The auction was organized by *Menatep* bank, which also won the bidding competition and received 45% of the shares with $159 million. In a separate investment competition, *Menatep* managed to obtain an additional 33% of the shares with $150 million. Three other banks that also took part in the competition immediately requested an investigation, which however, the government was reluctant to initiate.[75]

The main theft of the state enterprises, however, took place after voucher privatization was over and the third phase of privatization began.[76] According to the privatization program of 1994, given with a Presidential Decree in June that year, the rest of the shares of the

---

[74] Exact figures are not available because most enterprises refuse to give information about who are their shareholders (Bim, 1995).

[75] Privatization of the Yukos company is explained in Sailas (1996:201). Their description is mainly based on Russian press material. Illegalities and misconduct around Yukos and many other similar cases are public information. Publicity, however, did not seem to reduce the illegalities.

[76] Illegal spontaneous privatization can be called the first phase of privatization and voucher privatization the second.

state enterprises were going to be sold in bidding competitions.[77] The decree was an answer to the critics, who demanded that the state should also financially benefit from privatization (Kuorsalo *et al.*, 1999; Krüssmann, 1998). At least officially, the decree was a new attempt to find investors outside the companies and broaden their ownership structure. Criticism against the low incomes of privatization is justified when it comes to oil and gas and other similar companies, which are profitable even without considerable restructuring and also because of high world market prices. Selling such "crown jewels" could have given some desperately needed cash to the state for investments in infrastructure, as privatization in the Russian environment could not have given much financial benefit to the state. However, the presidential decree of 1994 was not implemented in practice and the government lost its role in the process completely.

After a short setback due to claims inside the government of reversing privatization and nationalizing the enterprises back to the state,[78] the new elite managed to implement the theft of the century. Vladimir Potanin, director of the Onexim bank,[79] proposed in March 1995 that instead of selling the shares of 29 prominent Russian state enterprises they would be given as a pledge to the banks against credits to the state. The plan was proposed by arguing that there was not enough money in the market and that the market

---

[77] The Duma left for summer vacation without accepting the new privatization program of the government. President Eltsin, therefore, introduced the privatization program with his decree.

[78] Vladimir Polevanov, during his short-lived period as Minister of Privatization, proposed the re-nationalization of some strategically important enterprises and gave statements against foreign investors (Kaser, 1995).

[79] The circles around the old foreign trade monopoly companies established the Onexim bank. It has good connections abroad including a daughter bank in Switzerland. It has been characterized as "a state bank" because it is the semi-official import-export bank of the government (Kuorsalo *et al.*, 1999). A bankruptcy petition was also raised against the Onexim bank after the banking crisis of 1998. The bank was, however, not ordered into bankruptcy because the Central Bank of Russia did not withdraw its license. In such situations, bankruptcy is impossible and the creditors have to sign a plan on reorganizing the bank's debts (17 February 2000, Supreme Arbitration Court's home page: http://www.arbitr.ru/akdi).

price would therefore drop and the enterprises would fall into foreign ownership (Kuorsalo *et al.*, 1999:25–30; Krüssmann, 1998).

The fear of foreign ownership and foreign contribution to restructuring, which includes unemployment, has been effectively used in Russian politics. The managers used it to support their first takeover and continued to fight to prevent outsiders from acquiring shares. The boost effect, which foreign capital could have given to the Russian economy has completely been neglected.[80] Even if Russian politicians do not have to take the opinions of the electors into account very much, foreign takeovers were such a threat in the public opinion, which made the politicians reluctant to make decisions that could have cost them their jobs. Thus, short-term effects of restructuring would not have been favorable for the politicians' careers either. Foreigners are mostly seen as intruders, who should not have any decision power in the Russian economy.

The problem with Russian privatization was indeed the lack of capital. Because of the lack of domestic capital, privatization did not increase the revenue side of the state budget, but made it difficult for the state to cope with new social costs with less income. The state and municipal authorities were given a lot of social expenses, which the enterprises had earlier taken care of. In this respect, privatization in countries in transition cannot be compared to privatization in established market economies, where the state has been able to gain money for budget expenditure. The loss of state property without any income led to a confiscating tax policy, since the taxation of private companies should have contributed to cover the expenditure of the social sector, the direct financing of which the enterprises got rid of. Therefore, enterprises that previously lacked capital ended up in an even more difficult situation, which was unfavorable for restructuring.

On 31 August 1995, President Eltsin approved the plan for giving the shares of the 29 enterprises as a pledge to the banks. It was

---

[80] A typical example was the Lada Togliatti factory, for which General Motors (GM) offered to pay considerably more than the insiders, who got the factory. GM offered to restructure the factory as well as develop the product to a world market level. The workers' collective started a strike against GM fearing the loss of their jobs and managed to turn GM down.

promised to arrange this through free auctions that were also open to foreigners for offers of credit. In practice, foreigners and other outsiders were not given anything as the winners of the auctions had been arranged beforehand. The crucial term of the contract between the government and the banks was that the banks were able to sell the shares, which were given for pledge, if the credit was not repaid in August 1996 (within less than one year). In practice, the deal meant that the "crown jewels" of Russia were donated to the banks (Kuorsalo *et al.*, 1999:25–30; Krüssmann, 1998).

3.3.2.2 Oligarchs Take Over Governmental Power

The donation of the 29 enterprises to the banks was neither a favorable result to the state, nor did it fit together with the liberalization ideals of the original transition program. Creating conglomerates of banks and enterprises capable of financing and managing business is an argument for favoring the banks in privatization.[81] The result was, however, a shift of power from the government in the economy to a new narrow and powerful circle of so-called *oligarchs*. This transfer of power may appear favorable from the standpoint of weak government theories. On the other hand, privatization and transition generally is a profound process, which would require not only a strong government but also one that is responsible to the people.

A narrow leading economic class may be dangerous not only to democratic development but also to the economy. Monopolistic markets with tight connections to the governmental sector effectively block any market impact. Successful entry into such markets is impossible without good connections to the governmental sector and protection of one of the monopolies. The Antimonopoly Committee proved to be too weak during both the second and third waves of privatization. Directors of the committee have openly admitted that their agency has been toothless (Krüssmann, 1998). Other interests of powerful interest groups have overridden the official antimonopoly policy.

---

[81] For instance, Stiglitz (1993) has emphasized the need to create financial markets.

Conglomerates, which are called Financial-Industrial Groups (FIGs) in Russia, are holding companies led by large banks with stakes in large industrial enterprises. Establishing holding companies was made possible with the Presidential Decree on Holding Companies of 16 November 1992, No. 1731. The elite banks and their holding companies are the key financial players—the Big Seven—controlling half of Russia's economy. These authorized banks have good political connections, industrial and media holdings and, of course, financial capital. Authorized banks are entitled to handle the funds of central and local governments. They may, for example, collect and transfer customs payments and tax revenues to the state budget. They have made huge profits in delaying budget transfers and allowing managers to use the money to invest in the government securities market. The status of a favored authorized bank cannot be obtained without good connections of the bank's management with the governmental level.[82]

---

[82] The Big Seven FIGs are: (1) *Alfa-group of Mikhail Fridman* and *Pyotr Aven*. It started as a trading company founded by graduates of the Moscow Steel and Alloys Institute in 1987. Alfa extended its activities to foreign trade and created connections to the Ministry of Foreign Economic Relations. The Alfa bank made profit on government treasury bills. It also handles funds of the State Customs Committee. One of Alfa's key holdings is Tyumen Oil. Its holdings are spread widely on different branches of industry and commerce. (2) *Inkombank* is led by *Vladimir Vinogradov*, who started his career in business developing commercial activities of the Komsomol. The bank handles accounts for the State Customs Committee and is the authorized bank for the city of Moscow. It has a lot of regional branches and regional governments as well as city councils as its customers. (3*) LogoVAZ* was founded by *Boris Berezovskii*, who started his business career in 1989 as the general director of the first private car dealership in Russia. It handles funds for Aeroflot and holds Obedinionny Bank, Oil Finance Company and Sibneft Oil. The group holds 38% of ORT Television, etc. (4) *Rosprom* or *Menatep* group was founded by a former Komsomol deputy secretary, *Mikhail Khordovskii*, who became engaged with Komsomol commercial activities. The bank was created in 1988 and is the authorized bank for the federal government. It has supported a lot of federal programs. It has a lot of holdings in the oil industry (Yukos, see section 3.3.2.1), the paper and pulp industry, metal trade and, of course, holdings in the media (38% of ORT, Literaturnaya gazeta, Moscow Times, etc.). (5) *Most* group is lead by *Vladimir Gusinskii*, a

In the presidential elections in the summer of 1996 the new elite—the *oligarchs*—financed President Eltsin's campaign because they were afraid of the rising popularity of the communists. The *oligarchs* had reason to fear that the communists would either have reversed privatization or at least started investigations on the illegalities of the process. The common interest led to a pact between the governmental power and the *oligarchs* lasting until the end of the economic collapse of August 1998. Former ministers became millionaires and the *oligarchs* obtained free entry to governmental power. During this period the conception *"robber baron capitalism"* became widely known.[83] Deputy Prime Minister Nemtsev's and President Eltsin's warnings to the robber barons no longer had any effect (Kuorsalo *et al.*, 1999). The robber barons managed to tame the *Kremlin* and not *vice versa*.

However, the Primakov government, which was appointed in the autumn 1998, acted differently from its predecessors. It started to defend state property and took before the court the sale of the shares of *Pugneftegas*, which the bank *Mapo* had received as a pledge against a short-term credit that was not repaid.[84] The Primakov government started an attack against the *robber barons* including a

---

former theater director, who started cooperatives and sold office supplies. The Most bank was established in 1989 to finance Gusinskii's office building renovation business. Several regional governments in Central European Russia are its customers. The Most group is especially active in media holdings (NTV). (6) *Onexim bank* was created by *Vladimir Potanin*, who originally came from the Soviet Foreign Trade Ministry. It is considered to be the most powerful bank in Russia (cf. footnote 79). (7) *SBS-Agro* is led by *Aleksandr Smolenskii*, an Austrian citizen, who came into business with the help of his ties to the Communist Party and government financial sources during *perestroika*. Acquiring the failing Agroprombank it obtained a lot of influence in the agricultural sector. This bank also steers industrial holdings and the media (RFE, 1998; Kuorsalo *et al.*, 1999).

[83] Deputy Prime Minister Nemtsev started to use the concept "robber capitalism" and made it widely known in Russian politics.

[84] The Arbitration Court of the City of Moscow held the contract void (9 December 1998). Also Procurator General Yurii Skuratov gave a report to the arbitration courts on October 1998 demanding them to pay attention to illegal bidding processes and possibilities to reverse illegal privatization (www.arbitr.ru/akdi).

warrant for the arrest of Boris Berezovskii and three other *oligarchs*. This was too much for the powerful businessmen and the *robber barons* started to hit back. As a result, Primakov fell from power and Berezovskii returned to politics boasting that he had managed to dismiss the government. After that, the theft was covered up with the constant change of governments (Kuorsalo *et al.*, 1999).

If the government had planned to regain its lost power over the economy with a pact with the financial and industrial circles, it succeeded partly. However, the negative effect of this pact was that the government became a hostage of the *oligarchs*. The pact was not an easy one. There were power struggles between the government and the *oligarchs* as well as between the different *oligarchs*. There were murders of bankers and mysterious raids to the premises of some companies.

After the banking crisis of August 1998, when most banks found themselves in financial difficulties, the government could decide which bank was to be saved. If the Central Bank withdraws the license of a bank, that bank can be made bankrupt. Otherwise it is saved and can continue with a reorganization plan. Inkombank (27 May 1999) and SBS-Agro (7 October 1999) were made bankrupt, but the Central Bank did not withdraw the license of Onexim bank.

3.3.2.3 *The Government Tries to Save Faces*

The attack of the Putin government on Chechnya also served as a good cover for economic misuses of the *oligarchs* and the bribery scandal connected with President Eltsin's family members. Prime Minister Putin was able to use the underlying Great Russian sentiments and encouraged hatred towards the Caucasians to draw attention away from the fact that it was actually a small group of influential Russians of different ethnic origins, not Caucasians, who robbed Russia and are responsible for her economic misery. In this respect, it is the distribution theory that best describes Russian privatization. But, since the interests of the state were not looked after, bargaining became more a total victory of the strongest in "jungle" circumstances. Formal rules were circumvented, neglected and ignored. The result was far from being Pareto optimal.

The change in president seemed to give new hope to the Russians, even though Mr. Putin came to the presidency without any economic program, only promising to put the economy in order. Just like the Weimar Republic before World War II, people wanted first and foremost order after chaos in the economy and politics and voted for somebody who promised to bring order. In chaotic circumstances, even war is an acceptable method "to bring order" and the frustration of the people is easy to project on an ethnic group. Restoring order, which Carl Schmitt predicted in the Weimar Republic, was given to Hitler to put into effect. The Russians trusted a former KGB officer to bring order. Tolonen (1996), who leans on Carl Schmitt in his point of view, considers that also in Russia order has to be restored before anything can be developed.

President Putin's restoring of order has been quite arbitrary. One of Mr. Putin's first decrees, which he gave on the first day of his Acting Presidency, was the decree (No. 1763, 31 December 1999) giving immunity to Eltsin as the former president. The scandal around President Eltsin's family and close assistants had decreased the credibility of the political system and his alliance with the *robber barons* does not increase trust on the origin of private property rights. President Putin may pick on some corrupted state officials as an example in order to tame the noise around the scandals and in that way try to increase the credibility of the political system. He may also increase centralism by attacking corruption on the regional level, because regional and local corruption nearer to the citizens seems to arouse more disapproval from the public than even worse corruption on the central government level. This fight is also a struggle on the state control of the economy between the central and the regional levels. In this struggle the central government is on the same side as the *oligarchs*, who prefer a monopoly in the Russian common market. It is quite obvious that the regional level will lose this struggle.

The majority of the citizens seem to hope that illegal privatization would be reversed. It is, however, not presumable that anything like that could happen. It could be an escalating process, which many of those who are in power have reason to fear. Reversing privatization may even be a stronger stroke on the credibility of the government than the *robber baron* privatization. It could break the economic structures again, since the old structures are already broken.

The *robber baron* privatization does not support the emergence of trust in the legal system either. When courts protect property rights, they can also be labeled as those, who protect the rich and the powerful. Only a small number of the illegalities in the privatization process were brought before the courts. Arresting, investigating or raiding premises seemed to be a game connected with the power struggle between the *oligarchs* as well as the *oligarchs* and governmental structures.

The *robber baron* privatization may still constitute a ticking time bomb in Russia. It should be borne in mind that economic inequality severely contradicts communist morals, which have been taught to Russian people during the seventy years of communism. When inequality is implemented illegally without the legal system being able to interfere, law appears toothless to ordinary citizens. On the other hand, toothless and arbitrary law in Russia seems to be an ordinary situation. For the development of the rule of law *robber baron* privatization as well as covering for it with operations such as the Chechen War have been serious drawbacks.

It is also fatal to Russia that injustices of the past have never been investigated and studied. Opening the files of the secret police, which took place in East Germany or even the truth-commissions in South Africa, has not even been considered in Russia. There was no shift of power to new democratic circles in Russia. Most of those who are in power also have a long and established communist past, often in the KGB. Investigating the past would therefore be dangerous. It is also a typical tradition in Russia that power cannot be challenged and that those who hold it are not responsible for the people. It is a question of mentality as well as political culture, which have developed in the absence of control from below. Therefore politics, which does not recognize the value of human life, can continue. It is quite sure that the Chechen War would not have happened, had the Russians really known and understood their history and past injustices towards the Chechens.

3.3.3 Theoretical Implications of the Results of the Privatization of Enterprises and Shock Therapy

3.3.3.1 A Virtual Economy and Gray Markets

Privatized enterprises form the core of the Russian economy. Many of them have a monopolistic position in the market. The author shares the idea with the so-called Austrian economists, according to whom it is small-scale business and entrepreneurship that is most important for a market economy to develop (cf., Kregel *et al.*, 1992). In Russia, there are also new small businesses especially in the service sector that do not have socialist inheritance in their business culture. They are, however, forced to function in the markets that are dominated by big privatized enterprises, which carry on bureaucratic management of the socialist type. The big companies can dictate the rules.

Small-scale business also has a lot of problems with criminal organizations and tax officials. Without good friends in the tax collecting sector, banking sector, illegal or legal private self-help, the business is likely to die before any legal protection from the court system can be used. The police do not give any protection either. The state should support small-scale industry and commerce both financially and in contributing to a better business climate. The heavy tax burden and complicated state bureaucracy increase the transaction costs of legal transactions. There are also a lot of small-scale enterprises, which have not registered and therefore function in the shadow economy. They live only to make short-term profit. Many companies have extended or moved their business to offshore sites.

There certainly have been considerable structural changes in the Russian economy. However, the changes have been different than what the reformers expected. Private ownership did not lead to improved efficiency, but to a situation which Gaddy and Ickes (1998) started to call a *virtual economy*. It is a mixture of pretended market economy and Soviet institutions in a new form. A virtual economy functions through the extensive use of barter, allowing fictitious prices of goods and services separated from their market values. A virtual economy effectively breaks the market-based price signals.

This system works well between firms and also with the taxing system. The government is also in great need of money. The firms are allowed to pay their taxes in barter. Building a new metro station can be a means of paying taxes, which the building company cannot otherwise afford. Problems arise only with respect to households. Households need cash to buy the necessary food and other products that are needed. The prices in ordinary shops are extremely high for ordinary citizens, yet the employees have to accept the continuous delay of their salaries being paid (Gaddy and Ickes, 1998). They have to rely on their networks of relatives, friends and their small garden plots.

This non-payment system is inherited from the socialist economy when money had no value and the industry was sub-sidized by under-priced raw materials and insufficient changes of capital. The manufacturing sector pretended to produce value but, in fact, destroyed it. Arbitrary pricing masked the system. Gaddy and Ickes (1998) see the roots of a virtual economy as lying in the maintenance of the socialist pretense. The big privatized companies have not been able to restructure for a cash payment system and a market economy. In mutual acceptance, the system can continue. Discontinuing the system is not needed by those who take part in it. On the contrary, discontinuing the system would ruin the whole economy. A virtual economy is actually the way the Russian economy has adapted to the changes.

Boiko (1997), a Russian economist who has paid attention to the same non-payment phenomenon, believes that the main reasons for this non-payment system are the monopolistic character of the economy and the weakness of political power. According to Boiko, the other typical feature of the Russian economy besides the non-payment system is the gray market, which Boiko himself calls the black market. In the Soviet Union, the shadow economy had an important role in correcting the errors of the planned system. Nowadays, the gray market is one way to earn cash, which both individuals and firms need. This cash should not, however, be officially shown anywhere in order to avoid paying tax. High prices in the market actually encourage gray market business.

The official statistics showed a drastic drop of production in Russian industry in 1994–1998. Depending on the source, the drop has been either from 20–25% or even 40–50%. As an example Boiko (1997) takes one firm, which produced ten times less in 1996 than in 1995. The amount of used raw material dropped 2.5 times.

The exchange of products dropped four times. Boiko suspects that the management of the company in this case either could not or forgot to hide the higher use of raw material compared to production. He also shows with statistics that in 1995 there were 61.5% more televisions, 22% more refrigerators, and 49% more automobiles sold in the market than officially produced or imported. This means that either smuggling of these products is immense or that the companies produce mostly hidden products for the gray market. He suggests, referring to the statistics and according to what he has heard from managers, that most of the exchange occur unlawfully on gray markets. It is, of course, impossible to estimate precisely how large the gray market sector actually is. According to the journal "Denki", 97% of the exchange of a typical Muscovite shop is on an illegal basis and only 3% flows through the official legal market.

3.3.3.2 Impacts of Insider and Robber Baron Privatization on the Industrial Structure

The Russian industrial sector is in great need of restructuring. The machinery is old and the premises in bad condition and as a result pollution is a great problem. This situation was largely blamed on socialist ownership and irresponsibility connected to it (e.g., Nove, 1977). Turning socialist enterprises into private companies has, however, not made any difference. Companies have not restructured production. There are both good and bad consequences. In the short run, it is good that jobs have not been lost but in the long run, continuous pollution is dangerous to the environment. This situation is due to the virtual economy, which anyhow manages to give some social security to the population. The low salaries are sometimes paid and production continues. Bankruptcy would not be in anyone's interest. The creditor would not receive anything and would only be in trouble himself in the chain of a virtual economy. In the long run, however, the virtual economy is going to destroy the Russian economy completely (Gaddy and Ickes, 1998).

It seems, however, that the situation has developed in a better direction paradoxically after the 1998 bank crisis. Prices of foreign products suddenly became too high for Russian citizens. The fall of domestic prices together with favorable oil market prices created devaluation, which has given a temporary boost to the Russian economy. This effect has also increased tax revenues and enabled companies to pay salaries. Salaries are, however, still as low as before and restructuring has not started. The gray market is not as favorable as before because the prices have come down. Transaction costs of formal production have diminished compared to informal production.

On the other hand, Russia experiences a wave of bankruptcies. Banks are especially in financial difficulties and the foundations of the monopolistic economy are shaking. Bankruptcy was made easier with the new bankruptcy law of 1 March 1998. In 1998, there were 10,000 bankruptcy cases in the Russian arbitration courts, which is twice as many as in 1997 (http://www.arbitr.ru/akdi). The banking system was created on an unsound basis. The collapse of the banks, however, does not shake the basis of the Russian virtual economy, since enterprises can operate with barter. Banks did not yet manage to gain any significant financial role in ordinary business transactions.[85]

It can also be claimed that the virtual economy helped to keep the Russian economy alive during the difficult transition period. If the government and the companies use the temporary boom caused by devaluation to invest in infrastructure and restructuring, the Russian economy would have a better chance in the future. Owner managers might be among those who have an interest in restructuring. This, however, is highly unexpected, even if there are exceptions. There is no investment wave yet to be seen even if Russia's second largest trading partner, according to the latest statistics, is Cyprus, which is the most important offshore site of Russian enterprises. The active role of offshore Russian firms only shows that laundered money has not completely abandoned Russian markets. If investing in infrastructure is not profitable in Russia,

---

[85] According to a series of case studies carried out by IIASA on the Russian forest sector, only a few enterprises used bank accounts for their payments (see Carlsson and Olsson, 1998a,b; Carlsson *et al.*, 1999a,b; Efremov *et al.*, 1999; Kleinhof *et al.*, 1999; Piipponen, 1999; Sokolova, 2000; Ivanova and Nygaard, 1999; Blam *et al.*, 2000).

laundered money is not going to be reinvested. Such investors are only interested in quick profits. An amnesty that has been suggested for those who repatriate laundered money is a short cut, which would have a new negative effect on legality.

For foreign investors, the Russian virtual economy is an obstacle to overcome to gain access to the market. Foreign firms have to pay taxes since they receive cash from abroad. They are also inspected more and the corrupted state officials would gladly receive bribes from them. Bribery, however, makes a foreign firm vulnerable. It can be thrown out from the market at any time, using illegal operations as the reason. Due to high barriers, foreign companies are not going to invest in restructuring the Russian industry either as they cannot be sure that they will profit in the long run. Unstable political and economic institutions favor only short-term quick profits. Without trust in business partners and political decision-makers, the desperately needed investments in restructuring are not going to emerge.

3.3.3.3 *Laissez Faire, Opportunism and Positive Law*

Shock therapy did not prove to work out in Russia. *Laissez faire* has not worked out anywhere. Emphasizing the abolition of state interference by Adam Smith and other early liberalists was historically connected with fighting against mercantilist state policy. The background of Russian shock therapy, the need to abolish the state governed economy, is actually quite similar to the situation that Adam Smith criticized. However, in European established market economies, transformation was gradual and the role of the state never became one of a Smithian night watcher. Poznanski (1992:91) describes post-communist liberalism as the "perverse" interpretation of liberal philosophy. It is largely deprived of its traditional concern for universal well-being and, instead, praises the "jungle" struggle for survival or "private warfare". It is no wonder that claims for restoring order have grown in Russia. These claims have also led to an increase in centralization and state bureaucracy, which were the evils that were supposed to have been crushed by privatization and liberalization. The power of the former ministries was broken but bureaucracy has now concentrated in the presidential administration (cf., chapter 2).

Russian privatization shows that the role of the government is important in the transition process. A weak government that cannot or does not bother to control the process only provides the chances of opportunistic behavior. Markets do not guide the process towards Pareto optimality because a functioning market does not exist yet. When the legal framework is vague, informal rules become more important. Legal rules were largely ignored and social networks counted more. Russian privatization did not lead to an efficient result. Insider groups were able to secure their positions and financial conglomerates, led by a few *oligarchs*, took over the earlier state monopoly in the economy. Privatization strengthened the role of informal institutions at the cost of formal legal rules. Privatization made it clear that informal social networks among the new elite are powerful, while the formal rules are weak and not respected. It was also a process that rather weakened than strengthened the development towards the rule of law. It proved that the political and economic elite does not show respect to the developing legal system as long as good relations among the elite can supersede the law.

Kelsen (1991) was right when he claimed that any political system must be based on positive law. The problem, however, is that creating positive law is not enough in a state where the legal and especially the political culture has not developed to respect it. Legality is especially important in connection with privatization because a lot of temptations exist for personal economic benefit. It is vitally important to control and limit opportunism, which is typical for human beings everywhere (Williamson, 1985). In the Russian privatization of enterprises, opportunism took over due to the lack of control and the strength of informal social networks among the *nomenklatura* and criminal organizations. There was a mutual understanding of opportunism in those circles because the window for personal opportunities was open to them.

Even if privatization (*privatizatsiya*) became petty stealing (*prikhvatizatsiya*) in common language, no one had to take the political responsibility. President Eltsin's resignation and apologies a few months before ending his presidency, was only a show covering the plan to give power to a reliable crown prince. And indeed, the people elected the crown prince, who is a good friend of many *oligarchs*. State power was lost to the *oligarchs* and instead of free markets economic oligarchy was created. Public choice does not play a significant role in Russia because people feel that there are no choices. The propaganda campaign of the new elite, masking their takeover with securing jobs and preventing foreign takeovers, was effective.

3.3.3.4 The Role of Legislation and the Rule of Law

Property law is still in the formation process. In Russia, the system of property rights is still developing and especially everything connected with private ownership is still unfamiliar. It is not clear what rights and duties an owner has and what duties and rights those have who can govern the private assets of other people. Control of private ownership in a country where private ownership is newly gained is a difficult question. Also, changing the public administration of state property into a modern system of state control does not happen easily. The omnipotence of the state is strongly vested in Russian mentality,[86] as is also the belief that bribery is the only effective way to affect it.[87] State officials act with this mentality and the government wants to regain its lost power. Since laws are not largely respected, regulations of the use of property may not be effective enough. Strong property rights require the rule of law and respect of formal legal rules. Economic growth cannot be sustainable before property rights are established and legally well protected.

The role of law in a transition process is twofold. Law should be obeyed but it is also an important practical tool in forming a new society. Privatization is especially an extremely delicate question,

---

[86] The Russian attitude to state power has been explained in her history. When European development led towards different power centers of the church and the state and growing opportunities to challenge power, Russian development led to one absolute power center, which came from God and could therefore not be challenged (e.g., Berman, 1983).

[87] In a survey comparing attitudes in Russia, the Czech Republic and Korea, 62% of the Russian respondents were likely to bribe when there was a delay in obtaining a government permit. While almost half of the Czech and Korean respondents would have written a letter to the head of the office, Russian respondents thought that would make no difference (Mishler and Rose, 1995).

which has to be handled in legal ways. It is a change that people have to accept. Privatization has to also correspond with other informal rules of society, otherwise law will lose its strength and will not be followed and the political and economic system will also lose the trust of the people. On the other hand, informal appropriation is inevitably going to become formal in the course of time. In established market economies, law usually changes from factual law to normative, positive law. However, in countries in transition the mechanism works the other way around. In Russia, the development of law is understood to occur in such a way that specialists draft laws, which the citizens are then supposed to obey. The rule of law is identified with "dictatorship of law" given from above. Business practices do not simply complement legal rules in Russia. Factual law in countries in transition usually contradicts legal rules because the rules of business have to adapt to the inadequate legal environment. The result is double standards, where the state tries to enforce formal legal rules with the short cut of the "dictatorship of law".

There is also a difference between changing positive law and fundamental legal principles. Drastic changes of positive law make it difficult for the citizens to adapt. But principles, whether they are metanorms as Eckhoff (1987) suggests or of independent character as Dworkin (1986) sees them, are much more difficult to change than ordinary norms of positive law. This is due to the fact that principles are institutional values, which are connected with the weight value and authority of the legal machinery (Tolonen, 1997). Therefore, principles that are not accepted by the citizens are not worth anything. Principles have to reflect the values and social norms of the people and the legal machinery should be able to apply them.

Transition changes almost all of the principles in the economic and political fields. Since the values in Russia are unclear, because they are transforming, there are still institutional and cultural hindrances on the way to strong property rights. Courts have an important role in applying new legal rules in compliance with social values and principles. Their newly gained independence from the political system has given them more power, which judges themselves seem to have realized. Their role should, however, not be exaggerated. If legal rules do not correspond with real circumstances, courts are regarded as bodies applying strange impractical rules, which are made for lawyers but not for businessmen or ordinary citizens. It is important that ordinary citizens understand and agree with the contents of legal rules. It is called a democratic rule of law.

3.4 Privatization of Apartments

During the socialist period apartments were also state property, which were given to the possession of the citizens. A new apartment had to be applied and queued for. The reforms made it possible for every citizen to privatize their apartments. A law containing the basic principles for privatizing state, municipal and enterprise housing was already passed on 4 July 1991. According to a Government Decree on Approval of the Tentative Regulations on Free Privatization of Housing in the Russian Federation (25 October 1993), a citizen could privatize the apartment where he lived without any charge. Privatization of an apartment is possible only once. It is not possible to sell the apartment and get another from the state and privatize it, too. At the same time, the rents of state apartments were increased as well as the payments for communal services in social housing (Decree of the Council of Ministers, September 1993). Apartments that belonged to privatized companies remained state property and could be privatized within the apartment privatization program.

Many citizens took advantage of the possibility to become private owners of the apartments in which they lived. Some were not so enthusiastic because an old apartment in bad condition or with dilapidated plumbing or electric wiring could become costly to the owner. Houseowners' associations or cooperatives where such costs can be shared, are still rare and do not function yet because it used to be the state that had to look after the housing system in a socialist society. A Law on Houseowners' Companies (*tovarishchestvo sobstvennikov zhilya*) came into force in June 1996. Since 1993, there was already a provisional regulation, approved by a presidential decree, on housing condominiums. During the transitional period, the state housing office continued to be in charge of the maintenance and housing services until the citizens could start their own association or hire a private firm.

Due to the lack of apartments in big cities, prices have risen quite high. The prospects of buying a bigger or better apartment are, however, not good for poor people or even for the new middle class. There is already a Law on Mortgages of July 1998, but a mortgage is not yet common in Russia. The banks do not give credits for buying an apartment. Neither do they provide credits to repair apartments. Those who have money have been able to invest in apartments and rent them for quite high rents because of the lack of housing and the pressure of migration to big cities. In such a situation, governmental price control does not work and the markets turn to the gray sector. According to the rent control regulation, invalids, pensioners and large groups of low-income people are not allowed to be charged more rent than half of one minimum salary per month.[88] This kind of regulation means that those groups of people have difficulties in finding new and better apartments because they are not popular tenants.

3.5 Property Rights and Immovable Property

3.5.1 Development of the Regulation of Land Property

3.5.1.1 *Background of the Land Law Concept*

The branch of law regulating property rights on land is called land law in Russia. The land law concept was introduced during the Soviet period and it developed to be the administrative regulations concerning land property. Nowadays, it is regarded as being partly public law (administrative) and partly civil (private) law regulation (Ikonitskaya, 1999b).

---

[88] Nowadays, the minimum wage is 83.49 rubles per month (less than $3), according to the Law on Minimum Wage of 1 January 1997. A new law on the minimum wage, which was passed in June 2000 (No. 82, F3), raised the minimum salary that the employers have to pay to 132 rubles from 1 July 2000, to 200 from 1 January 2001, and 300 rubles from 1 July 2001. The change, however, did not extend to using the minimum wage as a unit for calculating rents or company capital. It only affected the minimum salary that employers have to pay to their employees.

The German law from the second half of the 19th century significantly influenced the Russian civil (private) law. The German civil code (the Bürgerliches Gesetzbuch) was the model for the first Soviet civil code in 1922. However, the socialist economic system transformed the original model into a new form. The division between private and public law, which is a significant feature of continental law, was not important in the Soviet economic system because the sphere of private law was so insignificant. Questions concerning immovable property as well as contracts in the planned economy changed to the sphere of administrative (public) law.

The most important feature of German property law was the distinction between the law of obligations and property law (the law of things).[89] The law of obligations regulates an "obligational" relationship consisting of both rights and duties, which exist between contracting parties and them alone, while the law of property (things) regulates absolute rights and duties, which are vested in a single person protected against any other person questioning his title. Within the law of obligations, rights depend on the relationship, which is a bond of obligation between the parties. Obligational rights are relative, while rights concerning immovable property are absolute (Larenz, 1989:13). This distinction between the law of things and the law of obligations is inherited from Roman law and exists in every Germanic legal system including Nordic legal systems.[90] Immovable property was the basis of wealth of the ruling class both in ancient Rome and in pre-industrial Germany. It was therefore important to control and register changes of ownership and the most important use of land. Alienation of immovable property was not as important as the security of its ownership. Rules facilitating transactions of goods developed in the law of obligations in the sphere of contract law, where transactions were considered as functioning between contracting parties.

---

[89] In civil law countries, property law is a wider concept than in common law countries containing the law of obligations (contracts and torts), the law of things (property law) and commercial law as well as the property relations of family and inheritance law.

[90] In Nordic legal systems, the operative meaning of subjective rights as well as other legal concepts was reduced to a minimum due to the impact of Scandinavian realism (Helin, 1988:306).

In the Soviet Union, the distinction between the law of property and the law of obligations worked in its own way. Exchange was derived from the static property rights of socialist ownership. Property rights could not be exchangeable objects apart from the socialist rights vested in the means of production. Subjective rights were not rejected. Only the role of the relations in the sphere of the law of obligations was different. The relations between individuals were not as important as the "obligational" (contractual) relations between the subjects of the socialist economic system (Tolonen, 1976:88).

The concepts of subjects and objects of law are important in Russian law even today. Textbooks as well as the Civil Code are structured with these concepts. What these subjects and objects are seems to be treated as a question of definition by the legal system. It is not only returning to the roots but also path-dependency of legal history that some scholars (e.g., Efimova, 1998) have now started to emphasize the importance of the distinction between the law of obligations and the law of things in Russia.[91] The starting point of the distinction that static rights are more important and dynamic relations of exchange contribute to the static rights of ownership is quite understandable. Ownership used to be static in socialism and problems connected with dynamic rights are new.[92] Protection of new owners' rights is also important in Russia, since the concept of ownership has changed significantly after the emergence of a market economy.

In Russia, the role of property law changed and diminished after the October Revolution. In 1917, the Bolsheviks already passed a

---

[91] The theory of subjective rights regarding relative rights contributory to absolute rights was also developed in the Soviet Union towards the socialist direction (Ioffe, 1949).

[92] In Nordic countries, however, scholars of property law see that the increase of exchange in society has made the collisions of rights more important than the static right of the ownership of the owner to use his property freely. In dynamic relations the distinction does not work at all. Therefore, the old distinction is considered to be of hardly any significance. Both fields of law are concerned with the collisions in exchange situations. The law of property is developing into a general doctrine for explaining the protection of third parties in transactions (Kivimäki and Ylöstalo, 1981).

Decree on Land, abolishing private ownership of land. Before that, there were several forms of private ownership in Russia. There were fiefs, state and governmental land, land belonging to the church or to the monasteries, peasant land, and common property belonging to villages or municipalities (Korostelev, 1998:17). The Bolsheviks withdrew land from commercial exchange and its redistribution and use was regulated with administrative methods. Therefore, the land law concept was introduced to cover the relations to land as state property (Ikonitskaya, 1999b). The purpose of the land law was administering different types of land, which were all state property. The only exceptions were cooperative farms that were, in practice, also treated as state property. Administration of some types of land developed into their own branches of law. Forest law regulates the use of forests. Forests form the so-called forest fund of the country. Also waters form a water fund, which is divided into different types of waters with its own specific regulations (Ikonitskaya, 1999a).[93]

The first land code was passed in 1922 during the New Economic Policy (NEP) period[94] and only the general starting points of land use and land building were introduced by it. The new code of 15 December 1928 introduced socialist forms of land use, such as collective farms (*kolkhoz*) and socialist farms (*sovkhoz*). During the socialist period a more administrative point of view developed. Property became an administrative question, and the different roles of the state as the *imperium* and the *dominium* were mixed (Tolonen, 1976). Property was either local or state property, cooperative (*kolkhoz*) and forests, for example, were treated as a special type of state property with special administrative regulations. Therefore the idea, which is more or less clear in

---

[93] In current legislation, land is categorized into (1) land for agricultural use, (2) land of municipal areas, (3) land for industrial use, transport, energy, (4) land for nature protection, recreation or cultural historical significance, (5) forest fund, water fund, and (6) reserve land. The purpose of land use cannot be changed (Ikonitskaya, 1999a:182).

[94] NEP was launched by the Bolsheviks to save the Soviet economy from a total crush. Private entrepreneurship was allowed during the NEP period (1921–27). When Stalin managed to take power into his hands, the NEP was changed into a command economy (see Hosking, 1985; Nove, 1977).

western property law that the owner of the property has the same property rights irrespective of who he is, is not familiar in Russia. Since the state has the *imperium* on land, even its *dominium* is treated differently as different kinds of ownership are mixed up with the *imperium*. The absence of a market changed the nature of the law and new basic principles of legal theory developed.

Collectivization of land was a great human tragedy in Russia, where land was actually one of the reasons that gave rise to the revolution (Ikonitskaya, 1999b:16). The Bolsheviks who started to industrialize the country, however, saw the countryside as backward and its function was only to provide food for the industry. Forced collectivization, the terror against the *kulaks*—"the richer" peasants—who had owned one or two cows, led to disaster and hunger. According to Soviet statistics, which used to falsify production numbers, the Soviet countryside recovered in production only in the 1950s from the disaster of collectivization (Hosking, 1985). Psychologically, the disaster seems to have been even worse since it destroyed initiative in the countryside.

The state farms (*sovkhoz*) and collective farms (*kolkhoz*) were factories led by a manager. Their workers were allowed to cultivate small plots for their own consumption and later also for the *kolkhoz* markets of the towns and cities. Those markets were important in supplementing fresh vegetables and other groceries with better quality and higher prices than in state shops. Since the productivity of these plots was much higher than the land of collective or state farms, this fact could have been interpreted as proof of the superior efficiency of private farms. It should, however, not be forgotten that cultivating private plots had no risk, since the employees of the state and cooperative farms could use the equipment and working time of the farm for their own purposes. They did not have to invest anything in their plots. Successful cultivators of small plots of the socialist Soviet Union did not turn out to be successful private farmers of the new Russia. The reasons for this development are many, legislation being only one reason.

3.5.1.2 *Agrarian Land Reform of the Russian Federation*

Russian land reform started mainly as an agrarian reform. The first law to change the situation was the law "On the Land Reform" which was passed on 23 November 1990. Land was going to be distributed to new enterprises, individual farmers and agricultural cooperatives. The law aimed at creating favorable conditions for the development of alternative forms of agricultural business on an equal basis (Ikonitskaya, 1999b).

The reform introduced private ownership and payment for land property. The Soviet principle of no price for land was broken to create markets for land with the "Law on Public Fee for Land" of 11 October 1991. According to Ikonitskaya the right to possess agricultural land under private ownership was already introduced to Russian legislation as an amendment to the RSFSR constitution in article 12. The Law on Property of 24 October 1990 recognized the right of private ownership of land in the RSFSR as well as the new Land Code of the Russian Federation from 25 April 1991. According to the Land Code, land "can be transferred with a contract". Private ownership was in a way smuggled into the code. The word "private ownership" was not mentioned nor was the land "freely" transferable. The code, however, established private ownership and transferability and made them legal (Ikonitskaya, 2000a; Krüssmann, 1998).

Politically allotting land for private ownership in agriculture has been a bitterly disputed issue (see e.g., Kruglyi..., 1993:8; 1998:5). Private ownership has been received in different ways in the regions. Managers of state farms have often opposed the distribution of land to the employees. They have a lot of power in the countryside and the employees of the farms are dependent on their directors. The Agrarian Party has lobbied for the interests of the farm managers, who have closely allied with the Communists.

The Agrarian reform, however, aimed at redistribution of land. If the applicant for land was a worker of a state or collective farm, he was entitled to an allotment of land from his former farm. If he was a newcomer, land could be allotted from a specific stock of land, which was taken from the existing enterprises. According to the Federal Land Code, collective and state farms were to be distributed among the employees and pensioners of the farms. The farms were either distributed or a right for a share of the farm was established. This is common ownership with a right to have an allotment. The share of the farm could also be given as an investment to the reorganized privatized farm. Often the shares were not measured or the borders of the allotments made clear. Pensioners who were too old to cultivate themselves often gave the land to be used in the collective farm against the right to obtain agricultural products from the farm. Many other people, who preferred to move out of the farm to find a job somewhere else, did the same thing (Ikonitskaya, 2000a).

The governance structure of common property determines how clearly it allocates rights to members of the collective. Ostrom (1990) identifies a number of factors that contribute to long-enduring common property resources:
  • clearly defined borders,
  • congruence between rules and local conditions,
  • representative collective choice arrangements,
  • agents with an incentive to monitor use,
  • the gradual application of sanctions,
  • the availability of conflict-resolution mechanisms, and
  • the recognition of the collective by government authorities.
However, Ostrom points out that long endurance does not imply that the common property is being used efficiently.

Ostrom's list also includes factors, which are important in introducing private property rights. Clearly defined borders, congruence between rules and local conditions as well as the recognition of private property by government authorities is of significant importance in the Russian transition of property rights.

Unclear allotment was definitely a problem in Russian agrarian reform, but it seems that the lack of understanding of the reform among the employees of collective farms was even a worse problem. People were not prepared for the reform. The Soviet system, which had taught people to wait for everything to be given from the state, had destroyed initiative. Typically new farmers were newcomers from cities and not employees of the state or collective farms. The Moscow-based specialists, who planned the reform, probably had no clear understanding either of the problems of the countryside or the values and thinking habits of the local people. Thus, local authorities neither understood nor opposed the reforms. The managers of the farms, who were in key positions to monitor and apply the reform, were usually against it. The result was that the *kolkhoz* and the *sovkhoz* in practice prevailed. They were turned into joint stock companies led by the former managers. The reform failed to respond to any of the factors that, according to Ostrom, contribute to long endurance of common ownership.

New farms faced the same kind of problems in the Soviet Union at the same time as the cooperatives in industry and trade. A successful farmer was envied and even sabotage from neighbors was not rare. Most of the problems are, however, connected with unprofitability. New farms have difficulties obtaining seed or equipment or to sell the products, especially when the farm is remote. When the distribution channels are built for big state farms, it is difficult to buy or sell in smaller amounts. The prices paid by governmental agencies are kept low and they do not cover the expenses of the private farmers. When the farmers try to produce directly to town markets, the mafia is a nuisance. Credits for buying machinery are difficult to obtain in the absence of securities (Kaser, 1995; Krüssmann, 1998).

Development from this stage to private plots is a slow process. Most people have chosen to continue in the former collective farm as shareholders or simply to reject the land and move to the city. People are not motivated to start as private farmers because often neither the local authorities nor the local population support them in their business. In 1994, there were only 285,600 private farmers in Russia, owning an agricultural area of 11.8 million hectares. Family farms would need support both from the government sector and mutual cooperation. The state has, however, been more eager to support joint stock companies that were former state or collective farms (Kaser, 1995).

3.5.1.3 Land Reform and the Regulation of Land Markets

The Land Code of 1991 is, in principle, the most important law regulating land law. It deals with the right to ownership and other rights for land and allotment of the plot. The Land Code also deals with the rights and duties of use and protection of land, payment for the use, the general principles of carrying out the state land cadastre and state control for the use and protection of land as well as liability for infringement. The specific part of the Land Code deals with different types of land such as land for agricultural use, land of municipalities, land for industrial use, transport, etc. (see footnote 85). These are all considered as different types of land, which need different kinds of regulation.

After the Land Code of 1991 was adopted, considerable changes took place in Russia. The struggle between the president and the Supreme Soviet lead to the events of October 1993 at the White House and to the new constitution of 1993 with the ensuing extension of presidential powers. The president started to amend gaps of parliamentary legislation in the economic sphere with his decrees (*ukaz*). In this way, President Eltsin started to push economic reforms forward even without the consent of the parliament. In such crucial questions as property rights, a political balance should be found. Reforms, which are not commonly accepted, are usually diluted. Along with the privatization of enterprises the president also wanted to trigger land markets, since it was evident that a need existed for land markets (Ikonitskaya, 1999b). Actually, there was a need to change informal land markets into formal legal ones.

The following new decrees were issued in the land law sphere:
- "On the Sale of Land Plots to Citizens and to Juristic Persons under the Privatization of the State and Municipal Enterprises" (25 March 1992).
- "On Approval of the Procedure of the Sale of Land Plots under Privatization of the State and Municipal Enterprises, under Enlargement and Additional Construction of these Enterprises as well as of the Land Plots at the Disposal of the Citizens or of their Organizations for Entrepreneurial Activities" (14 June 1992).
- "On the Regulation of the Land Market and on the Development of the Agrarian Reform in Russia" (27 October 1993).
- "On Bringing the Land Legislation of the Russian Federation to Conformity with the Constitution of the Russian Federation" (24 December 1993).
- "On Implementation of the Constitutional Rights of the Citizens on Land" (7 March 1996).

These presidential decrees created a general legal land market, because they extended the rights of private ownership of the land to all sectors of the economy. The earlier agrarian reform was limited to the agricultural sector. The new constitution of 1993 abolished all of the restrictions for private ownership of the land in the Land

Code. Therefore, the decree of the president on "Bringing the Land Legislation in Conformity with the Constitution" made a considerable number of articles in the Land Code, as well as certain articles of the Law "On the Land Reform" invalid. Presidential decrees abolished the articles on the types of rights on the land plots, on the conditions to transfer the land plots in the ownership of the legal and natural persons and on the procedure of the allotment of the land plots to the citizens (Ikonitskaya, 2000b).

The right of foreigners to own land in Russia is not clear at all. According to presidential decrees on privatization (14 June 1992) foreigners (only juristic persons) can become the owners of land, which they acquire in connection with privatized enterprises. The current land code is, however, silent about foreigners' rights to own or use land in Russia. In practice, however, the rule is applied that a foreigner (a juristic person with foreign ownership) can acquire land for long term lease (Ikonitskaya, 2000b). In practice, leasing is mostly used also in domestic business (Hüper, 1998).

3.5.1.4 *The System of Russian Land Law in Transition*

According to Russian legal scholars, the new decrees and the new constitution created a legal vacuum in the land law (Ikonitskaya, 1999b). It was evident that a new Land Code was needed. The land law was amended and developed further by presidential decrees, which actually should have been based on a federal law. It took four years to draft a new code, not only because a new land code requires a lot of work with all the technical details, but also because private ownership was such a debated issue (Ikonitskaya, 2000a). However in 1997, the Land Code was approved by both the Duma and the Federal Council, but in a diluted form. Therefore, the president decided to use his power to veto the law. After the Duma elections of 2000, a new draft was introduced in the Duma on the initiative of a few deputies. This draft has started to advance in the Duma and it may become the new land code. It could, however, become an unclear and obscure law if preparation has been inadequate.

The Civil Code, which came into force in 1995, also contains rules on land issues. The connection between the Civil Code and the Land Code is also an important question. The Civil Code does not regulate the transfer of the rights on land. The Code, however, mentions that land may be in the ownership of the state, a municipality or a juristic person and that the rights of the land plots can be of various categories. The Code does not mention private persons as owners. Chapter 17 of the Civil Code on the ownership of land and other rights on land was decided in the Duma to come into force only after the adoption of a new land code. The reason for the decision was again the disputed right of private ownership of land (Ikonitskaya, 1999a).

Even with these contradictions, Russian land law would be complicated enough. The system becomes more unclear because, according to the constitution, the land law belongs to the joint powers of the federation and its subjects. According to the constitution (article 36), the federal law should regulate the conditions and the order of the use of the land. However, the constitution does not define "the conditions" and "the order" (principles of regulation) of the use of the land.

One of the most distinguished specialists of the land law, Ikonitskaya, basing her analysis on the current Land Code of 1991 and the draft, which did not come into force, considers that "the conditions" include the categories of the rights on land, payments for the allotment and the use of the land, accessory duties for the user of land in case the law specifies them, and the conditions for the deprivation of the rights for the use of the land. "The order" of the use of the land includes the more detailed rights and duties on the use of the land for specific purposes, the procedure of the state bodies' control of implementing the law, and the issues on the management of the land by state bodies. State management includes, for example, setting out the plan for the use of the land fund, carrying out the state land cadastre, and the issues on the organization of the use of the land.

According to Ikonitskaya's analysis, regional codes can supplement federal land law in details, but the principles of both the rights for ownership and use should be the same in every region as well as the principles of state control and registration of land property. In practice, however, there is quite different legislation in different parts of the country because land resources belong to the joint jurisdiction of the federation and its subjects. Malyi (1999), a constitutional lawyer representing the regions, sees that as long as there is no federal land code, the regions can pass their own laws.

As soon as the federal code is introduced, the regional laws should, however, not contradict the federal law. The regulations of the Civil Code belong to the exclusive competence of the federation. Therefore, the rules of the Civil Code cannot be supplemented let alone changed with regional legislation. So, there is not much left for the subjects of the federation to regulate.

Even if the new overwhelming federal land law is still missing, new federal codes concerning the use and ownership of other natural resources have been passed. The Forest Code regulating ownership and the use of forests as well as forest management, protection and registration was passed in 1997. A new Water Code came into force on 23 November 1995. The land covered with water, swamps or ice is also regulated as belonging to the water fund. The Code on Below Ground Natural Resources[95] from March 1995 regulates the alienation of minerals, oil and gas.

3.5.2 Types of Legal Property Rights of Immovable Property

3.5.2.1 *Rights of Ownership*

3.5.2.1.1 *Ownership of Agricultural Land*

One of the most debated issues after the collapse of socialism in the Soviet Union has been allowing private ownership of land. Land is still mostly state owned property. Those, who supported economic reforms, clearly saw that the agricultural sector, which is based on collective and state farms, is ineffective and hinders initiative. They saw that private ownership should be able to initiate changes and make agriculture more effective (Ikonitskaya, 1999b). Others, however, saw that especially small farms are nowadays ineffective in market economy countries and that therefore big farms should not be divided into smaller allotments.[96]

---

[95] The Russian name of this code is "*o nedrakh*", which means below ground natural resources (economically useful) material.

[96] Roundtable discussions in the legal journal *Gosudarstvo i pravo* (Bakunina, 1998a,b) show how legal specialists situated far from state farms derive their opinions from theories and scientific concepts, which do not have much to do with life in the countryside.

Article 9 of the federal constitution acknowledges private ownership stating that land may be in private, state, municipal or other forms of ownership. This article has later been criticized by many of those, who see that land should stay in state ownership (a roundtable discussion reported by Bakunina, 1998b). Those, who demand new forms of ownership, can always refer to the constitution. At the federal law level, however, private ownership is quite narrow. It was introduced in 1990 with the Law "On the Land Reform" in the agricultural sector. Private persons were able to become owners of land plots for the subsidiary smallholdings, gardening and buildings of dwelling houses. Furthermore, the lands of the reorganized state and collective farms were transferred into common ownership (with the right of alienating the allotment) of their employees and of the people who were engaged in all kinds of auxiliary services in the living areas where the farms were located.

In 1992, the circle of the persons who were allowed to own land plots was widened. Also those who had summer cottages (*dachas*), which they did not use for agricultural purposes, became owners of the land on which the cottage was located. Earlier use of the land for agrarian purposes was required for privatization. Furthermore, private persons engaged in private business in the non-agricultural sector were allowed to own land on which the enterprise was situated. Also juristic persons acquired the right to own land. Privatized firms were given the land on which the company was situated with the company itself. However, the question whether the right of natural (private) and juristic persons to own land can be extended to other land plots than those, which were in the use of privatized enterprises, remained unanswered. Therefore, it is not certain that buying new land for extending business is legal. From the standpoint of foreign investors the situation is a considerable risk (Krüssmann, 1998).

Ikonitskaya (2000b) represents an opinion according to which both natural and juristic persons have the right to own land in all sectors of the economy, irrespective of the origins of the ownership on land, except when the land according to the legislation may only be in the state or municipal ownership. This opinion is based on the list of the categories of persons and activities allowed to own land given in article 7 of the Land Code as well as on the decree of the president "On bringing the Land Legislation of the RF in

Conformity with the Constitution" and articles 212 and 214 of the Civil Code (Ikonitskaya, 2000b). The typical opinion in Russian jurisprudence is that if something is not especially allowed it is prohibited. The absence of a clear regulation allowing companies to buy land for business purposes therefore does not give enough security in transactions of land property. It gives local bureaucracy too much power and increases transaction costs.

There are, however, differences between the subjects of the federation. Regional laws are not consistent with federal legislation. For example, in Bashkortostan and in Sakha-Yakutia land is considered to be the common national property of the population. In Mari El, citizens may possess land for subsidiary smallholdings, gardening and building dwelling houses. Private ownership of farmland is, however, not allowed. On the other hand, there are regions such as Moscow, St. Petersburg and Karelia where private ownership is allowed (Ikonitskaya, 1999b).

It can also be claimed that not allowing private ownership is unconstitutional since the constitution allows all forms of ownership (Ikonitskaya, 1999b). The constitution also stipulates that the forms and rules of the use of the land are fixed by federal legislation (article 36.3). On the other hand, although allowing private ownership, federal legislation is obscure. In the absence of an up-to-date federal land code, the subjects of the federation interpret that they have a right to regulate on the forms of ownership. In some subjects of the federation, private ownership goes further than in federal legislation. For example, Karelia allowed private ownership without the inheritance right of forest land. The federal presidential administration has actively strived for the unification of legislation. The federal constitutional court has supported the tendency for unification leaning on the interpretation of the federal constitution. The subjects of the federation, however, would like to keep their newly gained right for their own legislation, which does not have to be unified under principles given from the federal level (cf., chapter 2).

There is also land in *municipal ownership*. According to article 215 of the Civil Code, municipal land property is the property of the rural and urban communities as well as other types of municipal units. It is, however, unclear what kind of land can be in municipal ownership (Ikonitskaya, 1999a; Brinchuk, 1999:188). It is also not clear, whether it is the subject of the federation that can decide what property is municipal and what belongs to the subject of the federation. This issue is not regulated in legislation. In practice, the subjects of the federation have decided whether or not to give land to municipal ownership (Ikonitskaya, 1999a).

According to the decree of the president on "Regulation of the Land Market", every owner of a land plot was given a certificate of ownership and those rights were also to be registered. This certificate was the proof of the right of ownership and the basic document for every transaction with the land plots. The certificate had to be used to register the right. Creating a new registration system and a land cadastre is, however, taking a long time. On the basis of a government decree (266 of 25 August 1992) and a presidential decree of 11 December 1993, the GKI and the State Committee of Land Resources and Land Management drafted a registration system. There was already a "Land Book", which was used in many localities (Butler and O'Leary, 1996). The Civil Code of 1995, which created a national registry of immovable property, superseded this intention.

After several attempts, a governmental registry on the rights on immovable property and transactions was created on 21 July 1997. Ownership, lease and other uses of land are registered as well as the different categories of land, the technical data and the economic value of land. The law regulates that a registration number should be given to every land plot. In the future, the register is intended to cover all of the property in the area of the whole federation. Nowadays, it is kept on regional levels.

Legislation and implementation of the regulation concerning the cadastre is still in transition. Nowadays, it is the State Committee of Land Resources and Land Management that takes care of the state land cadastre. Its activities are financed from the regional budget under a unified scheme. Regional or local committees on land resources and land management carry out the main work, the actual registering of data. The registration procedure is stipulated in the regulation on the procedure of the state land cadastre, which was approved by the Resolution of the Government of the Russian Federation on 25 February 1992. There is a new law from 21 January 2000 aiming at creating a complete land cadastre covering the whole area of the federation. The law stipulates that the country should be divided into cadastre units and a new administration arranged. This process has not yet started. Nowadays the cadastre contains only buildings. The process of including real estates is still going on.

Nowadays, the state registration is the only evidence of the existence of a registered right. A registered right can only be challenged in court. However, registering privatized apartments or buildings is not required as long as the property is not transferred. If the property is sold, it has to be previously registered in the name of the owner. Registration is only a technical question if all the documents proving the owner's right are in order. People, who are not planning to sell their property, have not bothered to register their right in order to avoid the costs and the trouble of registration.[97]

Before the Land Code and the Resolutions of the Government on Registration were adopted, there was a moratorium on the transactions on land and the registration of the transactions had been suspended. Nowadays, transactions are again permitted (Ikonitskaya, 1999b). Moratorium is quite logical from the point of view of clarity and the necessity to develop a reliable formal system. However, in spite of the moratorium, there were a lot of unclear or obscure transactions. When creating a new system of registration and cadastre is going on, the system cannot be completely reliable. If certificates were lost while registration was not yet possible, it is difficult to prove ownership and have it registered. In the former state and collective farms, where land is in common ownership but where every one has the right to alienate his own plot, the borders of the plots are not always drawn. Since unclear rules allow informal rules to supersede formal rules, corruption is likely to occur around registration and applying the rules for the right to alienate land property.

Another problem for creating a land market is that the regulation of the mortgage of the land plots was under formation for a long time. The Civil Code (article 334) of 1995 already mentioned the possibility of mortgage referring to a specific law, which only came into force on 16 July 1998. However, mortgages were temporarily regulated by a presidential decree "On the Additional Measures on

---

[97] This information was given by Maria Kotova, senior lawyer of the Solombala Paper and Pulp Company in Arkhangelsk on 21 August 2000.

the Development of Mortgage Credits" from 28 February 1996. The decree already contained a mandatory form of the contract of a mortgage and defined the content of the contract, rights and duties of the parties. Mortgage is, however, not yet much used in Russia. It is also difficult to obtain credits from the banks, which limits the possibilities of former collective farm workers or anybody without money or property to buy agricultural land or run an agricultural enterprise. Agricultural land is not valuable and is often badly transferable, except near big cities.

According to current legislation, a landowner has a duty to use the land effectively and according to specific purposes, to increase the fertility of the land and refrain from deteriorating the land, protect the land and follow the requirement for building. State bodies are not allowed to intervene in the activities of the owner, except when land legislation is infringed. The presidential decree on the regulation of land market grants the owners of land plots the right to sell, leave the land by inheritance, mortgage, lease and to invest land plots as shares in companies (Ikonitskaya, 1999a).

3.5.2.1.2   Ownership of Forests, Waters and Below Ground Resources

With the exception of land for agriculture and land for entrepreneurial use, which covers at least the land plot on which the enterprise building is situated, land is very rarely privately owned in Russia. The owner of natural resources is usually the state. According to Civil Code article 214, the state ownership of land is divided between federal property and the property of the subjects of the federation. How the division is drawn is still a largely disputed issue. The first attempt to draw the line was a presidential decree of 16 December 1993 on federal natural resources; the following property was regulated to be in federal ownership:
- plots for military defense and security of the country,
- land plots for the border guard, and plots of the federal energy, transport and space facilities,
- for the operation of nuclear power plants,
- for telecommunications and meteorological services, and
- objects of cultural and historical heritage, natural reserves as well as other objects in federal ownership.

The territories of national protection parks, national natural parks and other similar parks enjoying the protection of the state form a separate group of the federal property. Russian protection of nature is criticized by up-down legislation of aspirations, which was also typical for Soviet legislation (Greenspan-Bell, 2000). Also, the debate between the federation and its subjects hinders development of questions, which belong to the joint powers of the federation and the subjects. However, the principles of administering and monitoring nature protection have not changed. This means that the former institutional framework has not collapsed.

The debate between federal and regional state ownership has concentrated on the ownership of natural resources. In the Federation Treaties of 1992 all natural resources were given to the subjects of the federation. The constitution of 1993 regulated natural resources as belonging to the joint ownership of the federation and its subjects.[98] Most subjects of the federation have concluded a treaty on the division of rights and duties between the federation and the subject and some have gained ownership of their natural resources in this way. There is, however, a tendency of centralization going into the new federal legislation. The Forest Code of 1997 stipulated the ownership of forest resources to the federation. It seems that treaties between the federation and the subjects are superseded by new federal legislation and the ownership of natural resources is brought to the federal level. However, the income of the property is divided between the subject and the federation even when ownership belongs to the federation.

The Republic of Karelia and the Territory of Khabarovsk challenged the Federal Forest Code of 1997 in the Constitutional Court. Karelia referred to the fact that the Federal Treaty gives the right of ownership of forests to Karelia. In its decision from 9 January 1998, the Constitutional Court did not pay attention to the Federal Treaty but interpreted only the constitution. According to the court, the forests are still within joint jurisdiction since the Federal Forest Code

---

[98] The relationship between the Federal Treaty of 1992 and the constitution is a debated issue in constitutional law (cf., chapter 2). An environmental lawyer, Brinchuk (1999), sees the debate in a simple way claiming that the constitution substituted and avoided the Federal Treaty.

gives rights and duties to both the federation and the subjects. The court also saw that Karelia among others has participated in the legislative process and could have affected on passing the law. Furthermore, the court saw that not all of the forests belong to the federation, but only the forest fund. However, almost all of the productive forests, which are harvested, belong to the forest fund (cf., Forest Code article 8). Only parks and forests around municipalities do not belong to the forest fund. These forests, however, are supposed to be the property of the municipalities (cf., Ikonitskaya, 1999a; Brinchuk, 1999). The Federal Forest Code also stipulates that the transfer of ownership is also possible according to the rules of a federal law. Such a federal law, however, does not yet exist.

Article 46 of the Forest Code stipulates that the possession, use and right to decide on the forest fund belong to the federation. Unified investment policy, the means of payment for using the forest fund and the rules of using forest resources, are decided on the federal level. According to article 47, the subjects of the federation implement federal forest policy. They also participate in the possession and use of forests as well as decide on renting or leasing plots of forest for harvesting purposes. In practice, it is the subjects of the federation that control harvesting and give the permissions. Forests should, however, be used according to federal policy. The income is divided so that the federation receives 40% and the subject 60% of the lease or other rent of the forests (article 102). The division can be agreed in a different way in an agreement between the federation and the subject. Some subjects of the federation (26 of them) that do not have a lot of forests do not have to divide the income with the federation. This means that paradoxically only the owner holds the title without getting any income for the property.

There are also two kinds of tax payments that the user of the forest has to pay (article 103). One payment goes to the federal budget and the other to the subject of the federation. The federal payment is 5% of the value of the wood and is based on a presidential decree from 23 December 1993, No. 2271. There is also a special payment for exported wood (article 106).

The forest code divides forest land into three different categories, which were developed during the socialist system. The forests of the first group (article 56) can be of many different kinds, but usually they are areas that need special protection or are important for social purposes. Areas that are protected and where entrance is forbidden belong to the first group. Also forests that are evaluated as being the most valuable belong to the first category. Furthermore, forests that border on waters belong to the first group.

The second category of forests (article 57) contains areas that are situated near populated areas and transport routes. These forests are most often used for harvesting. Forests of the third category (article 58) are situated in areas of dense forest zones. These forests are mainly reserve forests and the ecological questions should be paid a lot of attention in using them. For the use of forests of the second and third categories, the subjects of the federation have more power than in the first category (Kommentarii..., 1997). The federal organs decide about the borders between different categories.

The categorization of forests has been criticized. There are demands in the subjects of the federation with vast forests that forests should be divided between the federation and the subjects. There have also been suggestions that forests situated near villages could be given to the common ownership of the people living there. In this way the local people could start to get used to private ownership.[99] If this form of ownership is introduced, monitoring and maintaining the borders becomes important and the arrangement should be in compliance with local values (Ostrom, 1990). Suggestions of common ownership may be overridden by the demands of municipalities. It is exactly the forests around settlements that have been extracted from the federal forest fund to the ownership of municipalities.

The idea of common ownership, both in the above-mentioned suggestion and in the agrarian reform, is that it might gradually lead to private ownership. Privatizing forests to private farmers would support private agriculture, since forests could give significant additional income to private farmers. Especially in northern areas, for example Finland, the income from forests is vitally important for farmers since agriculture there is otherwise unprofitable. In Russia, the institutional setup and especially the mentality hinder the introduction of private ownership. Privatizing forests might be

---

[99] These suggestions were presented in IIASA's policy exercise "Institutional Problems of Development of the Tomsk Forest Sector" in Tomsk held on 13–16 June 2000 (Carlsson and Olsson, 2001).

dangerous in Russia, if it were arranged in a similar way as privatizing state enterprises. Forests would soon be the property of a handful of *oligarchs*. Privatization of forests should, therefore, be well planned and targeted to support agriculture.

State forest management and the use of forests have not changed radically. The system did not collapse but continued to function in spite of transition. The only significant change in the forest sector has been the privatization of forestry companies. The new private owners are, however, usually the managers of those companies. Their policy to preserve the existing system is path-dependent. The centralization tendency nowadays prevents innovations. The whole system is run in a rather bureaucratic way on both federal and regional levels. At least in the forest sector, it is in nobody's interest to introduce private ownership. Harvesting with tickets functions in practice and owning forest property might only be a burden for the company. In the present situation powerful forest enterprises can control the harvesting system.

According to the Law on Below Ground Resources of 1995, minerals, oil, gas and all economically useful resources of the earth's crust (e.g., ground water) belong to the state. This is a joint ownership between the federation and its subjects. The use of these resources is governed together with the federation and the subject (articles 3 and 4). The policy to use these resources should be planned together with the federation and the subjects. According to the law the subjects of the federation should in practice have more power to decide on excavating activities, because licenses are decided on the regional level (article 30) or on the federal level with the consent of the executive power of the subject of the federation (article 11). Only licenses to use the continental shelf, which belongs to the ownership of the federation, are decided on the federal level without the consent of the subject of the federation.[100] The federation, however, govern the policy with federal programs, which the regional programs should follow.

There is no such concentrated federal administration for the whole so-called fund of below ground resources, which does exist

---

[100] In the legislation of some subjects of the federation, e.g., Sakha-Yakutia, also the continental shelf belongs to the ownership of the subject.

for forestry. But there are plans and suggestions to take minerals, oil, gas and other below ground natural resources more into federal control and to establish one federal service for all of them. Now, areas already exist where underground resources are defined to be of great federal importance (Pevsner, 1997). The president and the government of the federation decide a lot of issues concerning the policy for the use of oil, gas and minerals.

The longest period for a license for using below ground resources is 25 years. The Federal Law on Below Ground Natural Resources ("*o nedrakh*") regulates on the division of incomes from payments for use. The state collects incomes from those who participate in the auctions for licenses. The licensees also pay rent, income and excise tax. Incomes are divided between the federal, subject and local levels (article 42). From hydrocarbon raw material (e.g., oil and gas) the local level receives 30% and for others such as minerals 50%. Of hydrocarbon raw material the federation receives 40% and the subject 30% and for other than hydrocarbon resources the federation and the subject both receive 25%. In such autonomous areas, which are situated in the territory of a region or territory, the territory or the region receives half of the federal share.[101] Incomes from excavations on the territorial sea bottom are divided, 60% to the subject and 40% to the federal budget.

The ownership of waters is divided between the federation, subjects of the federation and municipalities. Inland waters that do not border foreign countries and do not belong to natural parks of federal protection are in the ownership and control of the subject of the federation, where the water is situated. Waters that are needed for military purposes, energy production or transportation may also belong to the federation. Also inner and territorial seas belong to the federation. Small waters inside municipalities belong to the municipality.[102]

---

[101] This arrangement guarantees that such regions as the Tyumen region containing one oil and one gas producing autonomous area receive a share from the profits (cf., section 2.3.1.3.2).

[102] Regional legislation does not, however, always comply with the Federal Water Code or the Law on Below Ground Resources.

An important issue among the other changes in Russia is the rights of indigenous peoples. Russian legislation has paid a lot of formal attention to the rights of "small peoples" (*malochislennye narody*) and indigenous peoples (*korennye narody*). There is a new federal law of 30 April 1999 on the guarantees of the rights of indigenous small peoples in the Russian federation listing all possible rights. Unfortunately, the "guarantees" only exist on paper. The law did not establish any mechanism for indigenous peoples to influence on the use of natural resources or on the protection of nature in their living areas. The new federal law is a typical example of the uselessness of formal rules when they cannot be effectuated. Such legislation only shows the good intentions of the legislators, but ignores practical and economic obstacles. Such a law is not credible. Indigenous peoples' rights of using land are also guaranteed, for example, in the Land Code permitting the tradi-tional use of land to indigenous peoples in their traditional areas. It is also allowed in natural parks of one type (*zemli prirodno-zapovednoigo zony*). The Law on Below Ground Resources generally states that a part of the regional budget revenue from below ground natural resources, which originates from the living areas of indigenous peoples should be used to develop social and economic circumstances of these people. There is, however, no effective monitoring by indigenous people for the proper imple-mentation of the rights, which are given to them in Russian legislation. Indigenous people have not yet organized themselves in such a way as in the Nordic countries and North America, where they already claim for restoring the ownership of the land.

3.5.2.2 *Other Rights on Land*

Other forms of the right on the land, besides the right of ownership, are regulated in the Civil Code. These are:
- the inheritable right of possession (article 214),
- the right of permanent use without a fixed term (article 216),
- the easement (article 216),
- the lease (article 607), and
- the gratuitous right of use (article 689).

The inheritable right of possession and the right of permanent use without a fixed period were created by the Civil Code and are stipulated in articles 266–270 of chapter 17. This chapter is, however, not yet current legislation, since it is going to enter into force only with the new Land Code. The Civil Code refers to land legislation. Current legislation mentions the inheritable right of possession only in connection with the land property for the subsidiary smallholdings, gardening and the building of dwelling houses. The law from 23 December 1992 regulates that land plots in possession that do not exceed certain standard limits can be inherited. The possessor can possess and use the land plot. He also has the right to build on the land and become the owner of immovable property on the building. Sale, mortgage or any other transactions, except lease of free use for a fixed time, are prohibited.

The right of permanent use without a fixed term is more limited than the inheritable right of possession. The holder of the land plot can agree upon building and using the land or a lease for a fixed period only with the approval of the owner.

Leasing land is regulated in chapter 34 of part two of the Civil Code, which provides the possibility for legislating special rules for leasing land plots. On the federal level there are, however, no such rules yet. In some subjects of the federation, rules of sale of the leasehold on the land plots exist. The Civil Code also stipulates that the maximum periods for the lease of certain categories of property can be limited in legislation. In the Land Code there was a limit of 50 years for leasing state owned lands and 5 years for leasing land owned by private persons. These articles are, however, not in force now because the decrees of the president abrogated them. In business practice, the most popular period for long-term lease is 49 years (Ikonitskaya, 2000b).

Easement is also an unregulated type of land use. It is regulated in the Civil Code in chapter 17, which has not yet entered into force. The Forest and Water Codes introduced easement in current Russian legislation.

Since forests are the property of the federation, plots of forest are leased for harvesting. Subjects of the federation decide over leasing the plots according to federal programs. Some subjects of the federation have also sold forests for private ownership, but after the Federal Forest Code of 1997 this is prohibited in federal legislation. Article 22 of the Forest Code stipulates that the forms of forest use are:

- lease (rent),
- use without compensation,
- license, and
- short-term use.

Leasing contracts are offered in auctions or they may be concluded with the administration of the subject of the federation without auction procedure. The representation of the federal organ on the subject level has to agree with the contract. Also, the decisions for use without compensation, which in practice means hunting, are done in the same way (Kommentarii..., 1997). The price depends on whether functioning markets exist or not. In Russian monopolistic markets, powerful companies can in practice influence the price.

Short-term use up to one year can be decided through auctions or simply by selling a ticket to harvest the forest on the plot, which is the most commonly used form of the use of forests. The decisions are made on the level of the subject of the federation. License agreements are made for both harvesting purposes and taking care of the plot. Such contracts are made on the federal level with the consent of the subject of the federation. Licenses are sold through auctions or competitive bidding. The term of the license can be from 1 to 49 years (Ikonitskaya, 1999a:237).

Natural (private) persons can also establish an easement on forest land (article 21). An easement is usually established for access to private property through forest land or for distribution of electricity (Kommentarii..., 1997, article 22).

The rights to use waters by those who do not own them are long-term use, short-term use and easement (Ikonitskaya, 1999a:241). Both long and short-term use is given through license agreements. Exploitation of peat is regulated in article 99 of the Water Code. An easement for both waters and forests can be founded by a contract or in court procedure. It can be established for using a road, taking water, etc.

There is also traditional common use of waters permitted in Russia. Swimming, fishing and taking household water is permitted in other than nature protection areas (Ikonitskaya, 1999a:240).

There are no regulations concerning the other rights on land by foreigners. In practice, foreigners can acquire land for long-term lease (Ikonitskaya, 2000b; Hüper, 1998).

Most of the other rights of land that are regulated in the Civil Code are new property rights, which have been included in Russian legislation with the Civil Code. Excluding lease, they are not yet widely used. The main reason for not using other forms of the right on the land is, of course, that chapter 17 of the Civil Code is not in force yet. Use rights are mostly rights to use state property, which is understood as a different kind of a property right than private property. The attitudes to state property still have a socialist flavor. Land was not understood to be property at all as it had no price and could not be sold or bought. Therefore, creating land markets was a decisive change. Land law, which derived from socialist principles, has been changed and amended, but seems to have preserved its original flavor of administrative law. This is especially typical in forest law, which is still based on the system established earlier. The regulation of land law, which has tried to be changed with new principles is, however, still unclear and has not been accepted in practice.

3.5.3 State Protection and Administration of Land Property

Russian land legislation guarantees the protection of the rights of all persons who use land plots. Any interference from state bodies is forbidden except in cases of violating land legislation. According to current legislation, state bodies that have unjustifiably intervened into the activities of the use of the land have to compensate the loss to the landholder. Such regulations limit the rights of the state also as a landowner. Protection of private ownership of the land is guaranteed in article 36 of the constitution. All transactions should be registered and state officials are in charge of the land registry.

One of the main principles before the economic reforms was the principle of the free use of land. The reformers, however, saw that free use of land leads to irrational use and encourages enterprises to hold more land than they are able to use.[103] Therefore, the payment for the use of the land was introduced in 1990 already during the

---

[103] A survey made by Hendley *et al.* (1997) proves this opinion.

Soviet period. At present the payment is regulated in the Land Code and by the law "On rent payment for land" of 11 October 1991.

Russian land legislation stipulates that payments for the use of land are land tax, the rent payment (of lease or license) and the regulated price of the land. The land tax on agricultural lands is calculated according to the quality, size and location of the land. The average amount of land tax per hectare is enacted in a specific annex to the law on payment for land. The tax for land in urban areas and land for other purposes is calculated according to different rules. There is also a long list of exemptions from the payment of land tax including areas for scientific institutions, public health services, nature preservation areas and veterans of wars, invalids of certain categories, people who suffered from radiation, etc.

Rent payment is determined in the lease contract. However, renting state or municipal lands is regulated and the authorities decide on the basic rates of the rent depending on the categories of the land plots and the categories of the leaseholders.

The land market price is also regulated because the land market is only being formed and because the state is afraid of speculation on land and of high prices. There is a so-called fixed price of land. This price is set by executive authorities of the subjects of the federation for the lands of different categories depending, for example, on the location of the land. The Resolution of the Government from 15 March 1997 does not clearly define which categories of natural and juristic persons have the right to buy state and municipal lands for a fixed price and who and what land has to be bought on the free market price (Ikonitskaya, 1999a:104). People entitled to a fixed price are at the mercy of civil servants, who apply the law. In practice, land is sold more eagerly to those who can pay.

One of the most important functions of the state administration of the use of the land is the territorial planning of the use of the land. It is however, not yet regulated by law. During the last few years, the planning of the use of the land has intensified and there are schemes for the use of the land on regional and local levels (Ikonitskaya, 2000b). The need for such planning has been realized on the local and regional levels. In the absence of a proper federal land code, the regions have taken more initiative and started to regulate land use themselves. Using the data of the land cadastre, which is still under formation, is mandatory in planning the use and protection of land. Planning the use of the land obviously suffers from the absence of a proper legal framework.

The state administration of land also includes the control over possible infringements of the land legislation. The State Committee on the Land Resources and Land Management[104] and other organizations of the executive power are responsible for controlling infringements. The executive officers of these institutions have powers to suspend any kind of building activity infringing land legislation, to give mandatory orders for the elimination of infringements and to impose fines. The land management also has the right to control procedures of the contests and actions on land and initiate court procedures for invalidating transactions contradicting current legislation. When property rights are unclear, the state authorities have a lot of power to interfere. Corruption is also likely to occur when monitoring is not based on clear regulation.

Besides the State Committee on the Land Resources and Land Management, also bodies of natural protection, the Ministry of Agriculture, planning and architecture offices, offices on the use of mineral resources and geological institutions as well as some other ministries and departments carry out monitoring of the land. The administration, management and environmental protection of other natural resources are carried out with even more different governmental bodies. The distribution of powers, especially with those governmental bodies engaged in environmental protection, management of natural resources and supervision of the use of natural resources, is unclear. Such an obscure situation causes a lot of trouble for enterprises, which have to cope with several different and usually contradictory standards of different state agencies (Kotova, 2001).

There is a tendency of trying to simplify the administration of natural resources especially with merging the tasks of different agencies under a new federal administrative or supervising unit. The Administration of Forests is currently being restructured. The State Committee of Environmental Questions and the Federal

---

[104] The State Committee of Land Resources and Land Management was founded in 1991.

Forest Service were liquidated and their tasks transferred to the Ministry of Natural Resources by a presidential decree No. 867 from 17 May 2000.[105] All the questions concerning the management of the forest fund is going to be concentrated there.

The state administration of land property and natural resources is experiencing a decisive change. The administrative command economy is changing towards land markets. State property, which was regarded as only administrative units, now has a price value and should provide profit. Such a change requires skills of modern planning and management. Old state officials may not be able to change their attitudes and change may, therefore, take time. In the present economic situation, when the state does not have enough money to support its huge bureaucracy any more, monitoring suffers and confiscatory rent-seeking policy is likely to appear in the administration to cover up the cost. Constant changes and continuous uncertainty also have similar side effects.

3.5.4 From Administrative to Court Control

Since land was not regarded as property and it all belonged to the overwhelming state, the disputes of land were between different state departments. Such disputes were administrative by nature and also handled as administrative disputes. With the changes it became clear that land disputes require court procedure. For some time both court and administrative procedures were in use, before a presidential decree of 24 December 1993 abolished the administrative procedure.

Land disputes can either go to ordinary courts or arbitration courts, which are Russian commercial courts. Disputes between enterprises (juristic persons) or enterprises and governmental bodies belong to the arbitration courts. However, if one of the parties of the dispute is a natural (private) person (not a juristic person) it is the ordinary court that has to decide over the dispute.

A suit can be raised against local or regional administration as well as against another juristic or natural person. Disputes in the

---

[105] The development of forest management structure from Soviet times to the 1990s is described in Carlsson *et al.* (1999a) and Piipponen (1999).

forest sector are between companies and they are therefore settled in the arbitration courts. Leasing contracts have been disputed even to the level of the Supreme Arbitration Court, which decided 21,524 leasing cases in 1998 and 24,734 cases in 1999 (Sudebno-arbitrazhnaya…, 2000).[106]

There have also been disputes concerning the payment for services of different governmental bodies. Such services as rendering harvesting tickets, allotting harvesting areas, services connected with the state cadastre are liable to be charged. State bodies offering these services can themselves decide on the payment. Such a system has led to high prices of services, which enterprises have started to challenge in the courts. The courts have considered such services, which are not based on law, as hidden taxation and declared them invalid (Kotova, 2001). The number of cases decided by the Supreme Arbitration Court concerning demanding too high payments on the use of the land back from state or municipal authorities was 2,325 in 1998 and 2,507 in 1999. The Supreme Arbitration Court has also decided cases concerning the authorities' refusals to register property rights or contracts.

3.6 Summary

Transition makes property rights insecure, especially when the forms of property rights are debated. In Russia enterprises were quickly privatized. The decision was political. Preparations were forgotten, when the main goal was privatization itself. There was already illegal and informal privatization going on without any legislative basis, a fact that also accelerated the start of the official program. From the legal point of view, the privatization of enterprises was not a success story. Legislation was superseded and ignored. Decrees became more important than the laws enacted by parliament since there was no political consensus on privatization and therefore no political commitment either. The final result of privatization was a complete theft of former state property. At that stage even presidential decrees did not count any more. The new

---

[106] These figures include leasing of all kinds of property.

Russian elite arranged a donation of the most valuable state enterprises to banks. A few big banks with holding companies led by *oligarchs* now have monopolistic power in the Russian economy. The government is their hostage but still controls who is admitted to the circle of the elite. Admittance to the circles occurs with state authorization. In financial difficulties the state can again decide, which bank is worth saving and which can be made bankrupt. The new elite also controls the media.

Incompetence and corruption are mostly considered as the reasons for the bad success in transforming Russia into a market economy (Åslund, 1999). Poor control leads to illegalities and opportunistic behavior. Many western advisers support this reasoning, which however, is too simple an explanation. The Russian economy and society are largely misunderstood, because of ignoring the past. "Social capital" and trust cannot be created through legislation and control. Social capital in Russian business was created in the shadow economy. Such businessmen had to know how to avoid the law and rely on the corruptness of state officials. State enterprises were run in a bureaucratic way. Managers were chosen according to their political merits or connections. Social networks and good personal relations were used in allocating the fruits of the socialist economy both legally and illegally.

Doubtful and partly illegal privatization may be a ticking time bomb in Russian society. At least it explains why people are dissatisfied and why trust does not exist in the political and economic system. The main problem of privatization was the lack of control, which gave opportunism a chance. It was, however, a path-dependent development managed by the network system of good relations between the *nomenklatura* circles. Who could have controlled the privatization process, when the controllers themselves belonged to the same circles and also wanted to get their piece of the cake?

Privatization did not bring economic efficiency. Transaction costs for producing formal profits are too high. Profits stay in the gray sector of the economy because of the fear of having to pay taxes or protection money to criminals or being taken over by foreign investors. The official economy keeps running as a pretense, a virtual economy with barter trade and artificial prices.

Restructuring has not started because the new elite still seems to be interested only in short-term gains. Such behavior is rational in the Russian environment. The most successful enterprises in the oil business provide profit without restructuring anyway. Former managers, who only wanted to guarantee that everything is going to continue as before, now own even less profitable enterprises. The most dangerous phenomenon for the economy is, however, the illegal flow of assets abroad. However, it may be that managers, who secured their positions, are now likely to be motivated to restructure in the long run to be able to keep the company going. Self-interested owner managers should, in principle, be more likely to restructure than private investors, who seek quicker profits.

The bank crisis of August 1998 also introduced bankruptcies in Russian business. It is, however, not certain that the wave of bankruptcies will abolish the most unhealthy enterprises from the market. Uncertainty continues and the enterprises try to secure their future with monopolizing aspirations and good contacts with the authorities and government circles. For small enterprises the environment is difficult for long-term business. The state does not pay enough attention in developing flourishing small and medium sized business.

Land property has not experienced the same radical reform as the privatization of companies. Agrarian reform aimed at introducing new forms of ownership and giving the possibility to the workers of state and collective farms to start their own private businesses. The reform was also necessary for new enterprises to be able to obtain land. Private property rights were, however, not clear enough. The aim of the reform was to offer choices by introducing a new form of common ownership, which could also have been used for allotting a plot for a family farm. In practice, redistribution of land proved to be unclear. The tragedy of the agrarian reform was that it was needed but too debated. It was introduced from above but in a diluted form. Managers of state farms and local officials opposed the reform and did not encourage people to take the initiative and start their own business. Private farms were not in the interest of the most important interest group of the countryside—the managers of state and collective farms. Private property of agricultural land has faced a lot of resistance also because of the fear of speculation on land. Such fear is not urgent in the deep countryside. But estates in Moscow and other big cities and their surroundings have become extremely expensive. State control of prices and rents has not been able to prevent the prices from rising.

Weak property rights in land property prevent the countryside from developing. Property rights cannot be made stronger by only developing the formal legal system. The hindrances for strong and effective property rights are institutional. The destruction of the countryside was so total in the socialist system that it is difficult to find incentives to make people develop those areas. The problems are both psychological and depend on the badly developed infrastructure. It is difficult to start a farming business when there are no distribution systems, electricity or equipment. The idealistic plans of legal and economic specialists for the positive results of re-introducing private ownership failed. The lack of initiative and risk-taking are results of rationality, which developed in the Soviet environment. This environment has not changed considerably in the countryside.

Russian agricultural reform has experienced almost all of the problems, which make property rights unclear and weak. Borderlines have not been drawn carefully. Alienation is still on an insecure basis. It is not clear who is entitled to buy and sell land property, and the registry is not yet reliable. Often local and regional administration has not been interested in the reform, which on the other hand, has given them power in the field of informal and weak property rights. Strong interest groups resist changes in fear of losing their power and influence. The lack of trust in the politicians and the persistence of changes is a significant hindrance for reforms.

Besides the agrarian reform, there have been no other programs for introducing private ownership on land property. Forests have not been privatized, as there seems to be a large consensus in the society that forests should remain state property. This is one way to prevent "the robber barons" taking this national property and destroying it. The privatization of forests to private farmers should, however, be considered. The income of forests would significantly support private agriculture. However, the destruction of forests is also possible when only the use of forests is permitted and when it is connected with bad control. The system of using forests has not changed considerably, even if forest enterprises were privatized to their managers. New payments have been introduced and there has been a dispute about dividing the profit between the central and the regional level. Even if the federation is the owner, the regional level receives more of the income from the use of forests. There is an administrative change taking place in the forest sector but it seems that the change is only organizational, not institutional. There is a tendency towards centralized administration to clear and simplify the rules.

Clarity of allocation is not yet on an acceptable level. The state registration and the cadastre are still unreliable. The costs of alienation may be too high due to corruption. Security against trespass is not good since the state administration has not yet adapted to the terms of a market economy. Violations of property rights are not protected enough in the administrative and executive levels. Disorder still gives criminal organizations too much power. The persistence of property rights is not protected and law changes all the time. For five years, it has been attempted to draft a new federal land code. In the meantime, the differences between the regions of Russia grow and a balance has not yet been found. When property rights remain unclear, the government loses its credibility. Foreign investments, especially, are not going to be made in such insecure circumstances.

There are still a lot of institutional remnants from the socialist period. Such remnants can be found in the peculiar concept of land law, which regards law as an administrative means. Also the whole concept of property is old-fashioned and has not yet adapted into dynamic relations in property rights. Introducing private property to an administrative system does not yet make a big difference. State property continues to be governed in an old administrative way. Introducing new payments easily leads to attempts of state agencies to charge too high fees to cover their administration costs. The role of the state as an owner has not changed. The state is still a privileged owner compared to others. The reforms brought land disputes from administrative tribunals to the courts that, in turn, have the important task of bringing equality among the different owners and stopping irresponsible management and corruption. It is, however, doubtful whether the courts have enough competence to solve all the new disputes that have not previously existed. The courts are now busy with bankruptcies and cases of frauds in privatization.

The most dangerous features of the socialist economy are the persistence of the gray market, stealing state property, and corruption. The persistence of these features does not create trust in the legal and political system. Rationality in an environment, where informal property rights dominate, is different from rationality connected with strong and efficient property rights. The absence of trust and the incapability of the political institutions to commit themselves to develop the property rights system are blocking the Russian economy from sustainable growth. If the politicians would commit themselves to firmly developing a strong property rights system, economic change should start to occur. The Russian experience also shows how political the property rights system is. A consensus is urgently needed as well as a commitment to make changes. However, Russian uncertainty prevents such commitments and the absence of credibility of any political commitment maintains uncertainty.

References

Books and Articles

Aarnio, Aulis (1989). *Laintulkinnan teoria. Yleisen oikeustieteen oppikirja (Theory of Interpretation of Law. A Textbook of Jurisprudence)*. Juva (in Finnish).

Alchian, Armen A. and Harold Demsetz (1973). The Property Rights Paradigms. *Journal of Economic History*, 33, pp. 16–27.

Åslund, A. (1995). *How Russia Became a Market Economy*. Brookings, Washington.

Åslund, A. (1997). Economic Causes of Crime in Russia. In: J. Sachs and K. Pistor (eds.) *The Rule of Law and Economic Reform in Russia*. Westview Press.

Åslund, A. (1999). Why Has Russia's Economic Transformation Been So Arduous? World Bank ABCDE Conference 1999.

Bakunina, T.S. (1998a). Pravovye problemy ratsionalnogo ispolzovaniya i ohrany selskokhozyaistvennykh zemel. Materialy kruglogo stola (A roundtable discussion). *Gosudarstvo i pravo*, No. 5, pp. 25–44 (in Russian).

Bakunina, T.S. (1998b). Pravovye problemy ratsionalnogo ispolzovaniya i ohrany selskokhozyaistvennykh zemel. Materialy kruglogo stola (A roundtable discussion). *Gosudarstvo i pravo*. No. 4, pp. 42–65 (in Russian).

Berman, Harold J. (1983). *Law and Revolution. The Formation of the Western Legal Tradition.* Harvard University Press.

Bim, Alexander S. (1995). Ownership and Control of Russian Enterprises and Strategies of Shareholders. *Communist Economies and Economic Transition*, Vol. 8, No. 4, pp. 471–500.

Blam, Y., L. Carlsson and M.-O. Olsson (2000). Institutions and the Emergence of Markets—Transition in the Irkutsk Forest Sector. Interim Report IR-00-017. International Institute for Applied Systems Analysis, Laxenburg, Austria.

Boiko, Ivan (1997). Nekotorye aspekty strukturnykh izmenenii v promyshlennosti Rossii v khode reformy. Published later in English titled: Mysteries and Puzzles of the Russian Economy. Business Research Development Center, Turku School of Economics and Business Administration, 13/1999.

Brinchuk, M.M. (1999). Ekologicheskoe pravo (pravo okruzhayushei sredy) (Ecological Law/Environmental Law). Institut gosudarstvo i prava RAN, Akademicheskii pravovoj universitet, Moscow. Yurist (in Russian).

Butler, Stephen B. and Sheila O'Leary (1996). Summary of Laws Relating to Housing and Urban Development in the Russian Federation. The Urban Institute, Washington.

Carlsson, L. and M.-O. Olsson (eds.) (1998a). Initial Analyses of the Institutional Framework of the Russian Forest Sector. Interim Report IR-98-027. International Institute for Applied Systems Analysis, Laxenburg, Austria.

Carlsson, Lars and Mats-Olov Olsson (1998b). Institutions and the Emergence of Markets—Transition in the Tomsk Forest Sector. IIASA Interim Report IR-98-084. International Institute for Applied Systems Analysis, Laxenburg, Austria.

Carlsson, L. and M.-O. Olsson (2001). Proceedings of IIASA's Policy Exercise "Institutional Problems of Development of the Tomsk Forest Sector". Meeting held in Tomsk on 13–16 June 2000 (preliminary title). Interim Report. International Institute for Applied Systems Analysis, Laxenburg, Austria (forthcoming).

Carlsson, L., N.-G. Lundgren and M.-O. Olsson (1999a). Forest Enterprises in Transition—Business Behavior in the Tomsk Forest Sector. Interim Report IR-99-010. International Institute for Applied Systems Analysis, Laxenburg, Austria.

Carlsson, L., N.-G. Lundgren, M.-O. Olsson and M.Y. Varakin (1999b). Institutions and the Emergence of Markets—Transition in the Arkhangelsk Forest Sector. Interim Report IR-99-021. International Institute for Applied Systems Analysis, Laxenburg, Austria.

Clarke, Simon and Veronika Kabalina (1995). Privatization and the Struggle for Law. In: David Leblang (ed.) *Russia in Transition.* Longman.

De Alessi, Louis (1983). Property Rights, Transaction Costs, and X-Efficiency. *American Economic Review*, 73:1, pp. 64–81.

Dworkin, Ronald (1986). *Law's Empire.* Harvard University Press, Cambridge, Mass.

Eckhoff, Thorstein (1987). *Rettskildelære (The Doctrine on Sources of Law).* Tano, Oslo (in Norwegian).

Efimova, L.G. (1998). O sootnoshenii veshchnikh i obyazatelstvennykh prav (About the interrelation of the rights on things and the rights on obligations). *Gosudarstvo i pravo,* No. 10, pp. 35–44 (in Russian).

Efremov, D.F., Carlsson, L., M-O. Olsson and A.S. Sheingauz (1999). Institutional Change and Transition in the Forest Sector of Khabarovsk Krai. Interim Report IR-99-068. International Institute for Applied Systems Analysis, Laxenburg, Austria.

Eggertsson, Thrainn (1990). *Economic Behavior and Institutions.* Cambridge University Press.

Elster, Jon (1993). The Necessity and Impossibility of Simultaneous Economic and Political Reform. In: D. Greenberg and S.N. Katz (eds.) *Constitutionalism and Democracy. Transitions in the Contemporary World.* Oxford University Press, New York, pp. 267–274.

Frye, T. (1997). Russian Privatization on the Limits of Credible Commitment. In: David L. Wilmer (ed.) *The Political Economy of Property Rights.* Cambridge University Press, pp. 84–108.

Furubotn, Eirik and Svetozar Pejovich (1972). Property Rights and Economic Theory: A Survey of Recent Literature. *Journal of Economic Literature,* 10:4, pp. 1137–62.

Gaddy, Clifford G. and Barry W. Ickes (1998). Beyond the Bailout: Time to Face Reality about Russia's "Virtual Economy". *Foreign Affairs,* 77, pp. 53–67.

Greenspan-Bell, Ruth (2000). Building Trust. Laying a Foundation for Environmental Regulation in the Former Soviet Bloc. *Environment,* March.

Gurkov, Igor (1998). Ownership and Control in Russian Privatized Companies: New Evidence from Repeated Survey. *Post-Communist Economies and Economic Transformation,* Vol. 10, No. 2, pp. 259–270.

Helin, Markku (1988). *Lainoppi ja metafysiikka (Jurisprudence and Metaphysics).* Finnish Lawyers' Publishing, Helsinki (in Finnish).

Hellivell, John F. (1994). Empirical Linkages between Democracy and Economic Growth. *British Journal of Political Science,* 24, pp. 225–248.

Hendley, Kathryn, Barry W. Ickes, Peter Murrell and Randi Ryterman (1997). Observations on the Use of Law by Russian Enterprises. *Post-Soviet Affairs,* No. 13, pp. 19–41.

Hohfeld, W.N. (1919). *Fundamental Legal Conceptions.* Yale University Press, New Haven.

Hosking, Geoffrey (1985). *A History of the Soviet Union.* Fontana Press/ Collins, Glasgow.

Hüper, Christine (1998). *Unternehmskauf in Russland (Acquisiton in Russia).* Berlin Spitz and Vienna Österreichische Verlag (in German).

Ikonitskaya, I.A. (1999a). Zemelnoe pravo Rossiiskoi Federatsii (Land Law of the Russian Federation). Uchebnik, Moskva, Yurist (in Russian).

Ikonitskaya, I.A. (1999b). Zemelnoe pravo Rossiiskoi Federatsii: Teoriya i tendentsii razvitiya (Land Law of the Russian Federation: Theory and Development Tendencies). Institut gosudarstvo i prava Rossiiskoi Akademii Nauk, Akademicheskii pravovoi universitet, Moscow (in Russian).

Ikonitskaya, I.A. (2000a). Interview, 3 April.

Ikonitskaya, I.A. (2000b). Land Law of the Russian Federation. In: Juha Tolonen and Boris Topornin (eds.) *Legal Foundations of Russian Economy*. Kikimora Publications, Series B 14, Helsinki, pp. 165–203.

Ioffe, O.S. (1949). Pravootnosheniya po sovetskomu grazhdanskomu pravu (Legal Relations According to Soviet Civil Law). Moscow (in Russian).

Ivanova, L. and V. Nygaard (1999). Institutions and the Emergence of Markets—Transition in the Murmansk Forest Sector. Interim Report IR-99-071. International Institute for Applied Systems Analysis, Laxenburg, Austria.

Jones, Anthony and William Moskoff (1991). *Koops: The Rebirth of Entrepreneurship in the Soviet Union*. Indiana University Press, USA.

Kaser, Michael (1995). Privatization in the CIS. In: Alan Smith (ed.) *Challenges for Russian Economic Reform*. The Royal Institute of International Affairs, London and The Brookings Institution, Washington DC, pp. 119–202.

Kelsen, Hans (1991). *General Theory of Norms*. Translated by Michael Hartney. Clarendon, Oxford.

Kivimäki, T.M. and Matti Ylöstalo (1981). *Suomen siviilioikeuden oppikirja (A Textbook of Finnish Civil Law)*. Yleinen osa, Juva (in Finnish).

Kleinhof, A.E., L. Carlsson and M.-O. Olsson (1999). The Forest Sector in Moscow Oblast. Interim Report IR-99-069. International Institute for Applied Systems Analysis, Laxenburg, Austria.

Knight, Jack (1992). *Institutions and Social Conflict*. Cambridge University Press, Cambridge.

Kommentarii k Lesnomu kodeksu Rossiiskoi Federatsii (1997). Red. S.A. Bogolyubov. Institut zakonadatelstvo i sravnitelnogo pravovedeniya pri Pravitelstve Rossiiskoi Federatsii (Commentary on the Forest Code of the Russian Federation). Infra M-Norma, Moscow (in Russian).

Kornai, Janos (1990). The Affinity Between Ownership Forms and Coordination Mechanisms: The Common Experience of Reform in Socialist Countries. *Journal of Economic Perspectives*, Vol. 4, No. 3, Summer, pp. 131–147.

Korostelev, S.V. (1998). Zemelnoe i lesnoe pravo (Land and Forest Law). Fond "Mezhdunarodno-pravovoi ekspertizy" Evropeiskii institut ekspertov. Izdatelstvo Mihailova V.A i Izdatelstvo Poluisk, St. Petersburg (in Russian).

Kotova, Maria (2001). Legal Problems of Forest Enterprises in Russia (preliminary title). Interim Report. International Institute of Applied Systems Analysis, Laxenburg, Austria (forthcoming).

Kregel, Jan, Egon Matzner and Gernot Grabher (eds.) (1992). *The Market Shock*. Austrian Academy of Sciences, Vienna.

Kruglyi stol (1993). Roundtable Discussion. *Gosudarstvo i pravo*, 8 (in Russian).

Kruglyi stol (1998). Roundtable Discussion. *Gosudarstvo i pravo*, 5 (in Russian).

Krüssmann, Thomas M. (1998). *Privatisierung und Umstrukturierung in Russland. Zur Rolle des Rechts als Instrument Struktureller Wirtschaftsreform im Übergang zur Marktwirtschaft (Privatization and Restructuring in Russia. The Role of Law as an Instrument of Economic Reform in Transition to a Market Economy)*. Berlin Spitz Verlag and Vienna Verlag Österreich (in German).

Kuorsalo, Anne, Ilmari Susiluoto and Martti Valkonen (1999). *Venäjä ja rosvokapitalismin haaksirikko (Russia and the Wreck of Robber Capitalism)*. Edita, Helsinki (in Finnish).

Larenz, Karl (1989). *Allgemeiner Teil des deutschen bürgerlichen Rechts*. Becks Verlag, München (in German).

Leblang, David (1996). Property Rights, Democracy and Economic Growth. *Political Research Quarterly*, Vol. 39, pp. 5–26.

Libecap, Gary D. and Steven N. Wiggins (1989). The Political Economy of Crude Oil Cartellization in the United States: 1933–1972. *Journal of Economic History*, 49:4, pp. 833–56.

Lipton, David and Jeffrey Sachs (1990). Privatization in Eastern Europe, The Case of Poland. Brookings Papers on Economic Activity, No. 2.

Lott, John R., Jr. (1987). The Effects of Nontransferable Property Rights on the Efficiency of Political Markets. *Journal of Public Economics*, 32:2, pp. 231–46.

Malyi, A.F. (1999). *Organy gosudarstvennoi vlasti oblasti: problemy organizatsii (The Organs of State Power of the Regions: Problems of Organization)*. Arkhangelsk. Izdatelstvo Pomorskogo gosudarstvennogo universiteta imeni M.V. Lomonosova (in Russian).

McFaul, Michael and Tova Perlmutter (eds.) (1995). *Privatization, Conversion and Enterprise Reform in Russia*. Westview Press, Boulder, Colorado.

Mishler, William and Richard Rose (1995). Trust, Distrust and Skepticism about Institutions of Civil Society. Studies in Public Policy, 252, Center for the Study of Public Policy, University of Strathclyde, United Kingdom.

Moore, John H. (1981). Agency Costs, Technological Change, and Soviet Central Planning. *Journal of Law and Economics*, 143:3, pp. 189–214.

Mozolin, V.P. (1992). Pravo sobstvennosti v Rossiiskoi Federatsii v period perekhoda k rynochnoi ekonomike (Property Law in the Russian Federation during the Period of Transition to a Market Economy). Rossiiskaya Akademiya Nauk, Institut gosudarstvo i pravo, Moscow (in Russian).

North, Douglass C. (1992). *Institutions, Institutional Change and Economic Performance*. Cambridge University Press, USA.

North, Douglass C. (1993). Institutions and Credible Commitment. *Journal of Institutional and Theoretical Economics*, 149:1, pp. 11–23.

North, Douglass C. and Robert Paul Thomas (1973). *The Rise of the Western World*. Cambridge University Press, Cambridge.

Nove, A. (1977). *The Soviet Economic System*. Allen and Unwin, London.

Olson, M. (1992). The Hidden Path to Successful Economy. In: Christopher Clague and Gordon C. Rausser (eds.) *The Emergence of Market Economies in Eastern Europe*. Basil Blackwell, Cambridge, Mass., pp. 55–76.

Ostrom, Elinor (1990). *Governing the Commons: The Evolution of Institutions for Collective Action*. Cambridge University Press, Cambridge.

Pevsner, M.E. (1997). Osnovanye napravleniya sovershenstvovaniya zakonodatelstva o nedrakh (The Basis of the Direction of Development of Legislation on the Natural Resources under the Earth). *Gosudarstvo i pravo*, No. 5, pp. 70–73.

Piipponen, Minna (1999). Transition in the Forest Sector of the Republic of Karelia. Interim Report IR-99-070. International Institute for Applied Systems Analysis, Laxenburg, Austria. Reprinted in *Fennia*, 177:2, pp. 185–233.

Poznanski, Kazimierz Z. (1992). Property Rights Perspective on Evolution of Communist-Type Economies. In: Kazimierz Poznanski (ed.) *Constructing Capitalism*. Westview Press, Colorado, USA.

Radygin, Alexander (1995). The Russian Model of Mass Privatization: Governmental Policy and First Results. In: Michal McFaul and Tova Perlmutter (eds.) with a foreword by Kenneth J. Arrow, *Privatization, Conversion, and Enterprise Reform in Russia*. Westview Press, Colorado, USA.

RFE (1998). The Big Seven—Russia's Financial Empires. Special Report of Radio Free Europe (RFE). In: Transition Newsletter, The World Bank Group. Available on the Internet: http://www.worldbank.org/ html/prddr/ trans/feb98/bigseven.htm.

Riker, William H. and David L. Weimer (1993). The Economic and Political Liberalization of Socialism: The Fundamental Problem of Property Rights. *Social Philosophy and Policy*, 10:2, pp. 79–102.

Riker, William H. and David L. Weimer (1995). The Political Economy of Transformation: Liberalization and Property Rights. In: Jeffrey S. Bank and Eric A. Hanushek (eds.) *Modern Political Economy: Old Topics, New Directions*. Cambridge University Press, Cambridge, pp. 80–107.

Rose, Richard (1998). Getting Things Done with Social Capital: New Russia Barometer VII. Studies in Public Policy 303, Center for the Study of Public Policy, University of Strathclyde.

Sachs, Jeffrey (1993). *Poland's Jump to the Market Economy*. MIT Press, Cambridge, Mass.

Sailas, Anne (1996). Venäjä opettelee markkinataloutta (Russia Learns Market Economy). In: Anne, Sailas, Ilmari Susiluoto and Martti Valkonen (eds.) *Venäjä—jättiläinen tuuliajolla (Russia—A Giant Adrift)*. Edita. Helsinki (in Finnish).

Simon, Herbert A. (1985). *Administrative Man*. Macmillan, New York.

Sokolova, N. (2000). Institutions and the Emergence of Markets—Transition in the Krasnoyarsk Forest Sector. Interim Report IR-00-028. International Institute for Applied Systems Analysis, Laxenburg, Austria.

Spiller, Pablo (1995). Regulatory Commitment and Utilities' Privatization: Implications for Future Comparative Research. In: Jeffrey S. Bank and Eric A. Hanushek (eds.) *Modern Political Economy: Old Topics, New Directions*. Cambridge University Press, Cambridge, pp. 80–107.

Stiglitz, J. (1993). Some Theoretical Aspects of the Privatization: Applications to Eastern Europe. In: Mario Baldassari, Luigi Paganetto and Edmund S. Phillips (eds.) *Privatization Processes in Eastern Europe*. MacMillan Press, United Kingdom.

Stiglitz, J. (1999). Whither Reform? Ten Years of the Transition. World Bank Annual Conference on Development Economics, 28–30 April 1999. Washington DC, USA.

Sudebno-arbitrazhnaya statistika (2000). Osnovnye pokozateli raboty arbitrazhnykh sydov Rossiiskoi Federatsii v 1998–1999 godah (Statistics of the Arbitration Courts). *Vestnik Vyshego Arbitrazhnogo Suda Rossiiskoi Federatsii*, No. 3. Available on the Internet: http://www.arbitr.ru/akdi/ (in Russian).

Tolonen, Hannu (1997). Mitä oikeus on? (What is Law?). *Oikeus*, No. 2, pp. 109–123 (in Finnish).

Tolonen, Juha Pentti (1976). Neuvostoliiton talousjärjestelmä ja sen oikeudelliset perusteet (The Economic System of the Soviet Union and its Legal Foundations). A Researches No. 48, Research Center of Social Sciences, University of Tampere (in Finnish).

Tolonen, Juha (1996). Legal Aspects of Transformation. A General View. Proceedings of International Symposium of Law, Economics and Business in the Melting Pot, 11–12 March 1996. Copenhagen Business School, Law Department and Tokai University Research Institute of Social Sciences, pp. 127–141.

Tomass, Mark (1999). A Decade of Conflicts in Czech Economic Transformation. *Journal of Economic Issues*, Vol. XXXIII, No. 2, June, pp. 315–325.

Torstensson, Johan (1994). Property Rights and Economic Growth: An Empirical Study. *Kyklos*, 47:2, pp. 231–47.

Vining, Aidan R. and David L. Weimer (1990). Government Supply and Government Failure: A Framework Based on Contestability. *Journal of Public Policy*, 10:1, pp. 1–22.

Vining, Aidan R. and Anthony E. Boardman (1992). Ownership versus Competition: Efficiency in Public Enterprise. *Public Choice*, 73:2, pp. 205–39.

Weimer, David L. (1997). The Political Economy or Property Rights. In: David L. Weimer (ed.) *The Political Economy of Property Rights. Institutional Change and Credibility in the Reform of Centrally Planned Economies*. Cambridge University Press, USA.

Wiles, P. (1977). *Economic Institutions Compared.* Basil Blackwell, Oxford.

Williamson, O.E. (1985). *Economic Institutions of Capitalism: Firms, Markets, Relational Contracting.* Free Press, New York.

Zitting, S. (1951). *Omistajanvaihdoksesta silmälläpitäen erityisesti lainhuudatuksen vaikutuksia (On the Change of Ownership).* Finnish Lawyers Association, Vammala (in Finnish).

Official Sources

Decree of the Council of Ministers of the Soviet Union No. 49 on Joint Ventures with Capitalist Firms of 13 January 1987 (Postanovlenie Soveta Ministrov SSSR ot 13 yanvarya 1987 f. No. 49 "O poryadke sozdaniya na territorii SSSR i deyatelnosti sovmestnykh predpriyatii s uchastiem sovetskikh organizatsii i firm kapitalisticheskikh i razvivayushchisya stran").

The Decree of the Russian Federation on Joint Stock Companies of 25 December 1990 (Polozhenie ob aktsionernykh obshchestvakh RSFSR ot 25 dekabrya 1990 g.).

Federal Law on Joint Stock Companies of 8 May 1996 (Ob aktsionernykh obshchestvah).

Law on Property in the Soviet Union of 6 March 1990 (Zakon SSSR o sobstvennosti v SSSR ot 6 marta 1990).

Federal Law on Property of the RSFSR of 24 December 1990 (Zakon RSFSR o sobstvennosti v RSFSR).

Law on State Enterprises of the Soviet Union of 30 June 1987 (Zakon SSSR o gosudarstvennom predpriyatii).

Law on Enterprises of the Soviet Union of 4 June 1990 (Zakon SSSR o predpriyatiyakh).

Law on Enterprises of Russia of 25 December 1990 (Zakon RSFSR o predpriyatiyakh i predprinimatelskoi deyatelnosti).

Decree of the Supreme Soviet on the Limitation of Privatization of 27 December 1990 (Postanovlenie Verkhovnogo Soveta RF "O razgranichenii gosudarstvennoi sobstvennosti v RF na federalnuyu sobstvennost, gosudarstvenuyu sobstvennost respublik v sostave okrugov, g. Moskvy i Sankt-Peterburga i munitsipalnuyu sobstvennost").

Law of the Russian Federation on Privatization of State and Municipal Enterprises in the Russian Federation of 3 July 1991 (O privatizatsii gosudarstvennykh i munitsipalnykh predpriyatii v Rossiiskoi Federatsii).

Law on Privatization of State Property and the Foundations of Privatization of Municipal Property in the Russian Federation of 21 July 1997 (O privatizatsii gosudarstvennogo imushchestva i ob osnovakh privatizatsii munitsipalnogo imushchestva v RF).

Presidential Decree on Corporatizing State Enterprises of 1 July 1992, No. 721 (Ob organizatsionnykh merakh po preobrazovaniyu gosudarstvennykh predpriyatii, dobrovolnykh obedinenii gosudarstvennykh predpriyatii v aktsionernye obshchestva).

The Privatization Program of 1993 (Ukaz Prezidenta RF o Gosudarstvennoi programme privatizatsii gosudarstvennykh i munitsipalnykh predpriyatii No. 2284 ot 24 dekabrya 1993 g.)

The Privatization Program of 1994 (Ukaz Prezidenta RF ob osnovnykh polozheniyakh gosudarstvennoi programmy privatizatsii gosudarstvennykh i munitsipalnykh predpriyatii posle 1 iyulya 1994 goda ot 22 iyuliya 1994 g. No. 1534).

Presidential Decree on Holding Companies of 16 November 1992, No. 1731.

Presidential Decree on Reforming State Enterprises of 23 May 1994, N. 1003 (Ukaz Prezidenta RF o reforme gosudarstvennykh predpriyatii).

Regulation on the State Committee of the Russian Federation for Administration of State Property of 4 December 1995 (Polozhenie o Gosudarstvennom Komitete RF po upravleniyu gosudarstvennym imushchestvom. Utverzhdeno postanovleniem Pravitelstva RF ot 4 dekabrya 1995 goda).

Regulation on the Russian Fund of Federal Property of 17 December 1993 (Polozhenie o Rossiiskom fonde federalnogo imushchestva. Utverzhdeno ukazom prezidenta PF ot 17 dekabrya 1993).

Law on Privatizing Apartments of 4 July 1991 (O privatizatsii zhilishchnogo fonda).

Law on Houseowners' Companies of 15 June 1996 (O tovarishchestvakh sobstvennikov zhilya).

Law on Minimum Wage of 13 June 2000 (O minimalnom razmere oplaty truda No. 82).

Law on Bankruptcy of 8 March 1998, No. 6, changed 6 June 2000 (O nesostoyatelnosti (bankrotstve).

Law on Bankruptcy of Banks of 25 February 1999, No. 40, changed 2 January 2000 (O nesostoyatelnosti (bankrotstve) kreditnykh organizatsii).

Law on Mortgages of 16 July 1998, No. 102 (Ob ipoteke (zaloge nedvizhimosti)).

Presidential Decree on the Additional Measures on the Development of Mortgage Credits of 28 February 1996.

Land Code of the Russian Socialist Federal Soviet Republic of 25 April 1999 (Zemelnyj kodeks RSFSR).

Grazhdanskii kodeks RF, chast pervaya ot 30 noyabrya 1994 g; chast vtoraya ot 26 yanvarya 1996 g. (The Civil Code of the Russian Federation, Parts I and II).

Federal Law on Changes and Amendments to the Law of the Russian Federation "On Below Ground Natural Resources" (Federalnyi zakon ot 3 marta 1995 g. 'O vneshenii izmenenii i dopolnenii v Zakon Rossiiskoi Federatsii "O nedrakh"').

Federal Law on the Continental Shelf of 30 November 1995 (Federalnyi zakon o kontinentalnom shelfe).

The Water Code of the Russian Federation of 16 November 1995 (Vodnyi kodeks RF).

The Forest Code of the Russian Federation of 21 January 1997 (Lesnoi kodeks RF).

Postanovlenie Konstitutsionnogo Suda Rossiiskoi Federatsii ot 9 yanvarya 1998 g. "Po delu o proverke konstitutsionnosti Lesnogo kodeksa Rossiiskoi Federatsii" 1998 No. 3 (Decision of the Constitutional Court of the Russian Federation on Constitutionality of the Forest Code of the Russian Federation).

Law on the Land Reform of 23 November 1990 (O Agrarnoi reforme).

Law on the Public Fee for Land of 11 October 1991 (VSRF No. 1738), changed 25 July 1998, No. 132 (O prave za zemlyu).

Law on the Right of the Citizens of the Russian Federation to Obtain for Private Ownership as well as For Sale Land Property for Personal Recreation, Gardening and Building of Private Dwelling of 23 December 1992 (O prave grazhdan Rossiiskoi Federatsii na poluchenie v chastnuyu sobstvennost i na prodazhu zemelnykh uchastkov dlya vedeniya lichnogo podsobnogo i dachnogo khozyaistva, sadovodsstva i individualnogo zhilishchnogo stroitelstva).

Decree of the President of the Russian Federation on the Procedure for Setting Norms for Giving Land Property to the Ownership of Citizens Without Payment of 2 March 1992, No. 11 (O poryadke ustanovleniya normy besplatnoi peredachi zemelnykh uchastkov v sobstvennost grazhdan).

Decree of the President of the Russian Federation on Selling Land Property to Citizens and Juridical Persons in connection with Privatization of State and Municipal Enterprises of 25 March 1992, No. 14 (O prodazhe zemelnykh uchastkov grazhdanam i yuridicheskim licham pri privatizatsii gosudarstvennykh i munitsipalnykh predpriyatii).

Presidential Decree on Approval of the Procedure of the Sale of Land Plots under Privatization of the State and Municipal Enterprises, under Enlargement and Additional Construction of these Enterprises as well as of the Land Plots at the Disposal of the Citizens or of their Organizations for Entrepreneurial Activities of 14 June 1992.

Presidential Decree on the Regulation of the Land Market and on the Development of the Agrarian Reform in Russia of 27 October 1993.

Presidential Decree on the Right of Ownership of Citizens and Juridical Persons on Land Property of Immovable Objects in Agricultural Areas of 14 February 1996, No. 198 (O prave sobstvennosti grazhdan i yuridicheskikh lits na zemelnye uchastki pod obektami nedvizhimosti v selskoi mestnosti).

Presidential Decree on Bringing the Land Legislation of the Russian Federation to Conformity with the Constitution of the Russian Federation of 24 December 1993.

Presidential Decree on Implementation of the Constitutional Rights of Citizens on Land of 1 March 1996, No. 11 (O realizatsii konstitutsionnykh prav grazhdan na zemlyu).

Government Decree on the Procedure to Introduce State Land Cadastre of 25 August 1992 (Polozhenie o poryadke vedeniya gosudarstvennogo zemelnogo kadastra. Utvezhdeno postanovleniem Pravitelstva).

Decree of the President on Land Registration of 11 December 1993, No. 2130 (O gosudarstvennom zemelnom kadastre i registratsii dokumentov o pravakh na nedvizhimost).

Law on Registration of Immovable Property of 21 July 1997, No. 122, changed 5 March 2001 (O gosudartvennom registratsii prav na nedvizhimoe imushchestvo i sdelok s nim).

Law on Land Cadastre of 2 January 2000, No. 28 (O gosudarstvennom zemelnom kadastre).

Law on Guaranteeing Rights of Indigenous Peoples of 30 April 1999, No. 82 (O garantiyakh prav korennykh malochislennykh narodov).

Law on Foreign Investments of 9 July 1999, No. 160 (Ob inostrannykh investitsiyakh v RF).

Presidential Decree on the Federal Natural Resources of 16 December 1993, No. 51 (O federalnykh prirodnykh resursakh).

Presidential Decree on the Structure of Federal Organs of the Executive Power of 17 May 2000, No. 867, changed 1 December 2000 (O strukture federalnykh organakh ispolnitelnoi vlasti).

4

RUSSIAN ENTERPRISES AND COMPANY LAW IN TRANSITION

4.1 Introduction

4.1.1 A Firm in Company Law and in Institutional Economics

Law defines a company as an organization regulated by certain legal rules. These rules are some kind of preconditions, which are set for the companies to be able to define them and then operate with legal methods. From the point of view of company law, companies differ from each other according to different company law regulations. However, legal regulations do not make a company. Each company has its own corporate culture within the framework of legal regulations. Thus, setting new regulations does not necessarily make companies function in a new way. Law is not only a simple and practical technical tool; it is much more. Law is an institution, which is connected with other institutions of society. Institutions are the rules of the game, of which law constitutes a significant part of the formal rules (North, 1992). The significance of law in each society is dependent on its connection with informal institutions. Law counts more in some societies than in others. Legal scholars representing legal realism express the same idea claiming that law is not only a system of norms. It becomes law only when it is implemented and when people feel that law binds them (Ross, 1966).

Legal studies, however, usually focus only on formal legal rules omitting other institutions and the interaction between them.

Specializing on legal regulation protects the autonomy of law and separates law from other social studies (see e.g., Hart, 1978; Kelsen, 1968). It can be claimed that law is to a large extent endogenous. Legal studies have built a system of concepts and their own methodology in studying legal rules. Such studies are needed in interpreting law in courts. Endogenous law, however, protects its boundaries and has difficulties in responding to the needs of a changing society. Law in itself is a good example of institutions, which resist change and tries to stick to its own stable rules and ways of thinking. Changes have to be transferred into this "legal language", before they have any chance of being accepted in the circle of lawyers, who guard the endogenous legal system. However, even if law is endogenous, it has to interact with the surrounding society and at least to some extent respond to its needs. Otherwise law will become insignificant and overruled by informal rules.

Company law is needed to define certain rules for business organizations, such as norms protecting minority groups in a company or third parties such as creditors or others whom companies may damage. In this respect the state also has important political aims and power to regulate business activities. The legislator can decide what principles should be followed in implementing company law. According to Tolonen (1974) the traditional ideological model, which understands that the company fulfills the will of the shareholders, is being displaced by a more dynamic theory. In this new approach the company is seen as a rational actor aiming at economic efficiency and other practical objectives, which should guide legal interpretation.

Tolonen's idea suggests that the aims of a company should be found outside the legal system of norms. Legal studies cannot answer the question: "What is a company?" Therefore economic and business studies have always affected the legislator. After Berle and Means (1967) established the concept of managerialism in the early 1930s in the United States, the focus of the legislator has been on regulating the relations between shareholders and managers. In economics, the institutional approach took a long step towards a new dynamic theory on the firm. It really tries to answer the question: "What is a firm and what are its aims?" while neoclassical economy focuses on markets and different variables, which may affect how they function. Coase's (1937) article on The Nature of the Firm gradually started to draw attention to a firm. Coase saw that a firm is a way of organizing activities and that the organization is chosen among different possibilities in order to reduce transaction costs. A firm is actually a nexus of contracts,[107] the organizing of which vary between contracting in a market without any organization and hierarchy, which draws the contracts within the organization. The nexus of contracts idea moves the focus from the relations between shareholders and managers to a broader understanding of a firm.

Coase's focus on a firm and transaction costs has created a wide range of studies. Transaction costs are not the only factor in choosing the organizing forms. Williamson (1985) has paid attention to governance structures. He found a lot of aspects that affect governance structures. There are behavioral aspects such as the assumption that human beings are "intendedly rational, but only limitedly so" (Simon, 1961). Therefore all forms of complex contracting are unavoidably incomplete. Another behavioral assumption is that human beings are given to opportunism. Their self-interest seeking leads them to opportunistic behavior if promises are not supported by credible commitments. These two assumptions suggest that economic activity has to be organized so as to economize on bounded rationality and simultaneously safeguarding the transactions in question against the hazards of opportunism (Williamson, 1988:68).

Williamson also identifies critical dimensions with respect to which transactions differ. The principal dimensions for the purposes of describing transactions are:

- the frequency with which they appear,
- the degree and type of uncertainty to which they are subject, and
- the conditions of asset specificity.

Contracting parties commit themselves in a credible way if they have specific assets. They can use the specific asset to tie their partner in business cooperation in a credible way. For instance, a contracting party may have special technological knowledge, a special site or specialized production capacity for a specific

---

[107] The nexus of contracts idea was later developed in the 1970s by Jensen and Meckling (1976) and Fama (1976) as well as Alchian and Demsetz (1972). It took several decades before Coase's articles started to interest other economists.

customer.[108] Asset specificity does not exist in occasional market contracts, but is connected with relations of mutual dependence.

Williamson also combines a process analysis to studies of organizations. It applies North's ideas of institutional change to a microlevel (cf., North, 1992; North and Thomas, 1973). Processes should be studied in connection with specific contracts. A process outcome is often an unanticipated consequence and also unwanted. For example, demands for control cause both greater control and make those, who are subject to control, adapt. The focus on process introduces a richer model of organization, which takes unanticipated adaptations into account. A "machine model" of organization cannot explain unwanted results.

4.1.2 Transition and a Firm

Economic and institutional theories have been developed in a market economy environment. This development can be described as a long process of learning (Tolonen, 1974). In market economies, types of firms have developed in practice. Company law has then responded to the needs to control and monitor, to sanction human opportunism. The most significant feature of a capitalist firm is that ownership and control are separated (Berle and Means, 1967). The managerial revolution occurred quite early in the United States and turned the focus of company law on corporate governance. The significance of the role of professional managers was identified and thus emphasized. Since the interests of managers differ from those of the owners, responsibility to shareholders also became an important issue of company law. Corporate governance has also later extended responsibility to other stakeholders.

The development of a firm has been totally different in socialist economies. In Russia, the October Revolution of 1917 disrupted the learning process of a market economy. In a planned economy enterprises were governed in an administrative manner. The whole economy worked like a huge hierarchy. Agency problems were

---

[108] Williamson (1996:105) distinguishes six types of asset specificity, namely, site specificity, physical asset specificity, human asset specificity, dedicated assets, brand name capital and temporal specificity.

great, because it was quite difficult for the state owner to control and monitor such a huge hierarchy. Managers found unwanted means to effectuate their own interests. They had to arrange production in such a way that it pretended to fulfill the plan, but under this umbrella managers treated the enterprises as their own. Privatization did lead to a managerial revolution, but this revolution did not separate ownership and control. On the contrary, managers became the main owners in most privatized companies. However, they did not turn into such entrepreneurs who created capitalism in the western world, but continued to survive in an economy that is neither a market economy nor a planned economy. Modern company law was then transplanted into this environment.

The Russian economy turned into that, which Gaddy and Ickes (1998) started to call a virtual economy. Socialist pretense has survived in a virtual economy, where signals of market prices are effectively blocked. A virtual economy pretends to create value, but destroys it in reality. Prices do not reflect the signals of the market and restructuring has not occurred. It is not certain that a virtual economy will eventually turn into a market economy. The problems of the Russian economy are institutional. Unwanted adaptations of the transition process have to be studied in their context. North and Thomas' (1973) focus on change in economic history shows that change is path-dependent. There is certain path-dependency vested in institutions making transition complicated to direct.

Abundant empirical data shows that the absence of trust is the main obstacle for development towards a functioning market economy, as well as being an obstacle toward the development of democracy and the rule of law.[109] In studying the development of enterprises, an institutional approach is therefore needed. When focusing on organizations in transition, Williamson's approach

---

[109] For example, Rose *et al.* (1999) and Kääriäinen and Furman (2000) found in surveys a low level of trust in institutions. Russian and foreign businessmen complained of the low respect of the law, contradictory legal rules and the high frequency of breaches of contract (IIASA survey on Russian forest sector referred to in Carlsson *et al.* (2000); interviews with businessmen in Lapland by Ollila (1999); and in case studies by Törnroos and Nieminen (1999)). In such an environment maintaining hierarchy is a more secure governance method than making market contracts.

has a lot to offer, even if transaction cost economizing may not seem to be the main objective of privatized large enterprises in Russia. The reason is the peculiar environment in which firms function. Therefore some basic assumptions of Coase's and Williamson's approach to firms such as private property and functioning markets do not completely apply to the Russian environment. However, Williamson's behavioral and dimensional assumptions seem to explain Russian institutional peculiarities.[110] Process analysis is also of vital importance in studying transition. Furthermore, Williamson's idea of asset specificity helps to understand the need for credible commitments in an environment where opportunism has to be controlled privately under great uncertainty. Fundamental transformation from opportunism to trust is needed, but it is not easy in the Russian environment.

Company law and courts also have their role to play in establishing trust in the legal system and contributing to the objective of reaching a market economy. According to the approach of agency theory on a firm as a nexus of treaties and Williamson's approach of governance structures, the role of the courts and the legal system on the whole is often exaggerated. This is due to the mainstream legal centralist standpoint, which emphasizes the role of the centralist court system above those, who operate in business. Of course, courts are always important as the ultimate place to appeal. They have *ex post* means to partly cover the damage and also establish rules that can be enforced *ex post*. "*However, courts are not available to enforce intrapersonal and intraorganizational agreements. Organizations can use lower-powered internal incentives and control instruments. Bureaucratic costs, of course, rise as a result*" (Williamson, 1988). Analysis of alternative modes of organization always requires an examination of context. In a transition economy the role of the courts extends to establish and enforce legal rules for a developing market economy. Even if the

---

[?] Williamson's approach has been criticized for ignoring the significance of [tru]st and emphasizing human opportunism (e.g., Granovetter, 1985; Etzioni, [19]8; Huemer, 1998). However, in Russia's rapidly changing "jungle [cap]italism" trust is mostly absent and protecting oneself from opportunism [bec]omes vitally important.

role of the courts is not powerful enough in this huge task as Williamson's approach suggests, company law has an important role to gradually enforce good corporate principles to protect outsider shareholders against the company insiders and creditors against fraudulent debtors. The legal centralist approach exaggerating the role of the courts should however be avoided. In the development towards a market economy, it is still crucial to change business life. It is here, where legal norms either function or not and where the rules in use develop.

4.1.3 National and International Company Law

The long socialist period abolished company law completely from Soviet law. Enterprises formed part of the state bureaucracy, the huge machine, which had abolished the market completely by drawing them inside a hierarchy. This development did not take place voluntarily to save transaction costs but through an authoritative order of the ruling Communist Party. Contracting within this hierarchy was done according to tight administrative rules in order to fulfill the state economic plan. Enterprises were juristic persons, but in practice they were only units of the state bureaucracy (Tolonen, 1976). They had only possession rights on the property with which they operated.

During *perestroika* the tight control of enterprises was eased to give them more economic decision power. Private entrepreneurship in small businesses became legal after being criminal for half a century. There were no forms of companies in the Soviet Union except cooperatives, which had previously been cooperatives in name only and were, in fact, governed by the state (Mozolin, 1992). Soviet managers, who had run state companies for their own benefit for a long time and had increased such activities along with decreasing state control, soon found new possibilities for rent-seeking. Parasitic cooperatives were founded alongside state enterprises. The state paid overheads, but the profits were channeled to parasitic private enterprises, the owners of which were the managers of the mother enterprise (Bim, 1995; Jones and Moskoff, 1991).

The first Russian decree by the government on joint stock companies was passed in December 1990. The forms of enterprises were also regulated in the law on Enterprises in December 1990.

The law determined several forms of enterprises, such as state enterprise, municipal enterprise, mixed enterprise (commandite), limited liability company/closed joint stock company, and open joint stock company. Cooperatives were not included in the list, which meant that they had to be transformed into other types of companies, usually joint stock companies. Privatization of state enterprises was effectuated on the above-mentioned legal basis. State enterprises had to be transformed to open joint stock companies and privatized according to a presidential decree on corporatizing (No. 721 of 1992). The decree contained a model of a company charter (articles).

A new Civil Code was passed on 30 November 1994. It determined the forms of companies in a new way differing from the earlier decree. A new Law on Joint Stock Companies was passed on 26 December 1996, 18 months after the main wave of privatization was over and after 75% of the state enterprises had been transformed into open joint stock companies with mainly private ownership. In 1998, a new Law on Limited Liability Companies was passed, which started a boom for limited liability companies. A limited liability company is popular in smaller and middle-sized companies, because its administration is regulated more flexibly than that of a joint stock company.

In drafting new company law Russian legislators have had a lot of models from developed market economies. Western countries have demanded modern company law legislation in Russia to make business in Russia more understandable for foreign investors. In the Partnership and Cooperation Treaty (1997) between the EU and the Russian Federation modern company law is one of the commitments, which Russia has promised to conduct. Thus, the example of EU company law directives is shown in current Russian legislation.

Company law even in the EU is still quite national by character. Each country has its own types of firms with different regulations.[111]

---

[111] According to Werlauff (1993) the differences in European company law are emphasized too much. Therefore he wrote a book focusing on the common nominators of European company law. In this way, he can actually show that company laws in European countries have a lot more in common than there are differences.

On the other hand, there is also a tendency to harmonize company law. EU directives aim at developing one type of company, which can fulfill the requirements of community directives. Harmonization is needed not only to integrate the European market but also because of the pressure of the globalization of competition in international markets. Corporate governance in an enterprise in market economies creates the decision-making process by balancing the interests of owners, managers and employees. In spite of different interests there is a common final objective, which is the profitability of the enterprise. Corporate governance has been arranged differently in Anglo-Saxon legal systems than in continental systems. The differences reflect the relative importance of different stakeholders in the economy in which they operate.

In the Anglo-Saxon one-tier system, there is a board of directors collectively responsible for the shareholders. In practice there may be a two-tier system inside the company in such a way that some of the directors are executive and others control. The shareholders' meeting chooses the directors, and usually the well-developed stock markets and skillful investors, who know the markets, can control and direct the decision-making of company management. In the German system there is a two-tier system of management with an executive board and a board consisting of representatives of interest groups, which are important for the company. Banks are the most important stakeholders, which appoint their representatives to the supervisory board. Employees are also regarded as an important stakeholder group in Germany. Employees' representation in the management and control of big companies is also guaranteed. The German *Mitbestimmung* system has raised a lot of resistance in the United Kingdom, where it is not understood at all. The fifth EU directive proposal for the structure of companies, which also contains workers' representation, is therefore frozen at the moment.

Even if company law is national by character, Russia has chosen to follow European models. However, there are still great differences due to differing business cultures. Company law is so new in Russia that most of the Russian lawyers do not include company law in the Russian system at all. Company law is regarded as part of the civil law concerning regulation of juristic persons.[112] Corporate governance is not an important issue yet, since managers keep shareholders in their control. It is not a difficult task, since managers themselves are usually majority shareholders. Thus the principle of equality of shareholders is not clear. There are also cultural differences. Russian managers are authoritarian and used to keeping the enterprise under their control without delegating power. Transforming formal regulations of company law to meet international standards is thus a much easier task than transforming authoritarian management culture and the economic environment.

4.1.4 Aim and Structure of this Chapter

This chapter focuses on Russian enterprises in transition. The approach to transition is on the enterprise level. The aimed objective of transition is to have capitalist firms in a market economy. There are, however, great institutional obstacles in reaching this objective. Special focus is on company law in its context. Does company law facilitate the change for enterprises or is it one of the obstacles? Or

---

[112] This differing approach occurs frequently in the Tacis/Tempus project, in which the author participates as a coordinator (Teaching comparative law Joint European Project (JEP) 10465-98: a consortium with Pomor State University, Arkhangelsk, Russia; University of Lapland, Rovaniemi, Finland; University of Umeå, Sweden; University of Abertay/Dundee, Scotland). Every time, when Western specialists use the concept corporate law or company law, the Russian specialists want to remind them that there is no such branch of law in the Russian legal system, but that the question is about the doctrine of juristic persons. Because the word company or the concept company law or corporate law is not used in Russia, Butler uses the word "association" instead of a company in his translations of Russian company laws (Butler and Gashi-Butler, 2000:introduction). Company law will, however, gradually become a new branch of law in Russia too. Also in Germany and other continental legal systems, company law emerged from the law of obligations. Because of rapid changes in the economic environment, Russian civil law doctrine should soon be able to develop to a more modern stage. The hindrance for doctrinal development is the deep-rooted legal positivism and conceptualism in Russian legal theory and dogmatics (see Nystén-Haarala, 1998 for a discussion about the continental roots of the Russian legal system).

does it have any effect at all? In studying the behavioral aspects of corporate governance, the nature of the process and other institutional explanations are taken into consideration. The focus is on what the ratio is and what the aims are of a Russian firm and how they are changing. What is the role of law in this process and does company law reflect the aims of a Russian firm?

The author shares the idea that efficient markets are built from below with assistance from the political structure but that the central figures in this development are the managers of individual firms (cf., Carlsson *et al.*, 1999). In establishing the rule of law, courts are important, but the legal centralist emphasis on courts must be rejected. In establishing the rule of law, civil society and informal institutions are at least as important as the formal hierarchy of norms.

First, we focus on the general development of company law in the Russian legal system. Company law is a totally new regulation, which has been drafted according to modern Western models. On the other hand, Russian "company law" also includes remnants from the socialist past. From the legal positivist point of view company law has to be integrated into the legal system and from the legal realist point of view company law should also be able to function sufficiently on the enterprise level. In the first section of this chapter we focus on the formal legal framework presenting the forms of companies and how they are founded and registered. The gap between formal legal rules and the rules in use is already met with the registration of companies.

The main concern of company law is the corporate governance aspect: regulating the responsibility of company management as well as the relations of different interest groups inside the firm. The relationship between shareholders or minority shareholders and owner managers is complicated and informal rules stemming from the socialist past still have an important role to play. Corporate governance, which stems from a quite different tradition and should start to change, is the second section. The rules for liability of losses and damages show how bad corporate governance is sanctioned within company law.

Russian enterprises are starting to orient themselves towards capitalist objectives such as maximizing profits. The third section of this chapter focuses on the transformation of Russian enterprises through studying the change of their aims. Comparing this transformation towards profitability with the stakeholder ideas in Western companies shows the contradicting requirements Russian enterprises must face and how profound the process of transformation actually is for them.

4.2 Forms of Companies (and Other Juristic Persons) in Russia

4.2.1 Juristic Persons According to the Civil Code

Only partnerships or companies are called commercial enterprises in Russia. According to the Civil Code, there are two types of partnerships: full and limited (commandite); and three types of companies: joint stock company, limited liability company, and company with additional liability. The division between partnerships and companies stems from Germany. Partnerships are associations of physical persons cooperating in business, while companies are combinations of capital (Komm./CC 1996).

All natural persons, who run a business, have to register as private entrepreneurs in the State Company register. These physical persons are allowed to run a business as private entrepreneurs without being a juristic person. These registered physical persons can also be partners in full or limited partnerships. Also a juristic person can be a partner in partnerships (CC 66§4.1). State and municipal administrative bodies cannot be partners in partnerships without a special stipulation in the law.

4.2.2 Partnerships in Russia

4.2.2.1 *Full Partnership (polnoe tovarishchestvo)*

Full partnership is defined in the Civil Code (§69). A full partnership is based on an agreement between partners, who are responsible for the obligations of the partnership with their whole property. The relations between the partners are based on confidence. Each partner is responsible also for each other's transactions and this liability cannot be limited in a contract (CC 75§). Each partner can represent the company. Power to represent the company and take care of the management can be divided in a contract. A new partner is also liable with his property for such obligations of the company, which have arisen already before his partnership. A partner, who has withdrawn from the partnership, is legally obligated for two years after withdrawal.

A full partnership is created by a partnership agreement (constituent or founding agreement). This founding agreement must contain the name of the partnership, the place of its location and the managing procedure, the amount and structure of joint capital, regulations for possible changes in the shares of the partners, regulations for capital investments and the liability for violation of this duty. A partnership must be registered and its legal capacity as a juristic person is attached to the moment of registration (CC §50 and 51).[113]

There is no minimum requirement for the amount of capital of the partnership. In this respect Russian regulation of partnerships follows the Anglo-Saxon model. In continental law the requirement for minimum capital is regarded as a rule protecting creditors. There is, however, no evidence that the absence of minimum capital requirements would have increased deceitful business in Anglo-Saxon countries (Memorandum..., 2000). Partners anyhow have full personal responsibility for the debts of the company. The absence of the minimum capital requirement makes starting a small business easier. Since it is still difficult to acquire credit from a bank in Russia to start a business, requirements for minimum capital might be an obstacle for starting small businesses.

Partners can agree upon sharing profit. If there is no agreement, profit or loss is divided according to each partner's share in the founding capital (CC 74§). The Civil Code also stipulates that partners must have the right to withdraw from the partnership (CC 77§). There is a term of notice of six months, which has to be followed unless there are especially worthy reasons for a shorter period. A withdrawing partner is entitled to compensation, which is defined according to the balance of the partnership (CC 78§).

---

[113] In Scandinavian countries, there was a principle that partnerships are created and also become juristic persons by the founding agreement. Registration only has a declaratory meaning. In Sweden, the law was recently changed (1995) and now requires partnerships to be registered to get the status of a juristic person.

A partner can also be excluded from the partnership. Other partners can demand this before the court, if they have a unanimous decision, which is based on a serious reason such as gross violation of duties or incapability of reasonable management (CC 76§).

4.2.2.2 Limited (Commandite) Partnership (tovarishchestvo na vere)

The Russian Civil Code also recognizes a limited partnership (§82) according to the German *Kommanditgesellschaft* example. In a limited partnership there are one or several silent partners (commanditaire) along with general partners, whose liability is similar to that in a full partnership. Silent partners are mainly investors, having a right to profit and a right to get information about the financial situation of the partnership. A silent partner bears the risk of losses within the amount of his investment. He has the right to withdraw and the right to transfer his share of the partnership to another silent partner. A silent partner can also be a juristic person and does not sign the founding agreement. He can for instance make a deposit agreement with the general partners. The anonymity of a silent partner is complete in Russian law.

Compared to western partnership regulations, a silent member has as few rights as possible in Russia. In some countries a silent partner may have the right to inspect as well as the right of action for disputing the accounts. Furthermore, there are issues contravening the partnership agreement or ordinary course of business that have to be decided with the consent of the silent partners. In Russia, however, the silent partner is clearly only an investor dependent on a partnership agreement, which he has not even signed himself. He only has the right to withdraw from the company.

4.2.3 Companies in Russia

4.2.3.1 Limited Liability Company (obshchestvo s ogranichennoj otvetstvennostyu)

A limited liability company is one of the forms of company regulated in the Civil Code. A new federal law on limited liability companies entered into force on 1 March 1998. The new law contains detailed regulation, but it also stipulates that the Civil

Code is applied to limited liability companies as well. The new law was drafted on the basis of the Civil Code regulations. After the new law came into force with more detailed regulation, a limited liability company became very popular in Russia. It seems to be a suitable form of company for small and medium-sized businesses, which is actually the purpose for which a limited liability company was originally created.

Members of a limited liability company are not personally liable for the commitments of the company, but bear the risk of losses within the costs of the contributions they have made. Typical for a limited liability company is the share of capital. Law determines a certain minimum capital for the company, which is a hundred times the minimum wage according to the law on minimum wage,[114] which is in force when the company is registered (14§). The investment of a member in the share of capital can be other items than money, e.g., securities, property and other rights, which can be evaluated in money.

The founding capital is divided into shares, which have been decided in the founding documents. These shares are determined in precise sums. The founding agreement must include the names of the founders, the size of the founding capital, the share of each of the members and the timetable within which the capital must be paid (12§). The agreement must also contain provisions in case the members do not pay their shares on time, the rules according to which the profit is shared as well as the governing bodies. The charter of the company may have more detailed regulations of, for example, the rights and obligations of the members, and the transfer of the share or rights of the shareholders' meeting.

The minimum capital requirement was adopted to emphasize the nature of a limited liability company as a company—a combination of capitals. In Germany, there is also a minimum requirement of DEM 50,000 (GmbHG 5§). In England, where the

---

[114] The minimum salary, which is used as an accounting unit is 83.49 rubles per month. According to a new Law on Minimum Salary, which was passed in June 2000, the amount was raised to 132 rubles in 2001, but it only affects the minimum salary, which employers have to pay. As a calculation unit, the amount stayed at the former level.

private company (PrC) corresponds to a Russian limited liability company, there are no minimum capital requirements. The minimum capital requirements have been criticized for hindering the free choice of the company form for small and medium-sized businesses. In Russia, the minimum capital requirement is, however, quite small to fulfill the purpose of protecting company creditors. Especially for a foreign investor the minimum requirement is low. Therefore, Russian company law specialists have suggested that the minimum capital for a limited liability company, with foreign ownership should be 1000 times the minimum salary (Sukhanov, 1998; Kommentarii…, 1998). This opinion is based on a Presidential Decree from 1994 on Registering State Subjects of Entrepreneurship (No. 1482). This decree is, however, usually not applied. If it were applied, it should also apply to joint stock companies with foreign shareholders. Special requirements for foreigners are also against the spirit of the new Foreign Investment Law of 1999, which aims at non-discrimination of foreign investors. Implementation and application of company law, however, vary in different regions and state bodies. There is also a widespread habit in Russian society of charging foreigners more than its own citizens. Therefore, companies with foreign ownership may face special requirements in founding a company.

There may also be an obligation for additional investment in the company, but this obligation has to be stipulated in the charter and decided at the members' meeting. This regulation resembles the English guarantee system. The members give a guarantee to pay more in certain circumstances. In an English private company the additional share is only connected to the liquidation of the company (Davies and Prentice, 1997). In Russia it is not limited to liquidation, but can materialize at any time.

The law on limited liability companies also sets limits for the number of members in the company. There has to be at least one member but not more than 50 members. The law thus allows one-man companies but only in the event that the member is not another one-man company. Allowing a one-man company has also been a gradual tendency in European company law. Germany allowed a one-man limited company in 1981 and England a one-man private company after the European Communities 12th Company Law Directive (89/667). Limiting the maximum number of members to 50 has been explained by the fact that too many members could make governing the company too difficult and cause conflicts (Kapkov, 1998:6). In Germany there are, however, no limits on the number of members, and there are also GmbH companies with a wide range of members (Lutter, 1998). In Russia limited liability companies are meant for small businesses. Big privatized enterprises were not even allowed the choice of having a limited liability company as their new form. They were all corporatized into joint stock companies and cannot change the form of the company as long as the state has unprivatized shares in the company (see chapter 3).

If the company charter (articles) does not forbid it, new members can be accepted to a limited liability company. The charter can also close the company to newcomers by stipulating that members do not have to accept newcomers (Kommentarii…, 1998). The closed nature and flexibility have made limited liability companies popular in Russia. They are good for small business and also quite practical for a big privatized joint stock company to start and channel profitable activities. A limited liability company is regarded as a daughter company, when another company governs 20% of the share of capital (CC 106§). In practice, the share of the company may be smaller and the share of its managers as private founders much more. In the charter (articles) the company can be closed to outsiders, which is not possible in open joint stock companies. Transferring more profitable activities to limited liability companies may be a possibility for former *nomenklatura* managers to continue business, if they have to abandon the non-profitable privatized joint stock company, and eliminate outsiders from the more profitable business. Limited liability companies are also preferred in foreign direct investments. The company may then be kept in foreign or shared ownership with carefully chosen reliable Russian partners.

4.2.3.2 Company with Additional Liability (obshchestvo s dopolnitelnoi otvetstvennostyu)

The Civil Code also recognizes a company with additional liability (CC 95§). It is a limited liability company but the liability is larger. The members have subsidiary liability for the debts of the company with their own property in the amount, which is for all of them equally multiplied to the cost of their contributions according to the charter. There is no special law on additional liability companies, but the law on limited liability companies mentions it (§56). Additional liability is also possible to arrange on an agreed amount and in agreed circumstances. The rules on the limited liability company shall otherwise be applied toward the additional liability company (CC 95 article). Companies of additional liability are not as popular as limited liability companies.

4.2.3.3 *Joint Stock Company (aktsionernoe obshchestvo)*

Joint stock companies are regulated in the Civil Code (96–104§§). The code stipulates that joint stock companies are also regulated in a Law on Joint Stock Companies, however, without regulating the relationship between the code and the law. The Law on Joint Stock Companies came into force in 1996. It regulates the foundation of the company, the legal position of companies and the legal rights and duties of shareholders. The law also contains rules on protecting shareholders' rights and benefits. The relationship between the code and special laws seems to be disputed among Russian scholars. Some regard the Civil Code as higher legislation in the hierarchy of norms and therefore prior to special laws. Braginskii (1998),[115] who sees that the Civil Code has priority before the Law on Joint Stock Companies, represents this approach. However, if the Civil Code were regarded as a general law and the Law on Joint Stock Companies as a special law, the latter would have priority according to the *lex specialis derogat legi generali* rule. The Law on Joint Stock Companies has also come into force later and would according to the rule *lex posterior derogat legi anteriori* also override the Civil Code.[116]

This dispute is not just theoretical as there are contradictory regulations in the code and the law. One example is the rules on

---

[115] Braginskii is one of the main drafters of the Civil Code.

[116] The hierarchial position of the codes and its consequences is a disputed issue among Russian civil lawyers. In a seminar in Vaasa 1997 preparing a book (Tolonen and Topornin, 2000), the leading specialists of Russian civil law from the Institute of State and Law of the Russian Academy of Sciences, Moscow, had a heated dispute on the issue with contradicting opinions.

increasing the charter capital. According to the Civil Code increasing the charter capital is an issue that is decided upon at the shareholders' meeting. The joint stock company law, however, regulates that deciding on increasing the charter capital can be transferred to the directors' board with a stipulation in the company charter. Another example is that buying one's own shares is not allowed in the Civil Code, but has been made possible in the Joint Stock Company Law. The nature of the supervisory board also changed in the Joint Stock Company Law because of taking into account the lobbying of the industrialist (Golubov, 1998:173).

According to Pistor (1997), letting the stipulations of the Civil Code concerning companies stay in force was a mistake and caused a lot of contradictions in company law. The situation is due to rapidly changing attitudes in a transforming society. The drafters of the Joint Stock Company Law focused more on companies than the drafters of the Civil Code. The Civil Code, however, contains the general doctrine of juristic persons, which is considered to be the starting point of further regulation. The coherence between the code and the new laws governing different forms of companies should, however, have been dealt with.[117] The legislator should have corrected the regulations of the Civil Code to correspond with the new Joint Stock Company Law.

The new Joint Stock Company Law took Russian company law closer to the European countries' legislation. Russian legislators already paid attention to European company law directives in the Civil Code (§97). Joint stock companies were divided into open and closed companies, which correspond to the division of public and private companies in the European Union. An open (public) company can offer its shares on the stock markets and is therefore subject to stricter rules for informing shareholders and the public. A closed (private) company does not function in stock markets. Other shareholders are entitled to purchase the shares, which a

---

[117] In his article concerning the contradictions between the Civil Code and the Joint Stock Company Law Golubov (1998), who was one of the drafters of the latter, explains that the drafters' starting point was to make the law and the code consistent, but that it was sometimes impossible. Golubov tries to explain the differences and underestimate their impact. Several times, however, he mentions that the Civil Code was not always clear.

shareholder is going to sell outside the company. There is no limit for the number of shareholders in an open company, while in a closed company there cannot be more than 50 shareholders. One-man companies are also allowed but, in the same way as in limited liability companies, the only shareholder cannot be a juristic person. The minimum number of shares is two but there is no limit for the nominal price of the share. The amount of charter capital in a closed company is at least 100 times the minimum wage, while in open companies it is 1000 times the minimum wage. Half of the capital has to be paid before registration and the rest within a year afterwards.[118] As in limited liability companies the share of capital can also be other items than money.

Apart from law, the activities of joint stock companies are regulated in the company charter (articles). The charter is the founding document of the company and is accepted in the founding meeting. A founding agreement can also exist, which is applied only to the relations between the founders.[119] The charter regulates the legal relation of the company to its shareholders and third persons. The registered charter binds the company, and all the changes to it become binding towards third parties as soon as they have been registered (14§). The law on joint stock companies only knows simultaneous subscription. Successive subscription is not possible at all.

According to the law (11§) everybody has a right to become acquainted with the charter (articles). In practice this requirement is not always fulfilled. Companies themselves do not want to give information about the ownership and relations within the company, and the registrar authorities have not always understood everybody's right to acquire knowledge about the charter (Clarke and Kabalina, 1995). Transparency, which is an important principle of European company law directives, is not included in the virtues of Russian companies. The reason is that in Europe transparency is

---

[118] The rule concerning paying the charter capital has been tightened in European Union countries where, according to the second company law directive (77/91), it has to be paid completely before registration of the company. In this respect Russia did not follow the EU company law directives but chose the older European rule.

[119] A regulation of the Supreme Courts on applying the Law on Joint Stock Companies, 2 April 1997, No. 4/8.

needed to attract investors, while in Russian companies portfolio investors are usually not needed and even information about company management is regarded as a trade secret, which competitors might use against the company.

The law lists all the information, which the charter (articles) must include. This list, though, is not complete. Other requirements, which are not contradictory to law, can be included. The charter (articles) must include general information about the company. It has to regulate the legal position of shareholders and the company bodies. Then there are non-mandatory rules in certain issues, such as the qualifications for a member of the directors' board. In drafting the charter (articles) the regulations of the law have to be followed strictly, otherwise the company cannot be registered. This has led to repetition of the rules of the Law on Joint Stock Companies. First, the text of the law concerning, for example, the bodies of the company is repeated word-by-word followed by the special company-wide regulations (Lehtinen, 1997). Charters (articles) have become standard documents in practice. Before entering into force of the joint stock company law, company charters (articles) had to fulfill the gaps in the law and create the legal position of the company (Lehtinen, 1997).

4.2.4 State and Municipal Enterprises (gosudarstvennye i munitsipalnye unitarnye predpriyatsiya)

State and municipal unitary enterprises are also included among commercial enterprises in Russia. However, they still have their own form of company, which is inherited from socialism. They are independent juristic persons; regulated both in the Civil Code (§§113–115) and in special legislation.[120] A unitary enterprise is defined as a commercial organization, which is not endowed with the right of ownership to the property that the owner (state or municipality) allotted to it. The property is entrusted to the unitary enterprise with either the so-called right of operative administration

---

[120] Decree on Federal State Unitary Enterprises based on the Right of Economic Jurisdiction of 6 December 1999; Decree on the Transfer of Federal State Unitary Enterprises to the Ownership of Subjects of the Russian Federation of 9 December 1999.

or economic management. These constructions are inherited from the socialist economy. Economic management means restrictions in the rights concerning immovable property. In operative management the restrictions concern all the property entrusted to the enterprise. In economic management the owner is not liable for the obligations of the unitary enterprise, while in operative administration the state is subsidiarily liable for the debts of its enterprise (Komm./CC 1996:141–146).

Unitary enterprises are not a dying form of juristic persons even if privatization changes state enterprises into open joint stock companies. Nowadays, municipalities have started to have a lot of economic activity and the form, which the law offers them for this activity, is a unitary enterprise.

4.3 Registration of Companies

Registration of companies is mentioned in the Civil Code. Legal norms governing registration can be found in a law stemming from the RFSFR and in the president's decree on the Regulations of the State Registration of the Enterprises and Individual Businessmen on the Territory of the Russian Federation of 1994. There are also rules on registration in special laws governing the different forms of companies.

According to the Civil Code the state registration is dealt with by the administration under the Ministry of Justice (CC 51§). However, this procedure is not functioning, as putting it into practice has failed. The Law on Enterprises regulates that the executive bodies of the Soviet of the People's deputies deal with registration. Such bodies no longer exist. In current practice registration occurs in the departments of local administration. Therefore there are different procedures for registration in different towns and municipalities.[121]

There are some exceptions from this procedure. The Ministry of Justice registers religious and social associations, even if the

---

[121] Lectures by Maria Kotova in the summer school of the Faculty of Law, Universtity of Lapland on 4 August 2000.

procedure does not work with companies. The Federal Ministry of Justice registers companies with foreign investment with the exception of oil and gas companies. The Central Bank of Russia registers banks (see footnote 121).

The application to register a company may be turned down for some reasons. If the company or members of the company have violated laws, the application may be turned down. Applications have also been rejected for reasons such as inexperience of the members or the existence of too many companies in the same branch. Antimonopoly bodies can also reject the application because of a dominant position or restrictions of competition. Antimonopoly regulations are, however, quite weak since positive social consequences can overweigh a dominant position. Social consequences can be jobs or new houses (see footnote 121). Actually, if antimonopoly regulations were strict, Russian industry and commerce would be split into smaller entities, since a dominant position is typical stemming from the socialist economy.

A registered company gets a stamp on the charter and a certificate proving that the company is a juristic person and has a right to conclude contracts. There are still unregistered companies, which do not have the right for legal actions. One way to find out whether the company is a juristic person and has the capacity for legal actions is to ask for the certificate. Nowadays, local executive bodies should also give information to everybody asking for it.

4.4 Corporate Governance in Russian Companies

4.4.1 Introduction

The current Russian Law on Joint Stock Companies has been praised as a long step towards company law of a market economy (Orlov, 1999). There is no doubt about this. As a formal system of norms it does not differ much from the company law of any western market economy. The law has clarified a lot of earlier unclear rules. However, the rules on corporate governance have been criticized as giving too little protection to the shareholders (Orlov, 1999; Pistor, 1997).

Corporate governance can be defined in different ways. The Advisory Group of the OECD, which produced a recommendation for corporate governance principles in 1999, defines corporate governance to "comprehend that structure of relationships and corresponding responsibilities among a core group consisting of shareholders, board members and managers designed to best foster the competitive performance required to achieve the corporation's primary objective."[122] This definition is a traditional Anglo-American view of the corporation, according to which the board members are solely responsible to the shareholders (Dignam and Galanis, 1999).

Corporate governance is a completely new issue in Russian civil law and even if, in practice, there have been a lot of infringements of shareholders' rights, corporate governance has not yet been included as an important issue of company law or actually the doctrine on juristic persons (cf., section 4.1.3). In Western countries, corporate governance has been the main issue due to several governance failures and misconduct in the recent past.[123] The reason for paying only marginal attention to corporate governance in Russian legal studies is due to the fact that legal scholars are not yet acquainted with such problems. Even corporate lawyers seldom come across with corporate governance, because the authoritarian management inherited from the communist period is still taken for granted.[124] Above all, shareholders' rights, which are the core of Western, especially Anglo-Saxon corporate law, did not even exist in the Soviet Union. Getting rid of Soviet state control emphasized

---

[122] The primary objective, according to the Advisory Group of the OECD (1999), is creating long-term economic profit.

[123] These failures have led to a lot of reports to provide standards of corporate governance. In the United Kingdom there are the Cadbury, Greenbury and Hampel Reports. The American Law Institute, the American Bar Association and the Business Roundtable have all passed their reports for US companies. France has the Vienot report, Australia the Borsch Report and so on.

[124] According to empirical research by Hendley *et al.* (1997), conducted in 1996 in fifteen enterprises in Moscow and Ekaterinburg analyzing questionnaires of sixty officials, even lawyers assumed the powers of the general director being stronger than the Joint Stock Company Law regulates. They were actually astonished to hear that the law regulates differently. It should be borne in mind that the law on joint stock companies of 1995 was still quite new when the empirical research was done.

the interests of the managers and employees. The managers saw privatization as freeing themselves from outside control. Shareholders, who are not managers or employees, are regarded as intruders, who should not invade "our company".

The discussion on corporate governance has had several approaches in market economies. In the United States, Berle and Means (1967) already noticed in the 1930s that division of ownership and control had led to a class of professional managers, who run the company for the benefit of the owners. The interests of managers and shareholders are partly conflicting when the managers are interested in increasing their salaries and other benefits, while the shareholders are interested in profit. Berle and Means's theory brought the concept of managerialism into organization studies and led to managerial corporate doctrine. The managerialist approach puts corporate management at the strategic center of the large firm. Because of their expertise and organizing resources, managers have the power to determine the processes of production and distribution to dominate hierarchical bureaucracies and represent the company to third parties. The power of managers was accepted and even facilitated in US company law.

There were, however, also those who denied the legitimacy of management's position claiming that managers were not accountable enough to higher authority. Realizing the conflict between shareholders and management has led to company law protecting shareholders' rights with detailed regulations. Rights of minority shareholders to challenge management and demand information stem from this origin.[125]

New economic theory, however, put forward a completely new approach displacing the management-centered concept of the firm. The nexus of treaties approach, which stemmed from Coase's ideas, did not regard a firm as a hierarchy where managers determine terms by fiat. They did not describe management as a hierarchical exercise but as a continuous process of negotiation of successive contracts (Alchian and Demsetz, 1972).

---

[125] According to Bratton (1989) anti-managerialists dominated law reviews in the United States in the 1970s. However, company law remained substantially pro-managerialist into the 1980s.

The contractual approach developed the agency theory. Agency costs have tried to be reduced in firm contracts. Jensen and Meckling (1976) developed the basic thesis of agency theory. According to them, managers act as agents to shareholder principals. Managers sell securities publicly to outside shareholder principals. The purchasing shareholders assume that the managers maximize their own welfare and will bid down the price of the securities. Thus management bears the costs of its own misconduct and has an incentive to discipline its own behavior. Management increases self-control and thereby increases the selling price of the corporation's securities by offering monitoring devices. These devices include independent supervisory directors and accountants as well as legal rules against self-dealing. Corporate governance was seen as a result of contracting and bargaining.

These new theories have led to demands for more flexible legal rules and allowing more to be decided with agreements between management and shareholders. The earlier approach, which in Germany and Scandinavian countries led to protective rules after some scandals and grave misuses, has experienced criticism and recommendations to replace formal binding rules with a more market-oriented approach.[126] When the stock markets developed and widened, a new group of skillful shareholders emerged, who invest in companies that are well run and give profit. They can affect the decisions of the managers by leaving the company and finding better firms for their investments. Therefore it can be claimed that in countries with a sufficiently developed stock market, it is the market that controls the power of the managers. The OECD Corporate Governance Principles rest on these market oriented ideas of the Anglo-Saxon model.

On the other hand, it can also be claimed that the stock markets are not well developed except in some countries such as the United

---

[126] A recent example is a Memorandum of the Ministry of Justice on Reforming the Joint Stock Companies Act in Finland (Memorandum..., 2000), which explains that there is a tendency to market regulated company law. The Finnish reform plans obviously follow the preparatory work that is being done in the British Department of Trade and Industry aiming at considerable flexibility at the cost of shareholders and creditors (see http://www.dti.gov.uk).

States and the United Kingdom. There are also opinions according to which the recent crisis in the financial markets caused by the Asian, Russian and Brazilian crises, casts doubt on the ability of the market to provide adequate and efficient prudential mechanisms (Dignam and Galanis, 1999). In continental European countries, such as Germany, it is often the interest groups, mainly banks, which control the management of companies. In the Anglo-American system the banks' rights to own shares or officially participate in corporate administration is restricted (Pistor, 1997). Stiglitz (1993) claims that banks are better controllers than shareholders. While shareholders' control is nominal, banks have managerial knowledge and can control with their credits. The most common criticism of the control of the banks is that the banks might act more for their own interests as lenders than in the shareholders' interest of profiting. There are both market control and network control countries. The interest group control is usually concentrated in the supervisory board controlling the managers (Nooteboom, 1999).[127]

In the dispute between the market control (exit) system and the network (voice) system, both sides have defended their approaches with cultural differences. Corporate law has developed within centuries and in different legal and corporate cultures. Quoting Tolonen (1974) it has been a long learning process. Russia has its own cultural features, which affect its formal rules and especially company culture. The Russian disrupted "learning process" has been quite different from the continuous western one.

---

[127] The third form of corporate control is the Japanese *keiretsu* system, which also is a network of banks and holding companies. Banks do not, however, play as important a role as in the German system. A *keiretsu* is a wide network of stakeholders such as business partners, government and local authorities. Employees are also regarded as an important stakeholder group. After the Asian economic crisis, Anglo-Saxon features have been adopted into Japanese company law.

4.4.2 Relations of Different Bodies of a Company in Russian Company Law

4.4.2.1 Bodies of Russian Joint stock Companies

The highest governing body of the company is **the shareholders' meeting**. Once a year there must be a general meeting of shareholders. There can also be additional meetings. The law on joint stock companies (48§) lists the issues that belong to the exclusive power of the shareholders' meeting and cannot be delegated to other bodies. In principle, decisions are made with a simple majority. There are issues, however, which according to the law require a qualified majority of three-quarters of the votes. Such issues are, for example, changes and amendments to the company charter (articles), reorganization of the company and liquidation of the company (49§).

Shareholders, who own at least 2% of the voting shares, can deliver two propositions to the general meeting agenda. An extraordinary meeting can be called according to a board of directors' decision on its own initiative, or on the initiative of the audit commission. An auditor, external auditor or shareholders, who own at least 10% of the voting shares, can also initiate an extraordinary meeting (55§). The shareholders' meeting is competent to make decisions, when more than half of the voting shares are represented (58§).

External voting is possible, except in decisions on the most important issues of the general meeting, such as the election of the executive bodies, audit commission and consideration of the annual report (§50). At the general meeting of a company with more than 100 shareholders voting on agenda matters is carried out only by ballots (60§). In a joint stock company with at least 50 shareholders, a board of directors must also be established (64§).

According to joint stock company law, **the board of directors** is a supervisory board responsible for the general management of the company except decision-making in issues, which are given to the exclusive power of the shareholders' meeting. If the number of shareholders who own issued shares with voting rights is less than 50, it can be stipulated in the company charter (articles) that the shareholders' meeting deals with the functions of the board of directors (64§). The shareholders' meeting chooses the members of the board of directors for one year. The law lists the issues, which belong to the exclusive decision power of the board of directors and cannot be transferred to the decision power of the executive body (the executive board or the general director) (65§).

The board of directors is a mixture of the British and German systems. The tasks of the board of directors resemble those of the executive board of directors in the German system of corporate governance.[128] The difference is that the executive board of directors is an obligatory body in a German-based system, while in Russia it is obligatory only in companies with more than 50 shareholders (open companies). The German system also has another administrative board as a supervisory body, which can be established in public joint stock companies. In Russia there is no such two-tier system, which draws outside directors or governors of different outside interest groups into the management of the company. The Russian board of directors has the functions of both the executive and the supervisory boards of the Scandinavian and German systems. In this respect it resembles the British board of directors. Directors of the executive body cannot form the majority of the board of directors. If the general director is the only executive, he cannot be the chairman of the supervisory board.

The functions of the board of directors are a bit unclear in Russian company law. The main reason for obscurities is that the Civil Code regulated the board of directors as a supervisory board in a more German style. The lobby group of Russian industrialists, however, wanted to make the board of directors a governing body resembling more the Anglo-Saxon system. The drafters of the Joint Stock Company Law took their opinions into consideration and made the board of directors a mixture of a supervisory and executive body (Golubov, 1998:173). The law, however, stipulates that it is a supervisory and governing body not an executive body (Golubov, 1998:171).

Russian joint stock company law allows several alternatives of a two-tier structure. There can be a board of directors (partly a

---

[128] Norway and Finland have the German-based two-tier system available for big companies, while Sweden and Denmark have a one-tier system with only one board of directors. Also, French joint stock companies have the option of a supervisory board (two-tier system).

supervisory body) and a general director or a structure with a supervisory board of directors, an executive board and a general director. The supervisory board in each alternative resembles more an executive than a supervisory body. The obscurity in the tasks of the different organs is probably due to the lack of tradition of a market economy type of corporate culture.

The executive body of the company is either one person as a **general director** or the **executive board** (or some other collective body mentioned in the charter). If the charter (articles) stipulates that there should be both a general director and an executive board, the authorities of both of them have to be regulated in the charter.[129] The general director is the chairman of the executive board of directors. The executive body takes care of the regular business of the company including ordinary legal actions and nomination of personnel. Founding or liquidating executive bodies belongs to the authority of the shareholders, if the charter does not stipulate this to the powers of the supervisory board of directors (69§). Large transactions, meaning purchasing or selling property in the value of more than 25% of the balance value of the company's property, belongs either to the powers of the board of directors or the shareholders' meeting (§§78–79).[130]

The shareholders' meeting chooses the **audit commission** or the auditor. Auditing takes place yearly. The audit commission or auditor himself can initiate additional auditing. Also the shareholders'

---

[129] However, according to Golubov (1998:174), the drafters of the Joint Stock Company Law saw that a collective board alone cannot be the executive body. It can only exist with the general director. This is again a contradiction to the Civil Code article 103, which allows three versions of executive management: an individual, collective, or both. The reasoning given by Golubov is that a collective body cannot be responsible for the executive tasks because it would make decision-making too complicated. Here, the opinion of the Russian drafters corresponds to the ideas of American corporate governanace with a lot of power concentrated in the hands of the managing director. In Scandinavian company law it is the executive board, which is obligatory in all joint stock companies, while a managing director is obligatory only in big open joint stock companies.

[130] According to the empirical study of Hendley *et al.* (1997) in Moscow and Ekaterinburg, most lawyers did not even know that a general director cannot make a decision alone on large transactions.

meeting or the board of directors can decide on extra auditing. A shareholder or shareholders possessing together at least 10% of the voting shares can demand extra auditing. Auditors must be outsiders and cannot be members of any of the company's bodies.

4.4.2.2 Comparative and Practical Aspects

In principle, the regulation of the Russian Law on Joint Stock Companies fulfills the minimum requirements of the OECD principles. However, the board of directors has more power than the shareholders' meeting compared to European company law regulations. Even if the Civil Code denies delegating issues placed within the exclusive authority of the general meeting to the executive bodies (103§), the Law on Joint Stock Companies does not stipulate questions concerning amendments to the charter in connection with an increase of the charter capital to the exclusive authority of the general meeting. Furthermore, the formation of the executive bodies is not within the exclusive power of the general meeting. On the other hand, the general meeting does not have the right to consider or adopt decisions regarding matters not referred to its authority. The shareholders' meeting does not have any authority to intervene the authority of the board of directors. Russian company law specialists consider that the law strictly restricts the authority of the general meeting (Komm./ZAO, 1996; Glushetskii, 1996). The administration of a joint stock company can be arranged in such a way that the directors can choose each other and increase the charter capital without consulting the shareholders' meeting (Orlov, 1999).

The power of the directors is also strengthened with the stipulation of the law that a decision of the general meeting with regard to, for example, the reorganization of the company, annual dividends and large-scale transactions as well as acquisition and redemption of issued shares by the company require the proposal of the board of directors (42§ and 49§). Even if the shareholders owning no less than 2% of the voting shares are entitled to submit not more than two proposals to the general meeting agenda, the board of directors can refuse to take the issues to the agenda. In such cases the shareholders may appeal to a court (53§). Likewise, the directors can refuse to call an extra shareholders' meeting on the proposal of shareholders owning at least 10% of the voting shares, in which case such a decision may be appealed to a court (55§). The role of the court is different than in Western countries' company law, since the board of directors has the right to refuse. Turning to the court is not merely requesting a declaratory action, but the opinion of the court. Rights of minority shareholders are therefore already, in principle, weaker than in Western countries.

In practice, the rights of minority shareholders are even weaker because the corporate culture in Russia is still highly management-centered.[131] In the Soviet Union soviet managerialism without shareholders existed. Managers were employees of the state. They were not always professionals, since they were chosen according to their political merits. It is the same directors, who now continue to control privatized companies. Turning to the court is a new right and the right of the courts to "interfere" in the management of the company is new to the directors, who already got used to dictatorial power after the collapse of the ill-functioning monitoring system of the state-owner.

In Western countries the role of the courts is usually regarded as minimal in company law. The courts are reluctant to interfere in the inner conflicts of companies (Pistor, 1997). In Russia the courts are the only bodies, which in principle could implant rules of modern company law into Russian corporate culture, but their opportunities to affect on corporate culture should not be exaggerated. It is very difficult for a court to also solve inner conflicts of companies in Russia. A court can give a final decision, but it does not guarantee that management practices of the company will change. It is also doubtful whether courts have such knowledge and ability to decide on inner conflicts of business organizations.

The board of directors can also dominate the shareholders in an open joint stock company with formal requirements. In the general

---

[131] A typical example of Russian corporate governance, reported in OECD proceedings (Brom, 1998), is the case of Novolipets Metallurgical Kombinat. The managers of this privatized company refused to allow a group of outside investors, together owning 40% of the shares of the company, appoint four of the nine members of the board of directors to represent their interests. Company management blocked the procedure claiming that the outside investors were intruders and managed to obtain their shares paying much less than they were worth.

meeting personal participation is not provided and the board of directors has effective means to hinder the use of the right of a shareholder to speak. They can effectively use the rules on the agenda. The opportunity of shareholders to effectively participate, which is one of their basic rights according to OECD principles, can be circumvented. Russian managers are masters in circumventing rules. In the Soviet Union they dominated workers' collectives. Managers made the decisions beforehand, which the working collectives were supposed to do. Also the labor union was under the managers' control, since there could not be conflicts of interests between managers and workers in socialism. Nowadays, when managers and workers own the majority of the shares together in most privatized companies, managers continue to treat the shareholders' meeting in a similar fashion to how they used to treat the workers' collective.[132] This kind of management is possible also because the labor union is weak in Russia. The labor union has always been dependent on both the government and the managers of the enterprises.

Many important principles of company law are not codified in Russian legislation. For instance, the principle of equality of shareholders is not directly codified. It is, of course, a significant part of the OECD principles and a clear principle in every western country as well. In the Russian legal system, codifying everything is important, because of the narrow doctrine on the sources of law. Neither court decisions nor legal studies are included in the sources of law (Alekseev, 1999).[133] The role of legislation is therefore extremely significant. Since there are still not always official

---

[132] Even the clear rule, one share–one vote proved to be difficult to follow. To make voting simple it often turned into one man–one vote rule with voting by raising hands, which was the old fashion of the production brigades (Pistor, 1997).

[133] Such a doctrine on the sources of law also diminishes the role of the courts. If the courts are given a task to transplant new company law legislation into practice, there should be more court cases and easily available. Court cases are almost never commented on in legal textbooks. Decisions of arbitration courts are published with comments in a series of books, which are sold out quickly. The Supreme Arbitration Court also has a webpage (http://www.arbitr.ru), and their cases can be found in other legal databanks, too.

preparatory works and even if there were, they have no value in interpreting legislation. The wording of the legal text becomes extremely important in interpretation. A principle, which is not codified, does not exist for Russian lawyers.

In a similar way the clear rule of the free right to sell shares is not clear at all in Russia, where the insiders try to keep companies in their control. Control over the shareholder register has given companies an opportunity to raise transaction costs for share trading. New shareholders are often required to pay for registration. Entry barriers are common. Companies frequently require not only documentation of the transaction, which in turn needs to be certified by a specially authorized firm with a notary's certified copy of the licenses of this firm attached, but also a variety of other documents. The shareholder may have to formally apply to open an account, powers of attorney by the seller or buyer, which has to be certified by a notary in case they send an agent to perform registration, as well as prove that taxes are paid on the transaction (Pistor, 1997:173). Abundant formal requirements are inherited from socialism. People simply continue to orient themselves according to these requirements without realizing that more simple rules might bring more flexibility and efficiency (Hendley *et al.*, 1997).

The legal rules protecting creditors are also weaker in Russian law than in Western countries. Both the division of a company and the decrease of the charter capital could be decided in the general meeting with only informing the creditors. It is also possible that, in principle, the company itself decides that it has no creditors and directly distributes its assets after the liquidation decision. There is only the requirement that the liquidation commission must publish the information beforehand. The creditors must be quite active—they have to keep an eye on the debtor. Banks, however, are creditors that look after their assets. Therefore it is important to create financial markets in Russia (Stiglitz, 1993). Financial markets are being created in Russia, but unfortunately in a very monopolistic way. In a very short time a small number of banks have managed to build up their own empires with the help of holding companies. Since the banks are weak in Russia and their power is based on holding companies controlled by a few businessmen, who are called *oligarch*s, it has been suggested that

Russian corporate control is going to develop into a direction, which is similar to the Japanese *keiretsu* system (Pistor, 1997).[134]

If creditors and shareholders did not exist earlier, employees did. They are therefore important stakeholders and actually at the core of corporate governance. According to socialist ideology, the workers in a way "owned" the enterprise where they worked since it was state property in their possession. This was one of the moral claims, which was used to support insider privatization (Bim, 1995). Employees, who used to think that the managers were responsible for arranging social benefits for them and look after their needs, were told that with the help of insider privatization they were able to keep their jobs. Therefore employees are still very important stakeholders.

Even if workers are an important group of stakeholders, workers' representation in the administration of the company was not arranged in the German way, let alone in the Yugoslav way. There was a discussion on including workers' participation according to the Yugoslav example, but this option was finally rejected (Krüssmann, 1998:289). In practice, however, those workers who own shares are represented in the administration of the company but managers effectively control them.

There are also serious gaps of transparency in Russian corporate practice. A lot of information, which is published in Western countries to ensure the potential investors of the good financial situation of the company, is regarded in Russia as trade secrets. Enterprises have refused to inform outsiders, who their shareholders are or to give information to minority (outsider) shareholders about the financial situation of the company. Such behavior casts a shadow on such companies, especially when it is widely known that illegal black market production is quite widespread. Managers, who have gained a lot of autonomy, have every incentive to convert firms' assets into their own because of limited future horizons (Stiglitz, 1993). Except for pure self-seeking, there are several rational reasons why Russian managers have to make informal profits and keep the company formally unprofitable. If they were to show profits, they

---

[134] The banks, which have gained a significant position in the markets, have managed to do this with the help of good connections to politicians (RFE, 1998).

would have to pay taxes, which are regarded as arbitrary and confiscatory in Russia. Double bookkeeping is common in order to avoid taxes.[135] Another reason to make informal profits is that criminal organizations might become interested in a profitable company. Managers also fear takeovers, especially those from foreigners. A company showing profit might start to interest investing shareholders, whose presence in the company may turn out to be disturbing (Gaddy and Ickes, 1998). There are no efficient stock markets in Russia, which could control the managers. A controlling network control system does not exist either.

4.4.2.3 Bodies of Limited Liability Companies

The administration of a limited liability company is possible to arrange in a much simpler form than that of a joint stock company. The supreme governing body is the general meeting of the members. The charter (articles) may provide the foundation of the board of directors. The executive body of the company can be either a board or one person. Members of the executive body must be natural persons, but not necessarily members of the company. Either an internal or external audit commission may be provided in the charter. An audit commission is, however, obligatory only for companies with more than 15 members (32§ and §§40–42).

Meetings of the members can be general or extraordinary. The latter can be initiated by the decision of the executive body, the board of directors, audit commission, auditor or members possessing at least 10% of the votes (35§). The article does not mention directly that also one member possessing at least 10% of the votes could initiate an extraordinary meeting. The wording of

---

[135] According to a survey conducted within the framework of the New Russian Barometer (Rose, 1998:16) 56% of the population are of the opinion that there is no need to pay taxes if you do not want to do so. If caught, 27% think the problem could be solved by paying bribes. The reason for such opinions is not simply low morals of the Russians. Such opinions reflect the arbitrary and contradictory tax legislation as well as the totally unrealistic and punitive tax penalty regime. Furthermore, taxation did not play a significant role in the Soviet system where the state allocated resources without being dependent on tax revenues. Paying taxes is simply a new duty.

the Joint Stock Company Law also allows the initiative of one shareholder. Tikhomirov (Kommentarii..., 1998) supports a narrow interpretation of the Law on Limited Liability Companies according to its wording. This issue is not clear.

The Law on Limited Liability Companies lists the issues, deciding which belongs to the exclusive power of the meeting of the members. These issues are:

- general direction over the activity of the company,
- changes to the charter including changes in the amount of the charter capital as well as the founding agreement,
- formation of the executive bodies and audit commission,
- approval of annual reports and bookkeeping balance sheets and the distribution of the profits,
- the decision on the reorganization and liquidation of the company, as well as
- other decisions provided by the law (32§).

The issues, which are placed within the exclusive authority, cannot be delegated to the executive body according to the Civil Code (91§). However, the decisions on the formation of the executive bodies as well as large-scale transactions, interested party transactions and organization of general meetings may be delegated by the charter to the board of directors according to §32 of the Law on Limited Liability Companies.[136]

Participation of a member in voting at the general meeting requires his registration. The general meeting is not allowed to adopt decisions on issues, which were not included in the agenda unless all members of the company are present. Most decisions should be adopted by the majority of votes of all company members. Amendments to the charter and some other issues,

---

[136] This is one of the disputed contradictions between the Civil Code and the Law on Limited Liability Companies. The same contradiction also exists between the Civil Code and the Joint Stock Company Law. Golubov (1998), however, explains that the Civil Code only prohibits delegating issues, which are placed within the authority of the shareholders' meeting to executive organs. The board of directors is, however, not an executive organ but a governing organ like the shareholders' meeting. On the other hand, Golubov does not mention that the board of directors also has executive tasks, even if it is called a governing (supervisory) body in the Joint Stock Company Law.

however, require a two-third majority of the members' votes. Decisions on amendments to the founding agreement as well as the reorganization and liquidation of the company have to be made unanimously. Other decisions except the approval of annual reports and the balance sheet can be adopted through external voting (38§).

In practice in small limited liability companies with a few members, the general meeting decides on even routine business, which usually belongs to the executive body (Kommentarii..., 1998). Members often accept a charter (articles), which determines too many issues to the authority of the general meeting. Then handling day-to-day business may suffer. The idea of the general meeting is that it would decide on matters, which affect the mutual benefit of all members (Kommentarii..., 1998).

The authority and decision-making of the executive bodies of the company is defined in the law, but it may be detailed in the charter as well as in a contract between the company and an external manager. Members of the board or the general director can be people other than members of the company, but they have to be natural persons. The general meeting chooses the board if the charter requires a board to be formed. A member of the company can appeal to a court, if he thinks that his rights or legal interests were violated by a decision of an executive body (§§40–43).

Exceptional for a limited liability company is that the so-called large-scale transactions can be delegated to the general director. This can be stipulated in the charter. In the absence of such a stipulation, it is the general meeting of the members that decides upon large-scale transactions. The charter may define such decisions also to the board of directors (46§). A limited liability company can be made much more manager-centered than a joint stock company.

A member of a limited liability company, who has not partici-pated in the general meeting or who has resisted the decision, has the right to bring an action before a court. He then has to consider the decision to be illegal or against the regulations of the charter. A shareholder of a joint stock company has a similar right. The time limit is two months. The court can hold such a decision as void, provided that it is illegal or against the rules of the charter and infringes upon the rights of the member or shareholder as well. In practice, the courts require that the infringement should be significant (Lehtinen, 1998).

The Law on Enterprises of 1990 defined a limited liability company and a closed joint stock company as the same type of company. Until the Law on Joint Stock Companies entered into force most companies with foreign ownership were limited liability companies. Closed joint stock companies began to be used after the joint stock company law regulated closed joint stock companies. A closed joint stock company has, however, after the Limited Liability Company Law came into force, become less popular because the joint stock company law includes a lot of general rules, which concern all joint stock companies. For a small company these rules are too clumsy. Limited liability company law allows the administration of the company to be arranged quite flexibly. It also allows completely closed companies, where no outsiders have to be accepted.

Limited liability companies are new companies having no long inheritance of socialist corporate culture, as do the privatized joint stock companies. Flexibility is important for small companies, but there may be difficulties in using flexible rules, since corporate governance of a market economy type is new and there is no experience with it. The Law on Limited Liability Companies also allows a management-centered administration, which encourages continuous use of old, socialist management traditions. Russian businessmen are only in the initial phase of the learning process, which in western market economies has lasted for centuries (cf., Tolonen, 1974).

We share the opinion of the so-called Austrian economics according to which small business is where Russian entrepreneurship can be found (e.g., Kregel *et al.*, 1992). It is entrepreneurship that can change Russia into a market economy not monopolistic privatized enterprises. Small entrepreneurs are, however, not such a lobby group as the managers of big companies. Entrepreneurship is not supported enough. Thus, attitudes are not favorable towards entrepreneurship. With profits small businesses have the same problem as big corporations. They cannot show profits so as to keep both tax authorities and criminal organizations at a distance. Also small business has tricks to make informal profits.

4.4.3 Liability of Managers, Shareholders and Members for Losses

4.4.3.1 *Liability of Shareholders and Members for Losses*

Neither the Law on Limited Liability Companies nor the Law on Joint Stock Companies contains a general rule on a member's or a shareholder's liability for losses. The rule of the Civil Code (53§) on liability for damages touches only on the liability of the representative of the company. It does not apply to a member or shareholder provided that he does not represent the company in legal actions. The Civil Code does not require willful action for the basis of liability. Negligence is enough to constitute liability. So, if a member or a shareholder represents the company and causes damage to the company, he is liable to pay damages if the other shareholders so demand.

Compared to regulations of company law in other countries, it is exceptional that Russian law does not regulate the liability of a shareholder or a member. For example, the German Limited Liability Companies Act contains a rule on the liability of a member towards the company. A member is liable to pay damages, if he has caused the damage with willful action or gross negligence (GmbHG 9a§). Usually other members are not allowed to receive damages in such cases. The Finnish Joint Stock Companies Act (OYL 15:3) also extends the liability of a shareholder towards other shareholders. The liability includes damages to the company, shareholders or third persons (Koski and af Schulten, 2000:353).

In the absence of a rule in law, liability for damage that a shareholder has caused to the company is regulated only in the charter (articles). The Civil Code is completely silent on, for example, the liability for not paying the share to the company capital. The code delegates the issue to the founding agreement of the company (89§). Likewise, the Law on Limited Liability Companies delegates regulating damages caused by not paying the share to the founding documents of the company to the company charter, which may include a regulation on such liability (12§).

The company charter of a limited liability company can extend the duties of a member considerably. He may have a duty to represent the company or participate in the administration. In such cases, his liability naturally falls under the 44§ of the Law on Limited Liability Companies concerning a manager's liability.

4.4.3.2 Managers' Liability for Losses

The §53.3 of the Civil Code contains a general rule on liability for losses. It stipulates that the members of the governing bodies of companies must act in good faith and reasonably. If they cause damage to the company, they are liable to pay damages, if not otherwise regulated in legislation or contracts. According to this general rule their liability is for negligence.

The Law on Limited Liability Companies contains a corresponding rule in §44. The general director, members of the board of directors and members of executive bodies have a personal liability. There is a narrow interpretation, according to which the list is complete and does not extend to, for example, a founder, auditor or a member of the audit commission. Both the regulations of the Civil Code and the one of the Law on Joint Stock Companies (71.2§) are interpreted in a similarly narrow way.

Good faith and reasonable behavior is defined to mean that the manager of a company must take care of the business as carefully as if it were his own and take the necessary precautions like an ordinary person in his position would take (Kommentarii..., 1998). The same rule stipulates further that in determining the grounds and extension of the liability, ordinary business practices and other relevant considerations must be taken into account. The Law on Joint Stock Companies regulates liability in a similar way. Ordinary business practice means that a manager shall look after the benefit of the company. He also has to make decisions carefully and with good business practice. These interpretations are quite similar to those of western company law. It is difficult to say whether there are differences in court practice. The benefit of the company as well as good business practice can be understood differently in Russia. Taking care of employment even at the cost of shareholders' rights to profit would probably be understood as good practice. The shareholders are not regarded as the core of the company, because previously the same company was explained as belonging to the workers, who possessed it as state property.

Both the Law on Limited Liability Companies (§44) and the Law on Joint Stock Companies (71§) require that a manager can be held responsible for damage, when he has caused it. The loss must be his fault and there has to be a causal relationship between the damage and the activity, which the director is at fault. The rule of the Joint Stock Company Law has been the model for the law of limited liability, while the model for the regulation of the Joint Stock Company Law has been the German regulations of directors' liability in joint stock companies (AktG 93§ and 116§, Ivanov, 1998).

The regulation on directors' liability has not been simple to apply. The general rule of the Civil Code requires responsibility for losses, which are caused by negligence. The law on joint stock companies, however, seems to assume intentional fault. The regulation of the Limited Liability Companies act is interpreted in the same way. At least in legal studies it has been suggested that a director is liable for damage, which he has caused intentionally, for instance, omission of his obligation to arrange reliable book-keeping (Glushetskii, 1996). The regulation is thus interpreted differently than in Germany, where liability to pay damages may already emerge through negligence (GmbHG 43§, Lutter *et al.*, 1987; Kraft and Kreutz, 2000). It has been suggested that the wording of the Joint Stock Company Law is unclear. The law mentions losses, which are caused by activities of a director who is at fault. It has been suggested that such wording, which emphasizes the fault, should be interpreted to concern situations, where managers have violated their obligations regulated in the law or the charter (Ivanov, 1998).

There is no limit for damages. The law assumes the principle of full compensation regulated in the Civil Code. According to §15 of the Civil Code both the physical damage and the loss (lost benefit) have to be compensated. In practice, the amount of the damages can be quite high (Sukhanov, 1998:42). On the other hand, the circle of those, who are entitled to receive damages, is narrow. Only the company can receive damages, not other shareholders, members or outsiders. For instance, according to Finnish company law (OYL 15:1-3) shareholders or creditors can also receive damages.

If there are several directors liable for the losses, then there is joint liability. The company can claim damages from any one of those, who are jointly liable or from all of them. A manager who has paid more than his share of the damages, however, has the right of recourse from the others, who are jointly liable (CC 325§). However, those persons, who did not take part in the administration or voted against it shall not bear liability (72.2§ ZAO). The right to bring the action for damages is held by the company or its members in a limited liability company (44§). In a joint stock company shareholders also have the right to bring the action for damages, but only provided that he or they own more than 1% of the shares of the company (71.5§). Since good faith and reasonable behavior is presumed in the Civil Code, it has been interpreted that it is the plaintiff, who has to prove that the manager deliberately caused the loss (Margolin, 1995:32).[137]

4.4.4 Personal Liability for Debts of the Company— Lifting the Corporate Veil

The main principle in companies is that a shareholder is not liable for the debts of the company, except with the value of his shares, and a member is liable only to the amount of his share in the capital. This is a principle separating companies from partnerships, where liability is unlimited. In limited liability companies this principle is not absolute, since there may be rules for additional responsibility.

A shareholder's or member's liability for debts is possible in some situations. If a member has not paid his share, the founders of the company are jointly liable to the amount of the unpaid share.[138] A member, who has invested property given as subscription in kind, may be held liable, if the subscription in kind has been evaluated

---

[137] According to general principles of western procedural law the burden of proof can be reversed only with a special stipulation in the law. In the absence of such a stipulation, the plaintiff is obliged to prove that the manager caused the loss deliberately. Margolin's way to argue his point indicates that the rules for using reversed burden of proof are not as clear in Russia as they should be in a rule of law country.

[138] There is already a decision of the Supreme Arbitration Court, in which the court held the members of a limited liability company jointly liable for 6 million rubles, which one of the members had not paid for his share (No. 5411/98).

too highly. Such liability is, however, limited to the real value of the subscription in kind. The joint liability of the too highly evaluated subscription in kind is limited to the next three years after registration of the company. Also an auditor or an outside expert can be held liable for his over-valuation. Their liability is also limited to three years. Such liability for overvaluation is also only subsidiary. The creditors have to collect a claim first towards the company. Furthermore, a member or a shareholder in a dominant position may be held personally liable for all the debts of the bankrupted company.

Both the Law on Limited Liability Companies (3.3§) and the Law on Joint Stock Companies (3.3§) include a regulation according to which a member, a shareholder or another person, who has a right to give binding orders or who has the possibility to direct its activities in some other ways, be held personally liable for its debts subsidiarily, if the bankruptcy of the company is due to his activities. This rule is a clear exception from the principle of limited liability. A member or a shareholder can be held personally liable to creditors of the company for the debts of the company. The liability of the member in a dominant position is identified to the liability of the company.[139]

A shareholder or a member owning 50% of the company has a dominant position. There has to be a direct causal relationship between indebtedness and the activity of the dominating owner (Komm./ZAO, 1996:35). The Law on Limited Liability Companies is silent about how the causal relationship can be detected, but the Law on Joint Stock Companies has a rule in 7.3§, which according to legal scholars can also be applied to limited liability companies. A causal relationship exists, when a person has used his dominating position in such a way that there has been a decision in the company, which caused the bankruptcy. It is also required that the person in a dominating position has acted knowing that his actions would cause bankruptcy (Komm./ZAO, 1996:35).

When a court sets a subsidiary liability on the debts of the company for a member or shareholder, it also has to determine the

---

[139] In common law countries the doctrine for making people behind the company liable is called *lifting the corporate veil* or *piercing the corporate veil*.

amount of the personal liability (Komm./ZAO, 1996:45). Since personal liability is subsidiary, the debtor has to try to collect the amount first from the company (399§ CC). The creditor can collect only the amount, which the company has not been able to pay. According to the Law on Bankruptcy (2§) the creditor can turn to the shareholder and demand payment after three months from the maturity of the debt.

The Russian regulation on piercing the corporate veil and making the dominating person of the company liable most corresponds to the French rule in the Bankruptcy Act. The corporate veil can be lifted if the creditors can prove that the dominating member actually caused indebtedness with his negligence. In England, the *Salomon v. A. Salomon Co. Ltd.* case from 1897 still constitutes the principle of separating the company from the owner. The decision admitted the right to separate the company from personal property even in small companies with practically only one active owner. In the Insolvency Act of 1986 it has been regulated that if it is found that the company intended to defraud the debtors or the company was used in an otherwise fraudulent way, then such a member can be held liable to add an amount, which the court finds fair. It is also required that the member has actually participated in a decision with a fraudulent aim. English courts have sometimes exceptionally held members liable for the debts of the company, reasoning the decisions with fraudulent trading (Davies and Prentice, 1997).

German courts have also held that the liability of a member of a GmbH company for the debts of the company can in some cases be personal and unlimited. However, a rule does not exist in the GmbHG about the principles of personal liability instead of the company. There is, however, an indirect rule of 32a§ in the GmbHG concerning indirect identification. If the company has not had enough capital and a member has granted a credit to the company when a bank would not have granted it the member may be held liable to the debts of the company (Hueck, 1991:368). Piercing the corporate veil is thus connected with an extraordinary situation, when the principle of limited liability is violated. A member can be held liable, when he mixes his own property with the property of the company, or misuses the form of the company (Lutter, 1998; Hueck, 1991).

The EU has issued a directive to give an entrepreneur an opportunity to do business in a one-man company within limited liability in all member countries (89/667 12th company law directive). The directive does not, however, prevent the member countries to regulate that in some extraordinary situations the corporate veil could be lifted and the person behind the company could be held liable (Werlauff, 1993). In most European countries, the rules allowing the corporate veil to be lifted have not been included in company law legislation but have developed in practice and are thus used quite exceptionally.[140]

Since the protection of creditors is much less effective in Russian than in English or German company law, it may be grounded to hold a member liable for the debts of the company in some situations in connection with bankruptcies. It will be seen in the future whether Russian courts are going to follow the inter-national rule on a wider liability in some extraordinary situations. At least written law clearly allows it.

In a virtual economy, bankruptcies are not for anyone's imme-diate need. Even unprofitable companies are kept going, because the creditor would not win anything in his positions where he is tied to a network, where everybody is indebted (Gaddy and Ickes, 1998). There are, however, more and more bankruptcies occurring in Russia. In the Russian extraordinary situation, it is obvious that bankruptcies are going to occur in the long term. For the time being it is small new companies that are more likely to become bankrupt than the big privatized ones, which function within a network of a virtual economy. In practice, this means that it is not the most unhealthy companies that become bankrupt, but those who do not find their place in a virtual economy. According to Bim (1995) the policy of managers refusing to restructure and operating partly in the black market is going to drive companies to bankruptcy, which in the long run can turn out to be good for the Russian economy. He assumes that bad management will abolish

---

[140] In Finland, there have recently been strong tendencies in the enforcement legislation and in the practice of bailiffs to try to lift the corporate veil especially for off-shore companies. This development has, however, not affected company law.

non-profitable companies from the market. For the managers themselves it may also be an opportunity to get rid of the unprofitable privatized company, when they already have been able to secure their future in a profitable new company, which has been created beside the unprofitable privatized company.

Even if the rules for personal liability of the managers exists, typical bad management of a virtual economy, would obviously not be considered as a deliberate action causing losses for the company. The courts might accept explanations, according to which the intention was to prevent unemployment or to take care of some other social duty. The widely spread habit to produce for the black market and share the profits among a small circle of insiders, is clearly criminal and causes losses both for the company and the tax collector. Such illegal activity seems to be regarded as a phenomenon connected with transition and is therefore tolerated as long as it remains hidden. The development of market structures and business culture should gradually correct the situation. Even so, the flourishing black market business is, however, also an institutional problem connected with widespread corruption, which is dangerous for the Russian economy and the development of society. Such circumstances keep the level of trust in business and politics low and hinder sustainable economic development.

4.5 Social Responsibilities of Russian Companies and the Stakeholder Theory

Making profit for the shareholders is clearly the main principle of a company in the company law of most market economy countries. This principle is often also explicitly declared in the legislation. This principle can be understood to stem from the point of view of protecting the shareholders' interests towards the managers' personal interests. Making profit is also understood as the special feature distinguishing commercial organizations from other economic organizations. It has, however, often been argued that multinational companies and other foreign developers have a responsibility to improve the material conditions of the people in whose territory they operate. As a matter of distributive justice it is thought that these companies should be sharing the acquired wealth with these people through the creation of 'collective goods', infrastructure development and compensation disbursements aimed at their benefit. This point of view has been called a 'stakeholder theory', the main idea of which is that the company should share the profits with affected 'non-shareholder' groups.

There have been tendencies in the developed world, especially in the United States towards such legislative development, which aims at sharing profits with the community (Lea, 1999). There are also codes of conduct for the multinationals.[141] Many multinationals, however, do not act according to the stakeholder theory. It seems that without enforceable legal rules, multinationals who are often in a position where they could make an affect on developing local business culture, still only tend to increase corruption in corrupted countries. A good example is Shell, which takes care of its public relations in developed countries, but actually finances Nigerian military dictatorship and politics oppressing the local population.[142] However, many see the development towards legislation supporting stakeholders' rights in the US as possible advancements for indigenous peoples and aboriginal groups. On the other hand, it can be shown that such duties result in the generation of excessive costs. Furthermore, such tendencies seem to lead to unrealistic expectations from the part of the stakeholders (Lea, 1999).

While the Western world discusses stakeholder theory, the post-communist world tries to transform companies to make a profit. Profiting companies could pay more taxes, which could be used for the benefit of the community. Soviet enterprises had a lot of social duties and they actually worked in a network of stakeholders. Especially after World War II the social duties of enterprises

---

[141] The most well-known codes of conduct are the OECD guidelines for multinational enterprises (OECD, 1986).

[142] There have been a lot of newspaper articles about Shell's poor human rights and environmental record in Nigeria, e.g., Adams (1995). The multinationals' support to Suharto's government violating human rights in Indonesia is also a well known story, e.g., Robinson and Thoenes (1998). British Petroleum has even been condemned by the European Parliament for funding death squads in Columbia. The ITT instigated the CIA's involvement in the removal of Alliende and his replacement by General Pinochet in Chile.

increased. They had to finance kindergartens, schools, housing, transport, medical care, and give their products (electricity and oil) freely to the local population. It was only a question of organizing the duties of the state, since enterprises were state bodies. They did not pay ordinary taxes but operated with different funds. There was often a town built around a big enterprise, which did not function simply as the only employer of the inhabitants, but also provided houses for the employees, maintained them and arranged all kinds of social services, including sports or other entertainment clubs for the local people. Drinking water supply or heating stations were often planned and constructed together with the large enterprises and on their costs, benefiting not only the company but also the surrounding community. Profit, on the other hand, was not important since enterprises had to fulfill production plans. Financial profit was not required (Commander and Jackman, 1995).

It is this tradition, which still gives an enterprise the opportunity to pay its taxes with its own products. A building company can build a school or a metro station, if it does not have cash. A virtual economy functions with barter and cash reserves are rare. Formal profits are not insignificant as in socialism; they are even a nuisance and avoided if possible.

Privatization of enterprises has changed the attitude towards social duties. Most of the social services were to be transferred to municipalities and private companies were to start functioning according to the rules of a market economy (Commander and Jackman, 1995). The presidential decree of 10 January 1993 prohibited privatizing social and cultural property together with the enterprises. According to the privatization program all these social and cultural "objects" and responsibilities had to be transferred to municipal authorities within six months from the confirmation of the privatization plan. Large enterprises are in a difficult situation where they, in principle, should start to restructure and make profit for the shareholders. It is a good reason to get rid of extra social costs. On the other hand, companies avoid taxpaying as much as possible. However, avoiding taxes is more acceptable in Russia than cutting down social benefits and causing unemployment to make the company profitable (see footnote 135, cf., Rose's opinion survey). Companies are at a crossroads, where they cannot completely abandon the old "taxpaying system" with the social benefits of socialism, but where they cannot start to show profit and pay ordinary taxes either.

Many social responsibilities of the enterprises were duties, which were based on legislation. Housing, for example, is still a duty of the enterprises, which have apartments on their accounts according to the Federal Housing Code. Because municipalities have not been able to take these duties on their own cost, companies have been forced to continue providing them. Often enterprises have founded joint companies with municipalities to take care of social responsibilities. The level of social services is negatively affected, since municipalities have not had the financial resources to take care of the infrastructure costs. Additional social duties are one factor, which makes transition to a market economy complicated and hinders restructuring. Enterprises, which try to get rid of their earlier social responsibilities, have ethical hindrances for restructuring that would make most of the population of the surrounding town unemployed and leave them without social benefits. Employees also prefer to keep their jobs, even if they are badly paid, because losing the job would lead to losing all of the other social benefits as well. Usually companies can still offer better social benefits for both their employees and their families than the municipality.

The relationship to employees is different in Russia and still carries on socialist inheritance. Both managers and workers are authoritarian. The latter expect the managers to take care of them. Earlier they received a lot of social benefits, health care and perhaps even holidays in the southern parts of the Soviet Union. Nowadays workers put their trust on the managers to maintain their jobs. Such attitudes can postpone restructuring, which in the end, however, is unavoidable.

Russian managers also differ from their Western counterparts. First of all, authoritarian management was a rule and authoritarian managers were respected among the workers. A manager delegating powers was regarded as a weak manager. Most directors are engineers, because production was important, while marketing did not play any role whatsoever. Therefore, knowledge about the economy is low among Russian managers, or actually economic skills, in the western meaning, are at a low level. Russian managers, however, do well in a virtual economy, where social skills connected with the network within which the enterprise works are of significant value. Those attempting to change the rules would definitely suffer. The loss of control during the *perestroika* period gave directors more power, which they used for "self-seeking with guile" as Williamson (1985) puts it. Self-made entrepreneurs are treated as "dishonest businessmen" in these established circles. With their monopoly position, big privatized enterprises can affect on small businesses, too. They can support those who agree to play along with their rules and who have good personal connections with them.

In the Soviet Union, environmental protection was badly arranged. Even if companies had to take care of the community, environmental questions were not paid any attention. There was the attitude that natural resources are abundant in Russia. Nowadays, the voices for environmental protection have grown. Citizens can openly discuss the health and environmental disasters caused by pollution. Still, when jobs are weighted against restructuring and environmentally better technology, jobs weigh more. The media, however, has had an important role in making environmental catastrophes public and affecting public opinion. There are also many international environmental movements such as Greenpeace operating in Russia nowadays. Their active role has sometimes had negative effects on public opinion. Super-power mentality does not accept foreigners to come and advise and show the obvious disadvantages of Russian society. On the other hand, this mentality easily buys the idea that foreigners have to finance environmental programs, which actually benefits them thereby reducing the environmental danger towards them.

Environmental protection is not well arranged in Russia from the enterprises' point of view. There are several authorities with their own requirements. The distribution of powers among governmental bodies is obscure.[143] It seems that the anxiety of the citizens has made the government increase control and found even more new bodies for environmental protection. Coordination between them

---

[143] There are examples of how complicated and contradictory rules affect companies in the forest sector in Maria Kotova's forthcoming paper (Kotova, 2001).

has, however, been forgotten. Environmental control also belongs to joint powers of the federation and its subjects, which causes additional problems. Regulations on different levels may differ considerably from each other.

There is a lot of bureaucratic environmental control, but it is not effective. Russian enterprises do not take environmental control seriously. Even foreign companies, which at home are required to take environmental protection into consideration, misuse Russian corrupt and ineffective environmental control. Examples are Finnish forest companies, which have harvested protected primeval forests in Karelia (see Piipponen, 1999). The case was made public by international environmental organizations. Globalization has reached Russia in both good and bad respects.

4.6 Summary

The role of the company is changing in Russia from an administrative unit of state administration to a profit-making unit of a market economy. The administrative unit and its governance by fiat correspond easily to the legal positivist idea of system of norms and endogenic technical definition of concepts. According to such thinking, changing technical rules will change the functioning of companies. However, companies and their corporate governance do not change only by changing formal rules. Experience from Russian companies in transition proves the weakness of legal positivism and the strength of legal realism. Corporate governance can be quite different in practice in different countries, even if the technical legal rules are almost similar.

Western company law is a product of a long-term learning process without significant interruptions. There have been misuses, which have affected on improving the formal regulation. There is a tendency from protecting shareholders and seeing them in the core of the company to a wider interpretation. Both stakeholder theory and a firm as a nexus of contracts saving transaction costs represent such a widening of the perspective. Shareholders have to give room to other stakeholders in the core of the company. A firm is regarded as a going concern, the aims of which should be understood in the context.

The Russian business environment differs from that of western market economies and therefore a firm is understood differently. Earlier there was a wider "stakeholder" approach, which regarded an enterprise as the unit responsible for the well being of the workers and the community at large. There is such a thing as Russian managerialism, which sees managers in the core of the company. Managers of former state enterprises privatized the enterprises for themselves in cooperation with employees. Since managers together with employees control the majority of the shares in most privatized companies, ownership and control are not divided in Russia. It reflects on a weak protection of minority shareholders and creditors. Directors managed to lobby company laws while they were drafted and further weakened the rights of minorities making the use of their rights technically complicated. Flexible rules that are now demanded even more in Western countries would not work in the Russian environment without an effective control system of the managers. Extremely formal rules can also be misused as barriers protecting managers' benefits. Russian managers have a long tradition for such a policy. They seem to treat other shareholders in a similar way as they manipulated workers' collectives before. Agency theory explains the behavior of Russian managers, who do not have to negotiate with their shareholders, yet. No one monitors the monitors, because there are no markets to control them.

Russian firms function in a virtual economy where networks and good connections matter and exchange is, to a great extent, barter. Bizarre taxation rules make profits costly and also encourage making informal profits as well as transferring capital abroad. It seems that company law has very little to do with actual corporate governance. With company law the legislator can transplant the formal system of norms into Russian society. Courts, of course, have a new role to control and help to plant new business culture. Their role should, however, not be exaggerated. A lot depends on the managers, who are in the core of Russian corporate governance. They have the power to start to restructure, which would be in the shareholders' long-term interests. Many shareholders, however, are also employees who do not wish to lose their jobs. Also a high burden of social responsibilities, which the companies have difficulties to get rid of, hinders restructuring.

Even if western economic theory does not fit into Russian concepts, it can still give new approaches to Russian company law. The logic of economic organization is different in Russia. Profits are costly and transaction costs are saved often with illegal methods. Restructuring has been postponed due to "an agreement" between managers and their workers. The latter helped the former to keep the enterprises in their control in order to maintain their jobs. Managers owe a lot to the workers and are therefore still reluctant to increase unemployment. The agreement of keeping things running as much in the old way as possible maintains a virtual economy. It cannot, however, last forever. Old style management will bankrupt the enterprises sooner or later. Managers still have an opportunity to survive, if they have managed to channel most of the profitable production to new companies. Old companies are actually more profitable than is shown. Since formal profits are costly, production is channeled to the informal sector. Before becoming bankrupt managers can "suck the company dry". Officially they do not cheat the workers in this way but maintain their jobs as long as possible. Company law has rules for sanctioning losses, which are deliberately caused to the company. Running the company into bankruptcy can also be sanctioned. It is, however, obvious that such rules can only be exceptionally used. Producing profits informally and double bookkeeping fulfills the definition of deliberately running a company to bankruptcy. It is, however, too common in Russia. In principle, exceptional personal liability of managers for losses has an exceptionally fertile soil in Russia.

Virtual economy networks diminish uncertainty with experienced methods. Asset specificity is involved in a simple way—scratch my back and I will scratch yours. Managers' self-seeking has no control.

Russian company law is a transplant, which does not meet with the current aims of companies functioning within a virtual economy. The forms of companies resemble German counterparts but also contain remnants from the socialist past. Transplanted company law introduced new models for governance structures, but old administrative methods prevailed on the side. Modern corporate law is structured for market control and rests on the assumption that ownership and control are divided and that shareholders have become moving investors. In Russia, shareholders are not the core of a company. The core is the majority of the shareholder managers, who are able to control the company effectively. The market does not govern them, because the framework of a virtual economy does not force restructuring or even make a profit. Shareholders are not investors. Insider shareholders only want to secure their position.

Because of insider privatization Russian companies are more closed than the law would allow. Information is given reluctantly, since companies do not compete for shareholders and good investors. However, there is a learning process going on. Some managers may understand the need for restructuring. The change is vested in small enterprises. The Russian economy is, however, dominated by big privatized enterprises. The state should encourage entrepreneurship, but the managers of big privatized enterprises are a significant lobby group, which can keep the economic policy favorable for them. The unholy alliance of government circles and the *oligarchs* keeps supporting unhealthy monopolistic enterprises.

Privatized former state enterprises have not emerged through contractual relations with private owners as economic theories explain firms, but have been created by state authority and now continue their life in a new private property form because of the will of the state. They are some kind of hybrids between administrative units of state bureaucracy and capitalist firms. On the other hand, there are also "new" small and medium-sized enterprises that have been started during the last ten years, which have been private from the beginning.

On the one hand, the development has been path-dependent but on the other, it has produced unwanted results. Modern company law is not perfect for a virtual economy, where it can be misused, neglected and ignored. The development also proves that the rationality of the legislator is bounded. No one can possess the required information and knowledge about the changing environment of Russian business. Russian company law regulation is not created to answer the immediate needs of current business, but for the future. In this way the legislator attempts to speed up the learning process towards a market economy. However, there always lies a danger in this kind of teaching businessmen. In the worst scenario, law loses its authority completely.

4.7 Further Discussion

Even if company law of modern market economies does not completely fit into the Russian environment it is, however, the only possible way to continue developing company law. For foreign investors it is easier when the regulations of company law are international.

There are some weaknesses in Russian company law, which should not be difficult to correct. For example, the requirements on companies to publish information should be tightened to ensure transparency. The equality of shareholders should be protected more efficiently by abolishing excessive formalities, which enable managers to make shareholders silent. The liquidation of a company without informing creditors should be made impossible. The provisions of the Civil Code should be made consistent with the later drafted Joint Stock Company Law and the Law on Limited Liability Companies.

An audit commission or an auditor should also be made obligatory in smaller limited liability companies. This would not make management more complicated but would protect creditors' interests. Management of close limited liability companies should not be made too flexible because it may encourage fraudulent business.

The development, which in European countries seems to go towards more flexible company law rules, does not fit into the Russian environment that has no effective control of managers. Flexible rules, which give managers more power, would only be used to keep minority shareholders silent in the absence of effective market control, which enables flexibility in more developed countries. On the other hand, there are formal rules that enable managers to silence minority shareholders, which should therefore be abolished. The control of managers is important in the Russian business environment.

Corporate governance should be studied and should be able to find its place as the most important issue of company law. Such development requires a change in legal thinking. Company law developed out of the law of obligations and used to be part of the doctrine of juristic persons also in Germany in the 19th century. The development towards separate company law occurred with the development of a market economy. The old fashioned legal positivism and conceptualist standpoint hinders the development of Russian law to reach the needs of a modern market economy. The most effective way in the long term is to educate legal scholars and university teachers.

Since it is the managers who are at the core of developing corporate culture, they should also be educated. This may be a difficult and complicated task because on the one hand Russian managers have to adapt to the environment of a virtual economy. On the other hand, Russian managers should start to think in terms of a market economy. Only investing in restructuring can save Russian companies in the long term. Responsible managers have realized this fact even if they have to work daily with problems, which are due to a virtual economy.

The problems with the management of companies are tightly connected with the attitudes of the managers. They should be able to understand that the shareholders have their rights, which cannot be neglected. Transparency is also in the long term the best policy for any company. Russian enterprises need strategic investments and not typical western portfolio investments. However, western investors, who are ready for strategic investments, might have experience in running companies and ideas for developing a Russian company to an internationally competitive level. Even if Russia is, in itself, a huge market area, globalization is a fact that even Russian companies cannot escape. On the other hand, it is understandable and acceptable that Russia wants to protect its own industry against competition during the transition period. There should, however, be better means available than hiding and distorting information either with the help of company law rules or circumventing them.

Even if corporate culture is not developed in the courts, they are important as a final resort in solving disputes. Judges, therefore, also need training and education. Even if there are specialized commercial courts (arbitration courts) in Russia, the general level of knowledge of the changing business environment is not one of the strongest among Russian judges. The attitude that lawyers teach businessmen should be exterminated completely. Lawyers and businessmen should be able to work together and understand the interests and objectives of one another.

References

Books and Articles

Adams, Paul (1995). Protests as Nigeria Condemns Minority Leader to Death. Financial Times, 1 November.

Alchian, Armen and Harold Demsetz (1972). Production, Information Costs and Economic Organization. *American Economic Review*, 62, pp. 777–795.

Alekseev, S.S. (1999). *Pravo. Azbuka, Teoriya, Filosofiya. Opyt kompleksnogo issledovaniya (Law, the Elements, Theory, Philosophy. Experience of Comprehensive Research)*. Statut, Moscow (in Russian).

Berle, Adolf and Gardiner C. Means (1967). *The Modern Corporation and the Private Property*. Revised version. First Edition 1932.

Bim, Alexander S. (1995). Ownership and Control of Russian Enterprises and Strategies of Shareholders. *Communist Economies and Economic Transition*, Vol. 8, No. 4, pp. 471–500.

Braginskii, M.I. (1998). Grazhdanskii kodeks. Chast pervaya. Tri goda spustya (kommentarii s uchetom prinyatykh izmenenii Grazhdanskogo kodeksa i novykh zakonodatelnykh aktov) (The Civil Code. Part 1. Three years from entering into force (Commentary regarding the changes of the code as well as new legislation)). *Khozyaistvo i pravo*, No. 1, pp. 3–20 (in Russian).

Bratton, William W. (1989). The "Nexus of Contracts" Corporation: A Critical Appraisal. *Cornell Law Review*, Vol. 74, pp. 407–465.

Brom, Karla (1998). Post-privatization Corporate Governance. In: *A Regional Approach to Industrial Restructuring in the Tomsk Region, Russian Federation*. OECD Proceedings, Paris, pp. 243–251.

Butler, William E. and Maryann Gashi-Butler (2000). *Russian Company Law. Basic Legislation*, Third Edition, Kluwer Law International, The Hague.

Carlsson, Lars, Nils-Gustav Lundgren and Mats-Olov Olsson (1999). Forest Enterprises in Transition—Business Behavior in the Tomsk Forest Sector. Interim Report IR-99-010. International Institute for Applied Systems Analysis, Laxenburg, Austria.

Carlsson, Lars, Nils-Gustav Lundgren and Mats-Olov Olsson (2000). Why is the Russian Bear Still Asleep After Ten Years of Transition? Interim Report IR-00-019. International Institute for Applied Systems Analysis, Laxenburg, Austria.

Clarke, Simon and Veronika Kabalina (1995). Privatization and the Struggle for Control of the Enterprise. In: Daniel Lane (ed.) *Russia in Transition*, Longman.

Coase, R.H. (1937). The Nature of the Firm. *Economica*, 4, November. Reprinted in R.H. Coase (1988). *The Firm, the Market, and the Law*. The University of Chicago Press, Chicago and London.

Commander, S. and R. Jackman (1995). Providing Social Benefits in Russia: Redefining the Roles of Firms and Government. Policy Research

Working Paper 1184, Economic Development Institute, The World Bank, Washington, DC.

Davies, Paul L. and D.D. Prentice (1997). *Gower's Principles of Modern Company Law*. Sixth Edition, London.

Dignam, Alan and Michael Galanis (1999). Governing the World: The Development of OECD's Corporate Governance Principles. *European Business Law Review*, September/October, pp. 369–406.

Etzioni, Amitai (1988). *The Moral Dimension: Toward a New Economics*. The Free Press, New York.

Fama, Eugene F. (1976). *Foundations of Finance*. Basic, New York.

Gaddy, Clifford G. and Barry W. Ickes (1998). Beyond the Bailout: Time to Face Reality about Russia's Virtual Economy. *Foreign Affairs*, 77, pp. 53–67.

Glushetskii, A. (1996). Organy upravleniya aktsionernogo obshchestva: vozmozhnye varianty (Organs of Administration of a Joint Stock Company: possible alternatives). *Ekonomika i Zhizn*, No. 9, pp. 38–39 (in Russian).

Golubov, G.D. (1998). Sootnosheniyai polozhenii Grazhdanskogo kodeksa i Zakona ob aktsionernykh obshchestvakh (The Relations between the Civil Code and the Law on Joint Stock Companies). In: *Grazhdanskii kodeks Rossii. Problemy. Teoriya. Praktika. Sbornik pamyati S.A. Khokhlova (The Russian Civil Code. Problems. Theory. Practice. A collection dedicated to the memory of S.A. Khokhlov)*. Mezhdunarodnyi tsentr finansovo-ekonomicheskogo razvitiya, Moscow, pp. 167–175 (in Russian).

Granovetter, M. (1985). Economic Action and Social Structure: The Problem of Embeddedness. *American Journal of Sociology*, 91, pp. 481–510.

Hart, H.L.A. (1978). *The Concept of Law*. Oxford University Press, Oxford.

Hendley, Kathryn, Barry W. Ickes, Peter Murrell and Randi Ryterman (1997). Observations of the Use of Law by Russian Enterprises. *Post-Soviet Affairs*, 13, pp. 19–41.

Hueck, Götz (1991). *Gesellschaftsrecht. Juristische Kurz-Lehrbücher (Company Law. Short Textbooks of Jurisprudence)*. 19th Revised Edition of the Works of Alfred Hueck. C.H. Beck, München (in German).

Huemer, Lars (1998). *Trust in Business Relations. Economic Logic or Social Interaction?* Borea förlag, Umeå.

Ivanov, I.L. (1998). Otvetstvennost upravlyayushchikh pered aktsionernym obshchestvom (opyt Rossii i Germanii) (Liability of Management for the Company (Russian and German experience)). *Gosudarstvo i pravo*, No. 11, pp. 94–102 (in Russian).

Jensen, Michael and William Meckling (1976). Theory of the Firm: Managerial Behavior, Agency Costs and Capital Structure. *Journal of Financial Economics*, 3, pp. 305–360.

Jones, Anthony and William Moskoff (1991). *Koops: The Rebirth of Entrepreneurship in the Soviet Union*. Indiana University Press, USA.

Kääriäinen, Kimmo and Dmitri Furman (2000). Religiya i politika v massovom russkom soznanii (Religion and Politics in the Russian Public Knowledge). In: K. Kääriäinen and D. Furman (eds) *Starye cerkvi, novye veruyushchie. Religiya v massovom soznanii postsovetskoj Rossii (Old Churches, New Believers. Religion in the Public Knowledge of Post-soviet Russia)*. Letnii sad, Moscow, pp. 49–78 (in Russian).

Kapkov, Aleksandr (1998). Chem ogranicheny obshchestva s ogranichennoi otvetstvennostyu (What is a limited liability company limited for?). Kommentarii. *Rossiiskaya gazeta*, No. 30 (in Russian).

Kelsen, Hans (1968). Puhdas oikeusoppi (Original title: *Reine Rechtslehre*) (Jurisprudence of Pure Law). Helsinki (in Finnish).

Komm./CC (1996). Kommentarii chasti pervoi grazhdanskogo kodeksa Rossiiskoi Federatsii dlya predprinimatelei (Commentary on the First Part of the Civil Code of the Russian Federation for Entrepreneurs). Collective of authors under M.I. Braginskii and V.D. Karpovich. Moscow. Redaktsiya zhurnala "Khozyaistvo i pravo" (in Russian).

Komm./ZAO (1996). Kommentarii k federalnomu zakonu ob aktsionernykh obshchestvakh (Commentary on the Federal Law on Joint Stock Companies). red. Tikhomirov, Yurinformtsentr, Moscow (in Russian).

Kommentarii… (1998). Kommentarii k federalnomu zakonu ob obshchestvakh s ogranichennoi otvetstvennostyu (Commentary on the Federal Law on Limited Liability Companies). red. Tikhomirov, Moscow (in Russian).

Koski, P. and G. af Schulten (2000). *Osakeyhtiölaki selityksin II, luvut 10–16 Kauppakaari Oyj. Lakimiesliiton kustannus. (Commentary on the Joint Stock Companies Act, Part II)*. Helsinki (in Finnish).

Kotova, Maria (2001). Legal Problems of Forest Enterprises in Russia (preliminary title). Interim Report. International Institute for Applied Systems Analysis, Laxenburg Austria (forthcoming).

Kraft, Alfons and Peter Kreutz (2000). *Gesellschaftsrecht (Company Law)*. Eleventh Revised Edition. Juristische Lernbücher 5, Neuwied, Luchterhand (in German).

Kregel, Jan, Egon Matzner and Gernot Grabher (eds.) (1992). *The Market Shock*. Austrian Academy of Sciences, Vienna.

Krüssmann, Thomas M. (1998). *Privatisierung und Umstrukturierung in Russland. Zur Rolle des Rechts als Instrument Struktureller Wirtschaftsreform im Übergang zur Marktwirtschaft (Privatization and Restructuring in Russia. The Role of Law as an Instrument of Economic Reform in Transition to a Market Economy)*. Berlin Spitz Verlag und Wien Verlag Österreich (in German).

Lea, David (1999). Corporate and Public Responsibility, Stakeholder Theory and the Developing World. *Business Ethics: A European Review,* Vol. 3, No. 3, July.

Lehtinen, Leena (1997). Venäläinen osakeyhtiö. Oikeudellisen perustan kehittyminen suunnitelmataloudesta markkinatalouteen siirtyvässä valtiossa yritysmuotojen ja erityisesti osakeyhtiön oikeudellisen aseman kannalta tarkasteltuna (Russian Joint Stock Company). Lakimiesliiton kustannus, Helsinki (in Finnish).

Lehtinen, Leena (1998). Venäjän rajavastuuyhtiöstä (About Russian Limited Liability Companies). *Defensor Legis*, No. 6, pp. 996–1005 (in Finnish).

Lutter, Marcus (1998). Limited Liability Companies and Private Companies. In: *International Encyclopedia of Comparative Law*, under the Auspices of the International Association of Legal Science. Editorial Committee by R. David, Chapter 2, pp. 1–199.

Lutter, Marcus, Peter Hommelhoff and Robert Fischer (Begr.) (1987). *GmbH-Gesetz. Kommentar (The Limited Liability Companies Act. A Commentary)*. 12th Revised Edition by Hommelhoff, Otto Schmidt, Köln (in German).

Margolin, M. (1995). Priobretenie aktsionernym obshchestvom sobstvennykh aktsii (Acquisition of own shares of the joint stock company). *Ekonomika i Zhizn*, 50, pp. 32- (in Russian).

Memorandum... (2000). Memorandum of the Ministry of Justice on Reforming the Joint Stock Companies Act in Finland. Ministry of Justice, Helsinki (in Finnish).

Mozolin, V.P. (1992). Pravo sobstvennosti v Rossiiskoi Federatsii v period perekhoda k rynochnoi ekonomike (Property Law in the Russian Federation during Transition to a Market Economy). Rossiiskaya Akademiya Nauk, Institut gosudarstvo i pravo, Moscow (in Russian).

Nooteboom, Bart (1999). Voice- and Exit-Based Forms of Corporate Control: Anglo-American, European and Japanese. *Journal of Economic Issues*, Vol. XXXIII, No. 4, December, pp. 845–860.

North, Douglass C. (1992). *Institutions, Institutional Change and Economic Performance*. Cambridge University Press, USA.

North, Douglass C. and Robert Paul Thomas (1973). *The Rise of the Western World*. Cambridge University Press, Cambridge.

Nystén-Haarala, Soili (1998). *The Long-term Contract. Contract Law and Contracting*. Finnish Lawyers' Publishing, Helsinki.

OECD (1986). OECD Guidelines for Multinational Enterprises. OECD, Paris.

OECD (1999) OECD Principles for Corporate Governance. Report of the Advisory Group of the OECD. The full text of the principles is available on the Internet: http://www.oecd.org/daf/governance/principles.htm.

Ollila, Timo (1999). Itä-Lapista Venäjälle. Tutkimus Itä-Lapin yritysten liiketoiminnasta Venäjän markkinoilla 1990-luvulla (Research of Business Activities of Enterprises of Eastern Lapland in the Russian Market in the 1990s). Working Paper 29, Publications of Social Sciences Center, University of Lapland (in Finnish).

Orlov, Vladimir (1999). *Entrepreneurship in Russia*. Finnish Lawyers' Publishing, Helsinki.

Piipponen, Minna (1999). Transition in the Forest Sector of the Republic of Karelia. Interim Report IR-99-070. International Institute for Applied Systems Analysis, Laxenburg, Austria. Reprinted in: *Fennia*, 177:2, pp. 185–233.

Pistor, Katharina (1997). Company Law and Corporate Governance in Russia. In: Jeffrey Sachs and Katharina Pistor (eds.), *The Rule of Law and Economic Reform in Russia*. Westview Press.

RFE (1998). The Big Seven—Russia's Financial Empires. Special Report of Radio Free Europe (RFE). In: Transition Newsletter, The World Bank Group. Available on the Internet: http://www.worldbank.org/html/prddr/trans/feb98/bigseven.htm.

Robinson, Gwen and Sander Thoenes (1998). Foreign Companies Need to Make New Friends in Post-Suharto Indonesia: Links to the Former President and His Web of Patronage Once Held the Key to Success But Now They Have Become a Curse. Financial Times, 1 June.

Rose, Richard (1998). Getting Things Done with Social Capital: New Russia Barometer VII. Studies in Public Policy 303, Center for the Study of Public Policy, University of Strathclyde, United Kingdom.

Rose, Richard, William Mishler and Christian Haerpfer (1999). *Democracy and its Alternatives*. Polity Press, Oxford.

Ross, Alf (1966). *Om ret øg retfærdighed (On Law and Justice)*. Copenhagen (in Danish). Available in English (1959) University of California Press, Berkeley.

Simon, Herbert (1961). *Administrative Behavior*. Second Edition. Macmillan, New York.

Stigliz, Joseph (1993). Some Theoretical Aspects of the Privatization: Applications to Eastern Europe. In: Mario Baldassari, Luigi Paganetto and Edmund S. Phillips (eds.) *Privatization Processes in Eastern Europe*. MacMillan Press, United Kingdom.

Sukhanov, E. (1998). Zakon ob obshchestvakh s ogranichennoi otvetstvennostyu (The Law on Limited Liability Companies). *Khozyaistvo i pravo*, No. 5, pp. 38–47 (in Russian).

Tolonen, Juha Pentti (1974). Der Allgemeine Erklärungshintergrund der Wirtschaftlichen Ordnung und seine Anwendung auf das Aktiengesellschaft. Rechtsvergleichende Untersuchung (The General Explanation of the Commercial Order and Applying it to the Joint Stock Company. A Comparative Research). Helsinki (in German).

Tolonen, Juha Pentti (1976). Neuvostoliiton talousjärjestelmä ja sen oikeudelliset perusteet (The Economic System of the Soviet Union and its Legal Foundation). Series A Researches, Research Center of Social Sciences, University of Tampere, Tampere, No. 48 (in Finnish).

Tolonen, Juha and Boris Topornin (eds.) (2000). *Legal Foundations of Russian Economy*. Series B 14. Kikimora Publications, Helsinki.

Törnroos, Jan-Åke and Jarmo Nieminen (eds.) (1999). *Business Entry in Eastern Europe. A Network and Learning Approach with Case Studies*. Series B 4. Kikimora Publications, Helsinki.

Werlauff, Erik (1993). *EC Company Law*. The Common Denominator for Business Undertakings in 12 States. Jurist og Økonomforbundets Forlag, Copenhagen.

Williamson, O.E. (1985). *Economic Institutions of Capitalism: Firms, Markets, Relational Contracting.* Free Press, New York.

Williamson, O.E. (1988). The Logic of Economic Organization. *Journal of Law, Economics, and Organization,* IV:1, pp. 65–93.

Williamson, O.E. (1996). *The Mechanisms of Governance.* Oxford University Press, New York.

Official Sources

Civil Code of the Russian Federation, Part 1 of 30 November 1994 and Part 2 of 26 January 1996 (Grazhdanskii kodeks RF, chast pervaya ot 30 noyabrya 1994 g. i chast vtoraya ot 26 yanvarya 1996 g.).

Federal Law on Joint Stock Companies of 26 December 1995 (Zakon ob aktsionernykh obshchestvakh).

The Decree of the RSFSR on Joint Stock Companies of 25 December 1990 (Polozhenie ob aktsionernykh obshchestvakh RSFSR ot 25 dekabrya 1990 g.).

Federal Law on Limited Liability Companies of 8 February 1998 (Zakon ob obshchestvakh s ogranichennoi otvetstvennostyu).

Law on State Enterprises of the Soviet Union of 30 June 1987 (Zakon SSSR o gosudarstvennom predpriyatii).

Law on Enterprises of the Soviet Union of 4 June 1990 (Zakon SSSR o predpriyatiyakh).

Law on Enterprises of Russia of 25 December 1990 (Zakon RSFSR o predpriyatiyakh i predprinimatelskoi deyatelnosti).

Federal Law on Privatization of State and Municipal Enterprises in the Russian Federation of 3 July 1991 (Zakon o privatizatsii gosudarstvennykh i munitsipalnykh predpriyatii v Rossiiskoi Federatsii).

Presidential Decree on Corporatizing State Enterprises of 1 July 1992, No. 721 (Ob organizatsionnykh merakh po preobrazovaniyu gosudarstvennykh predpriyatii, dobrovolnykh obedinenii gosudarstvennykh predpriyatii v aktsionernye obshchestva).

The Privatization Program of 1993 (Ukaz Prezidenta RF o Gosudarstvennoi programme privatizatsii gosudarstvennykh i munitsipalnykh predpriyatsii No. 2284 ot 24 dekabrya 1993 g.).

The Privatization Program of 1994 (Ukaz Prezidenta RF ob osnovnykh polozheniyah gosudarstvennoi programmy privatizatsii gosudarstvennykh i munitsipalnykh predpriyatsii posle 1 iyulya 1994 goda ot 22 iyuliya 1994 g. No. 1534).

Federal Law on Houseowners' Companies of 15 June 1996 (Zakon o tovarishchestvakh sobstvennikov zhilya).

President's Decree on State Registration of Enterprises and Individual Businessmen on the Territory of the Russian Federation of 8 July 1994, No. 1482. (Polozhenie o poryadke gosudarstvennoi registratsii subektov predprinimatelskoi deyatelnosti. Ukaz Prezidenta RF ot 8 iyulya 1994 g. No. 1482).

Law on Minimum Wage of 13 June 2000 (O minimalnom razmere oplaty truda No. 82).

Law on Bankruptcy of 8 March 1998 No. 6, changed 6 June 2000 (O nesostoyatelnosti (bankrotstve).

Law on Foreign Investments of the RSFSR of 4 July 1991 (Zakon RSFSR ob inostrannykh investitsiyakh v RSFSR).

Federal Law on Foreign Investments of 9 July 1999, No. 160 (Ob inostrannykh investitsiyakh v RF).

Decision of the Supreme Arbitration Court of the Russian Federation, No. 7841/98 (Postanovlenie prezidiuma vyshego arbitrazhnogo suda Rossiiskoi Federatsii 2 marta 1999, No. 7841/98).

Official Sources of Other Countries and the EU

The Finnish Joint Stock Company Act (Osakeyhtiölaki 29.9.1978/734).

The Finnish Partnerships Act (Laki avoimesta yhtiöstä ja kommandiittiyhtiöistä 29.4.1988/389).

The Swedish Joint Stock Company Act (Aktiebolagslagen 1.1.1975/130).

The Swedish Partnerships Act (Lag om handelsbolag och enkla bolag 1980/1102).

The German Limited Liability Company Act (Gesetz betreffend die Gesellschaften mit beschränkter Haftung 20.4.1892).

The German Joint Stock Company Act (Aktiengesetz).

The English Companies Act 1985.

Salomon v. Salomon and Company Ltd. (1897) A.C. 22 (H.L.).

The First Council Directive (68/151) 9.3.1968 ("The Publishing Directive").

The Second Council Directive (77/91) 13.6.1976 ("The Capital Directive").

The Twelfth Company Law Directive (89/667) 21.12.1989 ("One-Man Companies").

The Proposal for the Fifth Company law Directive (OJ NIO C 240, 9.9.1983) ("The Structure Directive Proposal").

5

SUMMARY

5.1 Rule of Law, Democracy and Centralism

Russian law is in transition and yet it is based on the legal positivist ideal of a normative stable system of norms. Transition is also governed according to the Kelsenian ideal of developing positive law for the courts to implement and make the legal basis of the society function. The rule of law would then start to function and develop democracy as well in the long run.

Even if law has an important role to play in transition, this role should not be exaggerated. Legislation, as a means of transformation, has its limitations. Law as "the formal rules of the game" must answer the needs of society and be able to fulfill its role as a true normative framework of that society. Law has to be acknowledged and implemented but should not be too far from the informal rules of the game. Law, which is not followed is not effective. The constant dilemma of law in transitional societies is that law, which is drafted for market economy circumstances, is ahead of the real situation in a transition economy. If law is too ahead of its time, it is not understandable and is therefore not followed. If law, on the other hand, is lagging behind it hinders the society in developing towards a market economy. As a means of transition, law is not the best because it usually represents stability reflecting the values and principles of society. In transition, law is treated as if it would be able to create new values and principles.

Russian law, which on the legislative level is almost as advanced as law in market economies, can be criticized heavily from the legal realist point of view. On the constitutional level rules are not acknowledged and transparent. The constitution of 1993 is being forced and used to serve re-centralization of the federation. Because the federation is politically on a weak basis, it is difficult to draft clear and transparent rules. The struggle between the center and the regions is mostly a political power struggle. The principles of a market economy are not understood on either level. It seems that the regions would more often like to have the power to raise a customs barrier and build the region with administrative methods. The ideas of a uniform federation are not more developed at the center either. Bureaucratic means of control are the only familiar methods for a developing economy. It seems that the economy is in nobody's control, but develops in a post-communist jungle of informal rules connected with corruption in both business and state and municipal authorities.

"A one-man above all" rule seems to be a tradition, which is difficult to obliterate. Presidential constitution and rule hinders the development of democracy. Even if presidential "dictatorship" may temporarily be a good solution for pushing changes through and guaranteeing a proper framework for the economy, it has a tendency of not remaining temporary. Russian history seems to be a history of constant extraordinary situations needing "a strong leader". A weak party system and corruption makes a one-man rule more efficient but, on the other hand, the weakness of parliament makes it difficult to develop democracy. The absence of a civil society is, however, the worst obstacle for democracy because without it there is no effective grass-root level control. Russian society is counting more on specialists than ordinary citizens.

It may also be true that democracy can hinder economic development towards a market economy because democracy easily blocks difficult decisions, which may have negative short-term effects on citizens. However, there is no guarantee that the one man leading the country would be competent enough to make the difficult decisions even with his army of specialists.

It seems that Russia is too deep in maintaining unity using all possible means that it cannot focus on the economy. Unity with force cannot bring any good results; it can only develop in a stable economy and from economic benefits. Russian unity is promoted with arms and superpower mentality. Threatening behavior with losing economic benefits does not seem to have a positive effect from the point of view of preserving the federation. Separatists are sure that leaving decision power, including the power to decide on economic development, in the center would not benefit their region. It can well be claimed that true decentralism is not going to develop in current circumstances. A natural collapse of the federation might, in the long run, force people into cooperation. If it would not, there are no real prerequisites for unity.

Strengthening centralism is not a modern answer to Russian problems. Decentralism is, however, difficult to develop if local bosses still regard themselves as medieval vassals. If decentralism does not develop, Russia is going to stay on the level of a late medieval state striving for unity in the form of the old ideal of the nation state. The ideal of centralism rests on the nation state idea of a modern state. A huge multinational federation cannot be unified in the same way as a nation state. Therefore the center has had to return to the soviet superpower ideology and forced unity. Old fashioned centralism cannot offer a prosperous future for Russia. Both collective choice and operational rules should be decentralized to make the Russian society function in a modern way. Only when Russian regions start to compete for investors and favoring entrepreneurship, can the economy start to function from a sound grass-root level.

5.2 Virtual Economy and Modern Business Legislation

Many reformers in Russia at the beginning of 1990s seemed to think that breaking down the planned economy would give room for markets to function on their own. Unfortunately free markets have not developed. Prices are not decided by markets. The old institutions and networks survive in a virtual economy, where the price of goods or property does not have any value. The absence of cash and the flow of currency abroad hinder the economy from developing. The virtual economy, corruption and old networks make it difficult for foreigners to invest and run business in Russia.

Therefore foreign investors have demanded a legal framework of a market economy. They have already got it, but only formally. Informal institutions still rule, decide prices and keep the markets closed. Insider privatization of companies strengthened the virtual economy and the old institutions. The absence of trust makes transaction costs high. Authorities are corrupt and business partners often unreliable. Courts, which are always the last resort, cannot offer compensation because court decisions cannot be implemented since dishonest businessmen can usually hide their incomes and property.

A good example of modern legislation is company law, which has been developed according to western models. However, it does not function in a market economy fashion. In the long run, however, company law rules are going to take root in Russian business. It is only a matter of time. Modern company law is at least a relief for western investors, who are allowed to manage their companies in a western way. With younger managers in control, big former state enterprises may also start to change their management methods.

5.3 Unclear Property Rights, Trust and Order

The unclear structure of property rights is one of the most difficult obstacles for an efficient economy. Unclear property rights is clearly a political question. There is no solid common foundation of values and principles in Russia's changing environment. The promotion of private ownership in the privatization of state enterprises glued an ugly label on private ownership. The often shameful methods, which brought the Russian economy into the hands of a few rich *oligarchs* and made the market extremely monopolistic, are not a good example in pushing forward the privatization of natural resources. However, if the countryside is going to be made a decent place for people to live, the privatization of natural resources is required to some extent. Farming without supporting sources of livelihood, such as forestry, is never going to be profitable.

There is, however, a real fear that those circles, which privatized enterprises for themselves, would do the same thing for natural resources as soon as the opportunity arises. Legal hindrances did not prevent them earlier. Corruption and close relations with state and local leadership can guarantee that even illegal informal property rights can be made legal as time passes. On the other hand, the *oligarchs* do not have to privatize natural resources for themselves. In the present situation monopolistic enterprises govern the markets for users' rights for natural resources belonging to state ownership. Actually the *oligarchs* can avoid the owner's official obligations and yet have easy access to natural resources. The same mentality, which existed during socialism and allowed irresponsible attitudes without taking sustainability of the environment into account, continues in a path-dependant way.

Clearly, the worst problem in Russia is the absence of trust. Authorities cannot be trusted and business partners are cheated for short-term gains. The reason behind the absence of trust is the lack of order. Without order no society can function properly. Restoring order by force and returning to "dictatorship of law" is only a short-term solution. Restoring order without trust is not going to work, unless it means a return to Stalin's methods. Even that alternative, order as well as economy, which is based on force, stops functioning as soon as forcing people ends. Attitudes and perception dating back to socialism can be handled with force and dictatorial methods, but that kind of ruling can only slow down the development of a civil society and a change in mentalities. It is the people, not the one man leadership of the country, who can change the trail.

Rules and regulations should be legitimate and not implemented simply by force. Attitudes and perceptions do not change easily, because change has to occur at all levels of society. If politicians and authorities are not trustworthy, why should people start to trust them? The change is not going to start from top-down. Everything should be done to make the change occur from bottom-up. When all the layers of society are properly and voluntarily interacting in change, trust can also gradually be created. Small and medium-sized entrepreneurship in industry, commerce and agriculture should be supported and given a chance. The fundamental transformation should take place on the grass-root level, where people have to find methods of establishing trust. Encouraging international business cooperation in small and medium-sized business, can spread values of entrepreneurship. However, a model of trust and fundamental transformation cannot be imported, because it is closely connected with culture and mentalities. Russian trust and responsibility for the future develops in the cultural environment under the conditions of her own socioeconomic development.

Russian transformation has counted too much on big privatized business, which has also been the most powerful interest group of Russian society. Small business and private agriculture should also be taken into account when formal rules are created. The only interest group that has been able to affect on drafting laws is the powerful group of Russian industrialists. Specialists, who draft laws for business, can be affected and they are not in principle against lobbying. However, the problems of the countryside are far from Moscow-based specialists and small and medium-sized businesses do not have channels to influence the development of their own business environment. The channels were ready only for the industrialists, who could change their role from state officials to private businessmen. All the informal networks were also in favor of the old *nomenklatura.* This unfortunate fact is also the greatest obstacle for the development of the countryside and agriculture.

5.4 From Legal Centralism to Fundamental Transformation?

It is some kind of an unfortunate paradox in Russia that in a rapidly changing society the point of view of legal studies is stable legal positivism. From such a standpoint the task of legal studies is to quickly create a normative system corresponding to modern needs. Law is reserved for lawyers, created through legislation and implemented by courts. The role of citizens is to obey the rules, which specialists have drafted for them. Keeping law autonomous and counting on legal centralism—the centralized court system to represent law in society—is a real obstacle of attitudes and perceptions in transformation.

Courts are definitely important in transition and their development should be supported. However, in changing circumstances the court system, which is based on stable legal positivist principles, cannot function properly. The problems of business usually emerge from changing circumstances, opportunism and the preference of short-term gains to long-term trustworthy business relations. Legal rules, which should be interpreted in a similar way in similar situations, often cannot give a good solution. Furthermore, even if the court decision would protect the cheated business partner, the decision could not be enforced. Legal centralist protection is therefore inadequate.

Even if courts are important, they cannot change society into a legalist path, if informal institutions and the environment are not favorable. A better enforcement system cannot do it either. Therefore lawyering should concentrate more on preventing legal disputes. Creating trust and preventing opportunism is most important in business cooperation. Such preventive tasks can be taken in cooperation with business economists, engineers and lawyers. If lawyers do not take preventive lawyering seriously, they will end up in their own absurd world of *ex post* lawyering, which does not help their clients any more.

Fundamental transformation cannot start only from above. It has to be done from below at the firm and operational level. Such an attitude is connected with legal realism and might gradually change the deeply rooted legal centralist standpoint. Interaction with all the different layers of society is important and it should gradually change the centralist attitudes of Russian society. Before change in attitudes can happen, the grass-root level of small and medium-sized business as well as civil society should be strengthened.

Index

KIKIMORA PUBLICATIONS

Series A

Temkina, Anna (1997): Russia in Transition: The Case of New Collective Actors and New Collective Actions. ISBN 951-45-7843-0

Мустонен, Петер (1998): Собственная его императорского величества канцелярия в механизме властвования института самодержца 1812–1858: К типологии основ имперского управления. ISBN 951-45-8074-5

3 Rosenholm, Arja (1999): Gendering Awakening : Femininity and the Russian Woman Question of the 1860s. ISBN 951-45-8892-4

4 Lonkila, Markku (1999): Social Networks in Post-Soviet Russia: Continuity and Change in the Everyday Life of St. Petersburg Teachers. ISBN 951-45-8911-4

5 Hanhinen, Sari (2001): Social Problems in Transition. Perceptions of Influential Groups in Estonia, Russia and Finland. USBN 951-45-9867-9

6 Vettenniemi, Erkki (2001): Surviving the Soviet Meat Grinder: The Politics of Finnish Gulag Memoirs. ISBN 951-45-9868-7

Series B

Vihavainen, Timo ja Takala, Irina (red.) (1998): В семье единой: Национальная политика партии большевиков и ее осуществление на Северо-Западе России в 1920–1950-е годы. ISBN 5-230

Granberg, Leo (ed.) (1998): The Snowbelt: Studies on the European North in Transition. ISBN 951-45-8253-5

Sutela, Pekka (1998): The Road to the Russian Market Economy: Selected Essays 1993–1998. ISBN 951-45-8409-0

4 Törnroos, Jan-Åke and Nieminen, Jarmo (eds.) (1999): Business Entry in Eastern Europe: A Network and Learning Approach with Case Studies. ISBN 951-45-8860-6

5 Miklóssy, Katalin (toim.) (1999): Syitä ja seurauksia: Jugoslavian hajoaminen ja seuraajavaltioiden nykytilanne: seminaari 8.4.1999, Helsinki. ISBN 951-45-8861-4

Винников, Александр (1998): Цена свободы. ISBN 5-89739-002-9

Лебина, Н. Б. (1999): Повседневная жизнь советского города : нормы и аномалии : 1920 и 1930 годы. ISBN 5-87516-133-7, 5-87940-004-0

8 Lejins, Atis (ed.) (1999): Baltic Security Prospects at the Turn of the 21st Century. ISBN 951-45-9067-8

9 Komulainen, Tuomas and Korhonen, Iikka (eds.) (2000): Russian Crisis and Its Effects. ISBN 951-45-9100-3

10 Salminen, Ari ja Temmes, Markku (2000): Transitioteoriaa etsimässä. ISBN 951-45-9238-7

11 Yanitsky, Oleg (2000): Russian Greens in a Risk Society: A Structural Analysis. ISBN 951-45-9226-3

12 Vihavainen, Timo ja Takala, Irina (toim.) (2000): Yhtä suurta perhettä: Bolševikkien kansallisuuspolitiikka Luoteis-Venäjällä 1920–1950-luvuilla. ISBN 951-45-9275-1

13 Oittinen, Vesa (ed.) (2000): Evald Ilyenkov's Philosophy Revisited. ISBN 951-45-9263-8

14 Tolonen, Juha and Topornin, Boris (eds.) (2000): Legal Foundations of Russian Economy. ISBN 951-45-9276-X

15 Kotiranta, Matti (ed.) (2000): Religious Transition in Russia. ISBN 951-45-9447-9

16 Kangaspuro, Markku (ed.) (2000): Russia: More different than most. ISBN 951-45-9423-1

18 Liljeström, Marianne, Rosenholm, Arja and Savkina, Irina (eds.) (2000): Models of Self. Russian Women's Autobiographical Texts. ISBN 951-45-9575-0

20 Nordenstreng, Kaarle, Vartanova, Elena and Zassoursky, Yassen (eds.) (2001): Russian Media Challenge. ISBN 951-45-9689-6

21 Nystén-Haarala, Soili (2001): Russian Law in Transition. Law and Institutional Change. ISBN 951-45-9902-0

23 Snellman, Hanna (2001): Khants' Time. ISBN 951-45-9997-7

Orders:
Aleksanteri Institute
P.O.Box 4
Fin-00014 University of Helsinki
Telephone +358-9-191 24175
Telefax +358-9-191 23822
E-mail: kikimora-publications@helsinki.fi
www.helsinki.fi/aleksanteri